Curriculum

Teaching the What, How, and Why of Living

Curriculum

Teaching the What,
How, and Why
of Living

Louise M. Berman
Jessie A. Roderick
University of Maryland

CHARLES E. MERRILL PUBLISHING COMPANY
A Bell & Howell Company
Columbus   Toronto   London   Sydney

Published by
Charles E. Merrill Publishing Company
A Bell & Howell Company
Columbus, Ohio 43216

The book was set in Palatino.

The Production Editor was Linda Hillis.

The cover was prepared by Will Chenoweth.

International Standard Book Number: 0–675–08480–6

Library of Congress Catalog Card Number: 76–45880

1 2 3 4 5 6 7—82 81 80 79 78 77

Printed in the United States of America

To those who are concerned about
the *what, how,* and *why* of living
and who wish to express this
concern in more explicit ways.

preface

This is a work about people and their lives—their decisions, their involvements, and their human contacts. This is also a book about schools; their practices and responsibilities. Indeed, the pervasive theme of this book is that schools can and should construct their curricular emphases so that persons can face up to their own humanness. Such self-awareness and confrontation enable persons to decide whether they will live primarily for their own comfort, convenience, and satisfaction, or whether they will obtain the prerequisite knowledge and skills to be contributing members to the larger world.

Several years ago, one of the authors of this text wrote *New Priorities in the Curriculum.* In the earlier book, eight skills were identified as being possible major emphases of the schools. The skills or processes sketched in broad outline included perceiving, deciding, valuing, knowing, communicating, and others. Since the earlier publication, the present authors have engaged in examining the skills or processes discussed in *New Priorities,* condensing them into a smaller number, and allowing the emergence of new emphases. A new, major thrust has been the examination of the educational setting to see how it can enhance the teaching of process skills. Another major emphasis has been attention to the problem of gathering information about what is transpiring when the critical skills of living are given high priority in schooling.

In times of economic abundance, but more especially in periods of economic recession, educators are prone to forget and neglect to plan for the full spectrum of human skills. Attention is frequently given to superficial and highly visible behaviors as opposed to the complex, interrelated aspects of human nature which make persons the unusual creatures that they are. This is a book which deals with aspects of persons that cannot be forgotten in any era.

Too long have we been concerned primarily and singularly with architectural designs of the schools, the trivia of teaching, modes of grouping children, and programs which may possess logic but lack punch. Too little have we been concerned with the very critical concepts about living which children and youth must have the opportunity to learn if their lives are to help right human wrongs. Too much have we been concerned about individual achievement in narrowly specified areas. Too little have we been concerned about the attainment of collaborative competence necessary to raise and fulfill human visions.

Unfortunately, although humankind is working toward a thoughtfully conceived view of men and women, a view which gives both sexes equal access, privileges, and rights, our language has not kept pace with our visions. Consequently, in this text the traditional form of the masculine gender will denote persons of both sexes.

In the pages that follow are proposals that invite the reader to contemplate teaching the *what, how,* and *why* of human existence. We urge the reader to examine our suggestions and the rationale behind them, to develop the concepts further, and ultimately to implement the curricular ideas. We trust such action will provide learners with opportunities to gain new insights about themselves and the reasons for their existence. This is what curriculum and teaching are all about.

acknowledgments

Our lives are constantly enhanced and enriched by other persons who make contributions in the moment of now. Such persons give of themselves and their talents in the form of the apt spoken comment, the telling written word, and the enabling giving of self through presence.

Our lives are also enriched by the rich legacies of those who have lived in moments past. Noble acts, discoveries improving the quality of life, and books rich in ideas energizing the mind are included in the heritage left us by persons who have lived earlier.

Because we have had the fortune of being enriched by so many persons, both those who have tailored or designed useful materials and those who have strengthened our lives in the interactive process, it is difficult to acknowledge adequately those who have contributed in any way to this book.

We are indebted to our professional colleagues, university students, and children who have assisted us in realizing the complexity rather than the simplicity of classrooms and teaching, and the inner and introspective rather than the obvious and superficial qualities of persons. We are also grateful to those persons who have knotty questions about curriculum development in a world demanding new modes of schooling.

We are indebted to the many authors whose ideas we have searched, mulled over, analyzed, and in many cases used. We appreciate permission to quote or paraphrase from the publications of the following authors and publishers:

Association for Supervision and Curriculum Development
George Braziller, Inc.
Center for Young Children, University of Maryland
Citation Press
Harper & Row Publishers, Inc.
Holt, Rinehart & Winston, Inc.

Macmillan Publishing Co., Inc.
Random House, Inc.
The Seabury Press, Inc.
Charles Scribner's Sons
Smithsonian Institution
Southern Illinois University Press
Springer Publishing Company
Carol A. Stevenson
The University of Chicago Press
The University of Michigan Press
Word Books
World Future Society

Although the designing of the ideological components of any book is critical, no work could come into being without the labor of those who give typing and editorial aid. Mrs. Loretta Germann gave invaluable assistance in assuming major responsibility for typing the manuscript, in obtaining clearances, and in giving editorial assistance. Despite the magnitude of the tasks, Mrs. Germann was always encouraging, supportive, and willing to accommodate our habit of frequently changing the manuscript. To Mrs. Rose Marie Dorn, Mrs. Barbara Germann, and Mrs. Loretta Southerland, we express our appreciation for their help in typing at critical periods along the way.

We are grateful to Charles E. Merrill Publishing Company for publishing this book. Although numerous persons are involved in producing a book, we especially wish to acknowledge Linda Hillis, Production Editor, for her valuable assistance.

Although we both enjoy the company of our families and friends, at times we found ourselves regretfully withdrawing from interaction with them in order to fulfill our commitments relative to the production of this book. We appreciate their willingness to understand our absences, but more especially we are grateful for the contributions they have made in our lives.

Despite the contributions and suggestions of others, only we can be held responsible for what is contained in the pages of this book. We trust our sharing of what we consider to be high priorities in the *what, how,* and *why* of living will be a stepping stone toward revamped practices in schooling.

contents

9   Decision: The What of Living   188

         Contexts Facilitating Decision-making
           Skill, 189
         Where to Look for Evidences of Decision
           Making, 189
         Context, Behaviors, and Recording
           Feedback, 192
         Context as Contributing to Communicating,
           Knowing, and Social Systems, 201
         In Retrospect, 204
         Suggestions for Further Reading, 204

10   Involvement: The How of Living   206

         Context Related to Involvement, 207
         A Rhythm of Involvement and
           Noninvolvement, 208
         Qualities of Contexts Facilitating
           Involvement, 209
         Context, Behaviors, and Recording
           Feedback, 210
         Involvement and Communicating, Knowing,
           and Social Systems, 221
         In Retrospect, 223
         Suggestions for Further Reading, 223

11   Peopling: The Why of Living   225

         Contexts for Peopling, 226
         Contexts Facilitating Peopling, 229
         Context, Behaviors, and Recording
           Feedback, 230
         Peopling and Communicating, 242
         Peopling and Knowing, 244
         Peopling and Social Systems, 248
         In Retrospect, 249
         Suggestions for Further Reading, 249

introduction

Teaching the What, How, and Why of Living

This book is written for those persons interested in exploring and designing alternatives to what is currently happening in schools. It is written not only for those who wish to teach the mechanics of reading but also for those who want to teach reading for the enhancement of the quality of living. This book is written not only for those concerned about whether school spaces should be "open" or "self-contained" but also for those concerned that persons learn to live on earth amiably and productively. It is not only for those who wish our young to learn basic principles and generalizations of bodies of knowledge but also for those concerned that humanity's combined wisdom be used to better rather than to destroy society.

The book is written for those who use current systems of evaluation and for those who are dissatisfied with our means of gathering and generating information about children and youth and are searching for new and better data-gathering procedures in keeping with more complex curricular goals. This book is written for those concerned about children from 5 to 18 and those interested in lifelong education. In essence, this book is written for those who are interested in providing settings where the person can develop skill in utilizing past impressions, present perceptions, and future hopes as resources in dealing with life's basic questions—the *what, how,* and *why* of living. This book is simultaneously a map and a plea. The map is a route by which renewed vigor and wisdom in searching moral and value-laden issues can be attained. The plea is for educators to commit themselves to greater leadership in the moral construction of society.

The capacity to become deliberately and intentionally involved in life can be dulled, heightened—or ignored. By ignoring a person's right to develop his personal power to the fullest, schools do the individual and the setting of which he is part a severe injustice. Those responsible for the education of the young have failed to provide settings in which persons can deal critically and responsibly with life's tough problems and questions and, by default, these persons do not develop the will and the competence to participate in collaborative efforts designed to enhance the well being of others.

To develop basic skills, such as deciding intelligently, becoming fully involved, and relating sensitively to others, is essential. The critical situations of the time are such that unless persons decide to be concerned, not only about themselves, but also about those in their immediate world, their local communities and the larger world, all stand to lose. One has only to look at what is happening in the world to realize that we can no longer afford to be unconcerned about the world's problems unless we are willing to face the threat of environmental deterioration to the degree that it is less than healthy for human habitation.

Because of the need to change the current thrust of schooling, the authors of this book have decided to delineate a program for children and youth in which major attention is given to such critical areas as decision making, involvement, and being concerned with people. This is not a book focusing upon the change process *per se.* Rather, it is a work which proposes alternative learnings and data-gathering and data-generating procedures compatible with the suggested foci for classroom settings.

If our orientation is accepted, then educators, instead of confining school experiences to the immediate classroom, will work toward making the larger world the classroom. Instead of focusing upon evaluative techniques, such as achievement tests that place persons in categories which they have difficulty shaking, educators will expand efforts to insure that data-gathering procedures are in line with a given purpose or classroom setting. It is because of a firm commitment to this latter task that a large portion of this book is devoted to new ways of gathering evidence about persons and their skills within the proposed critical curriculum areas.

Complacency, comfort, and conviviality only with those like our-selves must give way to outreach, compassion for the larger world, and concern that persons make the critical sacrifices necessary so that all may live fully. The schools, being gathering places of all levels of per-sons, can be prime initiators of this task.

The uncertainty of the times, the mobility of the population, and the inability to predict fully what the future holds for anyone necessitate the development of persons who can deal realistically, joyously, and in a transcendent manner with life and its many challenges. No parent or teacher can leave with the young the specific knowledge necessary to solve life's dilemmas. But those responsible for their education can provide opportunities for the young to acquire inner resources that enable them to deal effectively with the circumstances of living.

Purpose of Book

The purpose of this book is to provide the reader with the background and skills necessary for planning, implementing, and evaluating cur-ricula designed to enhance basic life skills of deciding, becoming in-volved, and relating sensitively to others.

Organization

Curriculum: Teaching the What, How, and Why of Living is divided into four parts. Part one is a discussion of aspects of the social context which prompted the writers to assume the curricular stance they take. Also included are definitions and assumptions useful to the reader. Part two contains theoretical background necessary to understanding the major emphases of the curriculum discussed in the book. Decision, The *What* of Man's Existence; Involvement, The *How* of Man's Existence; and Peopling, The *Why* of Man's Existence are each discussed in terms of definitions and major concepts. Part two also contains sections relating the major themes of deciding, becoming involved, and peopling to other necessary human skills of communicating, knowing, and dealing with social systems.

Part three, "Observing and Describing the *What, How,* and *Why* of Living," gives a rationale and specific techniques for describing progress in the basic skills outlined in part two. Considerable attention is given in part three to the topic of gathering information about persons in-teracting in settings since teaching the skills proposed in this work demands new ways of gathering evidence about growth. Part four on classroom practices is an application of parts two and three. Major concepts about the skills developed in part two are discussed in terms of classroom procedures. Specific activities which are designed to give the opportunity to learn the skills of decision making, involvement, and peopling are discussed in this section. Each of these activities contains a means of obtaining information or feedback about what is happening. Finally, a brief epilogue discusses jumping off points or thresholds for persons interested in implementing the ideas found in the book. The major jumping off points relate to making judgments about progress in process-related skills, teacher education, and collaborative efforts among educators.

Possible Uses
and Application

The organization of this work reflects the authors' purposes and hunches about how readers might best make use of the ideas in the book. However, each reader decides on the setting in which the material is utilized and applied, the time frame employed, and the manner in which the suggestions are adapted to specific ages and interest groups. The chart which follows suggests some ways a reader, depending on his or her purpose, might approach and utilize the material.

IF THE READER	THEN CONSIDER
desires a substantive background in a process such as decision or involvement,	part two or selected aspects of it.
seeks help in planning, implementing and evaluating a process skill,	appropriate chapters on that process skill found in parts two, three, and four.
seeks to understand the foundations of the book and the definitions employed,	part one.
wants to focus on the rationale and procedures for generating information on what transpires in the classroom setting,	part three.
wishes to see how communication facilitates describing what happens in the classroom setting.	chapter 7 on Communication.

is in a practicum or a situation   part four.
where he or she has to plan speci-
fic learning experiences for children and youth,

is a practitioner looking for new   the epilogue.
ideas or forward thrusts,

wants to study decision in terms   chapters 3 and 9.
of its substance and application,

wants to study involvement in   chapters 4 and 10.
terms of its substance and appli-
cation,

wants to study peopling in terms   chapters 5 and 11.
of its substance and application,

is a student of curriculum study-   the whole book.
ing the rationale, substance,
method, and research procedures inherent in curriculum
proposals,

part one

The Person in
the Social Setting

Persons simultaneously want the security of the past and the potential adventuresomeness of the future, the freedom of aloneness and the mutuality of compatible persons, the excitement of organizing and the stability of the organized. Persons have a need to break out of barriers and at the same time to be enclosed by familiar surroundings. Persons want to serve but at the same time to be served.

Because persons want and need the conditions for growth, expansion, and constant remaking, they tend to interact with persons, ideas, and institutions so that the self can be enhanced. They tend to want surroundings, places, organizations—a social context—which contribute to their well being.

At the same time, persons influence, or are influenced by social settings. Since institutions are made up of persons, they reflect the desires and purposes, the rules and regulations, the strategies for change, the "personality" that persons working within them have created. Social settings ordinarily reflect persons as composite, persons as collaborators, persons as network. Social settings are frequently unwieldy because they reflect the complexities of persons as they seek to organize themselves in space and time. They reflect the tension between persons' independent and interdependent longings.

The persistent interplay between the person and his setting is a theme of this book. The interplay can be constructive or destructive either through intent or carelessness. Persons and institutions stand to gain or lose depending upon the fruitfulness of the interplay.

The authors gave serious thought to the writing of chapter 1 for, at best, treatment of a topic as global as the social setting is an awesome task. In order to get a grasp of the topic, however, the authors over a period of time filed references on what appeared to be happening in the world. These references were then grouped into categories which reflected views of the media, such as newspapers, journals, television, and current books, on the persistent themes of our times. For example, the issue of mobility and the subsequent rootlessness seemed to be a recurring theme. Another theme involved apparent slave-master relationships. Themes which emerged from a content analysis of current issues are only briefly treated. Following the discussion of issues is a list of outcomes of persons and social settings interacting.

Chapter 2 is an attempt to delineate the nature of the person that the schools might assist in developing, to lay out certain basic assumptions relative to schooling and curriculum development, and to define terms used frequently in the book.

1

Persons and
Social Settings
Interacting

Perspective on Chapter 1

Theme: A partnership between the person and his social setting can mean a heightened existence for the person and new vitality in the setting.

Selected major points: (1) The social setting in which we live can be considered from several perspectives such as how the young are reared, the persistence of mobility and the lack of rootedness, and problems inherent in balancing societal power. (2) Because of the interaction between the person and the setting continuous change occurs.

As you read: (1) Think about the settings in which you live and interact. From your experiences what would you add to the list of perspectives from which the social setting can be viewed? (2) What would you add to the list of outcomes of persons and settings interacting?

The person is inextricably engulfed by his social setting. Simultaneously, however, he engulfs it. What is the social setting? At times it can be the world or some corner of it. It may be a place of occupation or a center for worship. It can be a cluster of homes or the steps of an apartment building on a city street. The social setting can be places, but it can also be the customs, traditions, mores, and ideologies which bind persons together. In other words, man's social environment includes the geographical spaces, the political persuasions, the ideological dynamics, and the institutional boundaries which affect how a person lives and moves. At times the outer limits of the social setting may be clear, but on other occasions, the social setting may appear to be a large amorphous mass over which the individual has little control—to say nothing of knowledge.

The central theme of the book—the interplay of the person and his setting—is highlighted throughout this chapter. Presented here are assumptions and different perspectives from which the social context can be viewed. The latter are areas about which the school should be concerned.

This chapter serves as a backdrop for the rest of the book in that illustrations are frequently drawn from the topics of this chapter or other topics that deal with the person's responsibility in the social setting. In addition, the chapter serves as a reminder to teachers and other educators that teaching and curriculum development do not take place in a vacuum. They take place in a very complex and complicated world in which education can serve as a useful force provided educators are astute observers and perceptive scholars of the many dimensions of the human condition.

Assumptions

The assumptions which underlie the remainder of the chapter are as follows:

1. Persons are free beings but they live in communities with others. Persons affect and are affected by the social organizations they have created. Persons can thoughtfully plan for the quality of life.
2. Persons need to expand their communities in breadth and depth. They need to cross boundaries to include persons of diverse characteristics and beliefs in their worlds.
3. Knowledge can take many forms. Persons are capable of generating it and utilizing it in dealing with the interplay of persons and social systems. Knowledge can involve the recognition of concrete events as well as the insights about contexts into which such events fit.
4. Persons should see as a major goal the giving of themselves in the service of others. The technological and industrial competencies

prized in past eras must give way to exploring how to assist persons in their living so that each serves, supports, and cares about the other.

Social Contexts

The social milieu in which persons live and interact can be considered from several perspectives. What follows are a few selected social contexts or aspects of them. A cursory consideration of certain of these social settings should assist the reader in understanding the suggestions and recommendations for curricular practice found in the rest of this work.

Rearing the young

It is trite to say that patterns of child rearing are changing in many parts of the world. The effects on children of increased movement of women to the job market, the emergence of more one-family homes, and the low status generally accorded child rearing are not known.

We have some information relative to multiple mother figures instead of one or a few. For example, Bowlby in his studies found that the child has a real need for closeness to the mother, and when prolonged separation takes place anxiety and other negative forces set in.[1] If a mother figure is important, do children growing up in day care centers, communes, or other new arrangements of persons acquire the qualities necessary to cope with the realities of everyday living? Or are such children given primarily custodial care which keeps them *off* the streets but without guidance *through* the streets by knowing and tender adults?

The setting in which parents do assume major responsibility for rearing their children needs exploring as do other types of child-rearing settings. Efforts could be directed toward finding means to give these parents feelings of satisfaction and rewards that they currently appear to be seeking through other channels.

Mobility and lack of rootedness

Citizens of the United States ordinarily are a mobile people. Complications arising from the energy crisis have slowed the rate of mobility to

---

1. John Bowlby, *Anxiety and Anger*, Vol. 2 of *Attachment and Loss* (New York: Basic Books, 1973).

some extent, but during the past decades Americans have tended to be on the move as potential professional and economic advancements seemed to point the way to a better life. Consider the young executive or the aging person seeking a place to call home.

Social settings are affected by and affect the mobile person.[2] The uncertainty of environments, partially caused by mobility and rootlessness, contributes to the complexity of the astute curriculum worker's task.

Balancing power

Recent literature is full of cases of the powerless seeking power. Nonwhite persons and women, realizing that they have had little power in their lives, seek aggressively to enter job markets previously closed to them. Students, used to following the dictates of university faculty and officials, search for means to participate in the decisions which affect their learning and living. Corporation workers, intolerant of decisions made by the few, interpenetrate organizations to have a voice in decisions affecting them. The purpose of such action is to acquire more responsibility for the whole of the work in which they are involved, preferring to see the relationship among the parts rather than perform some minuscule task. Nations, thought to be economically underdeveloped, have let the world know that they do not intend to receive what others deem good for them but wish to determine their own fate. The concept of balancing power can be found in almost all arenas.

The problem in balancing power is to help persons feel powerful in the situations of which they are part. Whether in a small social context such as the family, or a larger one such as an organization, persons must feel that their decisions and commitments make a difference so that individuals and the context interact in mutually beneficial ways. A person's feeling of power can alleviate disaffection, alienation, and disinterest. Balancing power can also help persons develop dynamism and commitment, essential ingredients to a democratic society.

Giving-receiving

If the balancing of power is considered a necessary factor in society, attention needs to be directed to settings in terms of their potential for

2. For further discussions of rootlessness and mobility see Eugene Jennings, "Mobiocentric Man," *Psychology Today,* 4:35, 36 ff, July 1970. According to Jennings, the mobiocentric man values action and movement which are his ultimate values. Also, see Vance Packard, "Nobody Knows My Name," *Today's Education* 62:22–28, September-October 1973.

enabling persons to give, receive, and deal with limiting circumstances.[3] In addition, thought also needs to be directed to how persons can influence the setting through their ability to give and receive.[4]

The setting can be designed in such a way that some persons are primarily recipients and some basically contributors, or attempts can be made to design contexts so that all persons have opportunities to give and to receive. Social settings which limit the potential for serving and being served are those in which channels do not exist for exerting individual initiative—the company in which the procedures are so formalized that a change cannot be brought about without going through several layers of "red tape," the school in which students do not feel they have a voice in making decisions which affect them, the family in which children cannot help establish the rules and procedures by which the individuals live together.

One answer to world and local dilemmas of giving and receiving is to develop persons with stamina and compassion so that innovative giving and receiving can take place in all contexts—from the smallest and simplest to the largest and most diversified. Concern for service enables giving of skill and self to the dilemmas of Africa, South America, North America, and home. A life in which one's skills are put to the service of others also enables self-growth and development, a prerequisite for psychologically healthy living.[5]

Living in multiple cultures

The person must deal with the problem of reconciling the many worlds in which he lives—the world of the family and those physically and psychologically close to him, including the milieu in which he must operate—in order to purchase the commodities necessary for sustenance. In addition, individuals can and should live in the world of outreach or the world in which the individual extends himself to do something for and with others.

The variety of worlds within which the individual lives requires two sets of competencies on the part of the person. He must be able to form close intimate relations with those near at hand. And he must under-

---

3. For an elaboration of the concepts of giving, receiving, and dealing with limiting circumstances, see Viktor E. Frankl, *The Doctor and the Soul: From Psychotherapy to Logotherapy* (New York: Alfred A. Knopf, 1955). Also see Frankl, *Man's Search for Meaning: An Introduction to Logotherapy* (New York: Simon and Schuster, 1959).

4. *Ibid.*

5. For a discussion of service in the life of an individual, see Walter Kaufmann, *Without Guilt and Justice: From Decidophobia to Autonomy* (New York: Peter H. Wyden, 1973), pp. 228–36.

stand the broader political and social settings so that he can gain points of entry for making an impact on the broader context.

Man and environment

For many years, humanity has behaved as though it could play god with its environment. Obviously current warnings, threats, and action steps are alerting us to the fact that our lack of concern for setting is affecting the inhabitants of today's and tomorrow's world. As a result humanity is attempting to rectify its mistakes.

Many students of ecology raise questions as to whether we really have looked at the interrelationships of our responses to ecological problems. Are we merely tinkering and attacking only one problem at a time when we should be attacking the problems in a dynamic inter-related manner? Reconciling the dilemma of our feeling that we have ultimate control of the earth without the necessary concern for the interconnectedness of the parts is a problem of our time.

Recently, persons in many quarters have taken a new perspective on the environment. From learning to modify diets to planning for saving our trees, our streams, and our oceans, in our personal and public lives we must give renewed emphasis to the interrelatedness of ourselves and environment if either is to endure.

Sharing resources

Related to the problems of the interconnectedness of humanity and its environment is the problem of the allocation of resources. The gap between the rich and the poor which has always been present is widening and polarizing. Brown says:

> In effect, our world today is in reality two worlds, one rich, one poor; one literate, one largely illiterate; one industrial and urban, one agrarian and rural; one overfed and overweight, one hungry and malnourished; one affluent and consumption-oriented, one poverty stricken and survival-oriented.[6]

If the world is to survive, each person, including the young person, needs to share not only with his family and nearby neighbors but also with his neighbors around the world. Worldwide sharing at a funda-mental and pervasive level is critical in a shrinking world. In addition to providing opportunities for the young to have an awareness of what

6. Lester R. Brown, *World Without Borders* (New York: Vintage Books, 1972), p. 41.

is happening in other parts of the world and to share their own resources, schools and universities can determine their role in the development of some part of the world. Philosophically, children and youth
need opportunities to learn as much as possible about "man as man, of
different ways of being human,"[7] with the intent of finding points to
assist others when a need warrants aid.

Old and new institutions

The American culture has been geared to movement, to growth, to
change. Democracies are characterized by dynamism. Through hard
work and a competitive spirit, America managed to achieve many
goods. But in so doing, persons were trampled underfoot, the value of
law was questioned, and competitiveness was placed above cooperation.
Too many persons and too few resources—these and other issues
created problems. Therefore, now we hear ... Stop the population
growth! Stop accepting tradition and precedent without thinking! Stop
thinking goods will bring good happiness and success! Stop doing things
to divide when a new kind of cohesiveness must be found!

The problem exists of how to achieve cohesiveness, movement, improvement, and ideological excellence in a world in which a need per-
sists to achieve new corporate arrangements among persons—
arrangements which build upon rather than denigrate man's need to be
involved in causes larger than himself. Service, both individual and
corporate, must be central to the goals of persons and institutions if old
institutions are to be changed and new ones developed which cater to
society's deepest problems.

Outcomes

If persons and settings are revitalized through their constant interactions, what are some of the outcomes? A few are mentioned and briefly
discussed.

Common and emerging symbols

One of the advantages of the interaction of the person and his setting
is that a need is promoted for common symbols. It is not necessary for
each person to invent his own system of language, his own quantitative

---

7. Robert Leestma, "Reflections on the Internationalization of Higher Education," in
The International Role of the Universities in the 1970's: Conference Proceedings(Amherst:
University of Massachusetts, 1973), pp. 125–45.

system, his own set of religious symbols, or his own symbols for interpreting art experience. Procedures can be established so that symbols and their meanings have commonality among various persons.

At the same time, individuals have the opportunity to add to or delete from the symbolic system when the need arises. As new causes emerge or as old institutions become obsolete, symbol systems can change.

Stability and movement

Since institutions, by virtue of their complexity, ordinarily move more slowly than individuals, institutions usually provide a degree of stability to societies. Most persons need to feel that there are stable elements in their lives even if they tend to be highly mobile or eager for rapid change.

Individuals can facilitate or hinder the stability of an institution by virtue of their own contributions to it. If individuals select to change the focus of a setting frequently, obviously the rate of its change will be more rapid than if they allow tradition and precedent to be the sole determinants of behavior within the setting.

Effective interplay between institutions and persons places each individual in a position of constantly assessing the movement of institutions and working out changes which enhance both the person and the social setting of which he is part.

Rootedness and branching

Related to the first two outcomes is the concept of rootedness and branching. Social settings, because they ordinarily emerge over a period of time can provide the individual with roots which enable branching to occur. Institutions provide the vehicles through which a person can explore the past and can look in depth at critical issues of our time and how they relate to past incidents of a similar type.

For example, schools can build compendia of practices that succeed and those that fail when rootedness is prized. Thus, schools can branch off in new directions but simultaneously build upon past history and knowledge. Similarly, individuals can branch off into new activities, new friendships, new thoughts when branching is prized. Without the roots of old friendships, old places to which one can return, the results of branching may be only short-lived.

Individuality and mutuality

Man is not meant to live alone. The person who tries to do so often loses some of his peculiarly human qualities. Through interacting in the social setting, persons have an opportunity to share ideas, to grow, and to take cooperative action. Such action enables persons to realize that although they can accomplish tasks alone, certain tasks are more adequately carried out through bringing to bear the expertise of many.

Families provide an excellent vehicle for children and youth to learn mutuality. Sharing experiences enables the child to learn the satisfactions and dissatisfactions that can come from working with others on a joint venture.

Those persons who prize the concept of mutuality can better understand and prize the concept of aloneness. Aloneness permits a person to come to grips with himself and to develop increased self-awareness which is necessary if mutuality is to operate at a real and vital level.

Inner discipline and outer procedures

Persons can learn that purposes can be carried out more effectively when self-discipline coupled with stated procedures accompany action. Such concepts frequently are lost in our current thinking relative to "humanistic" institutions or schools. The concept of *self*-discipline is integral to the literature on creativity. Order and procedure are necessary for any individual or group to function well over a period of time. It is only when a predisposition to make order the key element in life predominates that it becomes a deterrent to good functioning.

Desire for new competences

If persons are to provide service within their social settings, they need to feel they have competences which are useful in the setting. At the same time they need to see the setting as one that provides a stimulus to persons to develop new competences. Through having the opportunity to utilize skills and gain new ones, persons mature and grow. Institutions and other places where persons live and work together become relevant and vital when persons are given opportunities to continuously utilize old competences and develop new ones.

Consideration and achievement of alternative destinies

Because of the diversity of persons who are part of any social setting, it is possible for them jointly to consider immediate and long-term destinies and what it would take to make them realities. Not only the goals but means to achieve them are appropriately considered within social settings.

For example, institutions for the young can begin to prepare individuals to consider problems of destiny, to learn to spell out what is involved in any given destiny, and to recognize the means by which the considered destinies may be achieved. Young children can begin to consider factors that partially cause persons to be artistic, to be athletic, to be social, to be wealthy, and to be poor. Then students can begin to plan with their fellows for the achievement of what is important to them—at least at the time.

The social setting can be a backdrop against which persons can look at alternative destinies. It can also provide a friendly or hostile setting for persons to achieve what matters to them.

Diversity of persons and common meeting places

Provided social settings honor diversity, persons of different backgrounds can assist in the multiplication of ideas through the interaction of mind with mind. Persons representing a variety of personalities, commitments, and schools of thought need a forum or a common meeting place if democratic thought and action are to prevail. The setting can seek to obliterate differences in persons or meeting places can blend the idiosyncracies and diverse gifts which persons bring so that newness and freshness characterize the settings of which persons are part.

Social settings can be exciting as well as functional when persons are encouraged to participate fully in the common meeting place. When diversity is prized, the individual feels freedom to utilize his own idiosyncratic tendencies on projects of mutual concern. The results of such creative efforts can contribute far more to other persons than if diversity and creativity were not prized.

In Retrospect

The larger context in which curriculum is developed is exceedingly complex, necessitating a familiarity with and an ability to act upon critical issues within the social setting. The person and the social setting are in constant interaction, the one having a bearing upon the other. It is because of this persistent interplay that educators cannot neglect the larger world in planning learning opportunities for children and youth.

Suggestions for Further Reading

Amara, Roy C. "Some Features of the World of 1994." *The Futurist* 8: 129–30, June 1974.

Argyris, Chris. *Integrating the Individual and the Organization.* New York: John Wiley, 1964.

Beck, Carlton E. and others. *Education for Relevance: The Schools and Social Change.* Boston: Houghton-Mifflin, 1968.

Bowlby, John. *Attachment and Loss.* 2 vols. New York: Basic Books, 1969 and 1973.

Brown, Lester R. *World Without Borders.* New York: Vintage Books, 1972.

Carpenter, Edmund, and Ken Heyman, Photographer. *They Became What They Beheld.* New York: Ballantine Books, 1970.

Center for New Schools. "Strengthening Alternative High Schools." *Harvard Educational Review* 42: 313–50, August 1972.

Charnofsky, Stanley. *Educating the Powerless.* Belmont, Cal.: Wadsworth, 1971.

Conger, D. Stuart. "Social Inventions." *The Futurist* 7: 149–58, August 1973.

Della-Dora, Delmo, and James E. House, eds. *Education for an Open Society.* 1974 Yearbook. Washington, D.C.: Association for Supervision and Curriculum Development, 1974.

DeMott, Benjamin. *Surviving the 70's.* New York: E. P. Dutton, 1971.

Etzioni, Amitai. *The Active Society: A Theory of Societal and Political Processes.* New York: Free Press and London: Collier-Macmillan, 1968.

Frankl, Viktor E. Translated by Ilse Lasch. *Man's Search for Meaning: An Introduction to Logotherapy.* New York: Alfred A. Knopf, 1955.

Frankl, Viktor E. Translated by Richard and Clara Winston. *The Doctor and the Soul: From Psychotherapy to Logotherapy.* New York: Simon and Schuster, 1959.

Gordon, Theodore, J. "Some Crises That Will Determine the World of 1994." *The Futurist* 8: 115–21, June 1974.

Howe, James W. and the staff of the Overseas Development Council. *The U.S. and the Developing World: Agenda for Action 1974.* New York: Praeger Publishers, Published for the Overseas Development Council, 1974.

Kaufmann, Walter. *Without Guilt and Justice: From Decidophobia to Autonomy.* New York: Peter H. Wyden, 1973.

Keen, Sam. *To A Dancing God.* New York: Harper & Row, 1970.

Klein, Donald. "Community: Who Needs It?" *Psychology Today* 3: 32–35, December 1969.

May, Rollo. *Power and Innocence: A Search for the Sources of Violence.* New York: W. W. Norton, 1972.

Means, Richard L. *The Ethical Imperative: The Crisis in American Values.* Garden City, N.Y.: Anchor Books, 1970.

Millar, Jayne C. *Focusing on Global Poverty and Development: A Resource Book for Educators.* Washington, D.C.: Overseas Development Council, 1974.

O'Meara, Thomas F. and Donald M. Weisser, eds. *Projections: Shaping an American Theology for the Future.* Garden City, N.Y.: Image Books, 1970.

Packard, Vance. *A Nation of Strangers.* New York: David McKay, 1973.

Patai, Raphael. *The Arab Mind.* New York: Charles Scribner's, 1973.

Platt, John R. *Perception and Change: Projections for Survival.* Ann Arbor: University of Michigan Press, 1970.

Platt, John. "World Transformation: Changes in Belief Systems." *The Futurist* 8: 124, 125, June 1974.

Raskin, Marcus G. *Being and Doing.* New York: Random House, 1971.

Reich, Charles A. *The Greening of America.* New York: Random House, 1970.

Royce, Joseph R. *The Encapsulated Man: An Interdisciplinary Essay on the Search for Meaning.* New York: Van Nostrand Reinhold, 1964.

Slater, Philip. *The Pursuit of Loneliness: American Culture at the Breaking Point.* Boston: Beacon Press, 1970.

Stein, Herman D., ed. *Social Theory and Social Invention.* Cleveland: Press of Case Western Reserve University, 1968.

Verhoeven, Cornelis. *The Philosophy of Wonder: An Introduction and Incitement to Philosophy.* New York: Macmillan 1972.

2

The Person and
Schooling

Perspective on Chapter 2

Theme: Persons can live responsibly, responsively, and decisively.

Selected major points: (1) Schooling can be a major force for providing settings where persons can learn to make intelligent decisions, become involved in worthwhile activities, and interrelate in human ways with their fellows. (2) Assumptions and definitions integral to the ideas in subsequent chapters are introduced.

As you read: (1) Think about the concept of the process-oriented person. With what aspects of our description do you agree or disagree? (2) Read the definitions carefully and then browse through the rest of the book to see where the terms are developed more fully.

Education has a dual purpose: (1) to help persons develop internal qualities necessary to meeting the problems of living and of life, and (2) to enable individuals to gain the moral courage and stamina to carry out what they perceive to be their own commitments in relation to themselves and others. The schools are successful to the degree that they assist the young in acquiring the intellectual appetite to achieve wisdom necessary to fulfill their visions and fortitude to move in paths mutually beneficial to self and others.

Current literature is replete with ideas relative to helping the person live more "humanistically." Yet those responsible for educating youth frequently lack the skill to help persons deal with the complex concepts which emerge when the emphasis is upon the individual within a society and the mutually enhancing benefits which can accrue when the dynamic interplay of the person and society are acknowledged.

Since schools are responsible to the public, they must be responsible for their expenditures of time, money, and resources in terms of what happens to children and youth. A need exists, therefore, for schools not only to teach low level cognitive skills for which procedures of accountability are easily outlined, but also to teach and obtain feedback on concepts which are more demanding and related to the realities of life.

The remainder of this chapter outlines a view of persons who are simultaneously equipped to develop themselves and to contribute to the society of which they are part. The person who can engage in both of these processes we have chosen to call "process-oriented."[1] Following the view of the person are statements of basic assumptions about schooling as it relates to the person. Finally, the reader is introduced to terms used frequently in the book.

Toward Process-Oriented Persons

Persons can live fully, creating and recreating their own peculiar human qualities or they can live with only a very partial awareness of what they can do with the stuff of life. The opportunities which make up the potential of each person's existence become available as the person becomes aware that he can act responsibly, decisively, and responsively within the setting that he finds himself. Too frequently persons are duped into believing that they can do little to control their feelings, behavior, and actions. These authors believe that persons can obtain a certain amount of control over their environment and can live lives characterized by continuous growth in basic human qualities. What kinds of qualities might a process-oriented person exhibit?

---

1. Throughout the book, the process-oriented person is the basis for the curricular suggestions. It should be noted that many terms are used as synonyms for this person and for the curricular recommendations. For example, "process-oriented personal qualities," "process skills," "a living-based curriculum," "a curriculum based upon basic human functions" are among the terms used.

First, the process-oriented individual has a fully developed range of perceptual skills. He sees what others see—and much more. Because his perceptions are accompanied by faith in what can be, the process-oriented person has a friendliness to the unknown as well as sharp vision relative to what is. Consequently, his perceptions and observations are usually rich and complex. Carpenter has indicated that it is observation that teaches—not experience.[2] Persons differ because they have different ways of perceiving, selecting, classifying, and patterning reality. The process-oriented person wonders about his observations and is not driven by a persistent need for stability.[3]

Complexity of vision adds depth, richness, and awe to life. The person's perceptions come not only through his eyes but also through touch, sound, taste, and smell. He has the ability to utilize a wide-angled lens at times for breadth of perspective, but he can also use a microscope to get depth and detail. Because of this wealth of perceptions and the colorful blends and mixes he gets when perceptions are placed in juxtaposition the process-oriented person is simultaneously creative and misunderstood. His perceptions are much more extensive and unusual than his less process-oriented counterpart. The person takes in not only the beauty of the single rose but also the patterning, color, and fragrance of the setting from which the rose was plucked.

Second, the process-oriented person tilts his life toward others in order that they may receive what he wishes to give.[4] Contrary to much contemporary thinking and writing, he considers the good of others as very critical. His life is a constant reaching out, tilting toward, and contributing to the well-being of others. The giving person is aware that his gifts must be appropriate to the needs of others; therefore, he gives with an awareness of the total context and the probable readiness of the receiver to be receptive to what he is offering.

The person is aware that when there is no readiness to receive a gift or when an inappropriate gift is extended, the humanness of both the giver and the receiver may be lessened. Thus, persistent questions of the process-oriented person are: In what direction am I tilting? Who is tilting toward me? What gifts shall I give and take in order to make worthwhile contributions in my own living?

---

2. Edmund Carpenter, *They Became What They Beheld,* photography by Ken Heyman (New York: Ballantine Books, 1970), pages not numbered.

3. For a discussion of wonder as it relates to observation, see Cornelis Verhoeven, *The Philosophy of Wonder: An Introduction and Incitement to Philosophy,* trans. Mary Foran (New York: Macmillan, 1972).

4. For a discussion of the nature of giving, see *ibid.,* pp. 166–71. Verhoeven discusses the nature of the giver, the receiver, and the gift. Among his points is the notion that the giver of a gift is present by the giving and in the gift. A gift has value when it has meaning for the recipient.

Third, the process-oriented person is an acting individual. His stimuli, knowledge, and sensitivities are constantly transformed into new visions, dreams, and ultimately actions. His behavior is purposive.[5] His perceptions may become structured so that they provide information upon which to build a path to achieving ends—ends primarily focused upon the good of others. Since, as we indicated earlier, the process-oriented person perceives richly, his actions transcend ordinary courses of behavior. He does what other persons do—and more! Because he has gained a reasonable amount of control of himself, and to some extent his environment, he is able to transcend expectations both in terms of his present behavior and his future planning. His actions are full of the unanticipated, unexpected, and the unpredictable. Persons do not see the variety of factors which he takes into account in his performance.[6]

In addition to transcending what is, the process-oriented person has a capacity to transform his data so that his responses are cloaked in meaningfulness. In other words, the process-oriented person is oriented to the depths of reality even though he may be able to see beyond it. Consequently, his responses serve as a linkage between the most pressing need of the existing situation and the most worthwhile visions that those persons within the situation hold. Catalyst, yet sustainer, the process-oriented person serves as a bridge between the mundane, fragmented, and trivial aspects of life and the image of what may be.

Fourth, the process-oriented person is aware of a cauldron of possibilities, only a small fraction of which are visible. Because of the vastness of the perceptual powers of this person and the transforming and transcending powers which he possesses, at a given moment a minute portion of this person's internal processes are observable. He cannot possibly speak of all his inward images. Thus, the principle of interiorization is critical to the understanding of the process-oriented person. Although he is open, sharing of himself, and communicative, the explosion of possibilities which he sees in each day means that much of him is hidden from the astute observer's eye.

Fifth, the process-oriented individual operates on the assumption that he is the best monitor of his own behavior. Although he may seek the opinions of others, he is not overly concerned about their approval. He resents regulations or standards imposed upon him for which he can see little reason. However, when allowed to determine his own goals,

---

5. That purposive behavior is part of process is discussed in Terry Borton, *Reach, Touch, Teach: Student Concerns and Process Education* (New York: McGraw-Hill, 1970), p. 76.

6. Although we are dealing here with persons who transcend, Amitai Etzioni discusses social units which transcend in *The Active Society: A Theory of Societal and Political Process* (New York: Free Press, 1968), pp. 32–34.

to regulate the use of his own time, and to establish his own relations with others, the process-oriented person thrives.

Sixth, the process-oriented person flourishes in an environment in which his peculiarly human qualities are used for the enhancement of others. He receives his richest satisfaction from the realization that, not only does the world contribute to him, but also that he can interact in mutually enhancing ways with the persons in his world.

Finally, the process-oriented person lives a life characterized by flair, humor, and ease. He has learned to accept life with its exciting dimensions so that each day possesses for him the elements of a new poem to be written, a new story to be told, a new view to be shared, a new encounter with a person to be loved. Because of his intense excitement about life, the process-oriented person invites others to join in the search for making life more full of meaning for self and others.

Basic Assumptions about
Persons and Schooling

If we accept the view of the person just described, then the tasks facing the schools may be different than if the person is not highlighted or if an alternative view of the person is held. The assumptions which are critical and peculiar to this work are now briefly discussed.

The person and curriculum development

Inherent in our view of the person is the concept that man is a dynamic organism capable of deciding, becoming involved, and interrelating with his fellows in humane ways. Although alternative views of the person exist, we are concerned about the dynamic elements in a person's nature and what the school can do to facilitate their development. It is assumed that the curriculum takes special directions when attention is given to the inner dynamics of persons and how these affect individual and interdependent efforts.

The school as one influence

We recognize that the school constitutes only one source of influence upon the student. Since the person is a dynamic being, always interacting with his environment and interconnecting his perceptions, it is difficult to describe cause and effect relationships for the process-oriented person. The school, however, can delineate areas in which it feels it can make major contributions to the life of the student and those in which it can make only minor contributions. The school can play a major part in teaching the qualities of the process-oriented person. How the person applies these qualities to many aspects of living within such institutions as the family or the church may be out of the purview of the school.

Communication as foundation

Communication, unlike many of the skills discussed in this work, is an *observable* process and as such is foundational to this book. Communication, both verbal and nonverbal, is the vehicle through which information is gathered about the other processes. It is the process by which persons acquire new skills and also the channel for recording what is transpiring between an individual and his environment. This information provides the bases for next steps in curriculum planning.

Furthermore, the communication process as discussed in this book is *inter*active and *trans*active. Communication is *not* seen primarily as a *re*active process. Transactive communication occurs when persons who interact with each other feel that they can control their destinies, at least to some degree. Transactive communication can take place between teacher and child, child and child, child and group, and teacher and group. Obviously if parents, community workers, aides, and others are brought into the classroom, transactive rather than reactive communication can be encouraged. Through the communication process teachers can begin to gather information about what students have learned in their experiences in settings designed to encourage growth in process-oriented skills.

Reality and curricular decisions

Since communication is foundational to the curriculum ideas proposed, realities as they exist in the moment of now provide one base for curricular decisions. We are calling the perception of reality feedback; and it is this coding of reality in diaries, category systems, or coding procedures that provides the material for curricular decisions. The assumption that feedback is critical to curricular decision making allows the person's common and idiosyncratic behaviors to emerge and be utilized in planning next steps in the curriculum development process.

Curriculum and teaching

Curriculum and teaching are closely interrelated. Teaching is concerned with the moment of now in the teaching-learning situation, whereas curriculum includes the anticipatory and retrospective aspects of teaching-learning as well as the moment of now. Teaching has to do with how the teacher provides learning opportunities for what she wants to happen and accounts for the unanticipated. Teaching also takes place when teachers record on-the-spot happenings in the classroom in order to plan for next steps. Curriculum development takes place when, in retrospect, the teacher analyzes her on-the-spot feedback, couples it with her own goals, and plans new sets of learning opportunities.

What we have been saying might be diagrammed roughly as shown in figure 2-1.

FIGURE 2–1. *Relation of Curriculum to Teaching*

Time (as seen on a continuum)	Factor	Curriculum	Teaching
Anticipation	Thinking about what one expects or desires to happen	X	
	Thinking about what will actually happen	X	
Moment of now	Providing learning opportunities for what one wants to happen	X	X
	Accounting for the unexpected	X	X
	Recording what is actually trans-piring in the setting	X	X
Retrospection	Analyzing on-the-spot feedback	X	
	Planning new learning oppor-tunities based upon feedback and purposes and goals	X	

Basically, those concerned about curriculum and teaching need to answer the following questions:

What should be the planned happenings in the classroom?

How does one establish the setting so that the student can participate in his knowing and that unplanned as well as planned events can occur and be accounted for?

How does one achieve feedback about what is occurring in the classroom?

What does one do with the information one gathers from answering the above questions?

The concept of match

A curriculum proposal should possess a match between the view of the person upon which the proposal is built, the recommended teaching-

learning environment or activities, and the suggested research and evaluation procedures. In this work obtaining feedback relative to what is
happening in the classroom is the link between what is proposed in the
curriculum design and what actually transpires in the classroom. Obtaining feedback is also a major tool recommended for research and
evaluation procedures.

Constant refinement

Curriculum designs demand constant development, refinement, implementation, and testing. Because the curricular ideas in this book are
built upon a view of the person which considers his complexity as well
as his simplicity, developing a tight curricular design is difficult.

School systems, state departments of instruction, and parents are
asking educators to work out systems of reporting and appraising what
is happening in schools. When a school moves from a curriculum focused upon the separate subjects to curricular foci such as the ones we
are advocating, the accountability procedures may be difficult to establish. Many of the procedures employed in other types of curricular
designs cannot be transferred to our foci. This book is an attempt to set
forth ways to approximate knowledge relative to the curriculum thrust
proposed and ultimately to gain more refined knowledge when the
person in all his complexity is considered as central to curriculum designs.

Introduction to Terms

Certain terms are now briefly introduced. Fuller development of them
is found in subsequent chapters.

Three components of the book should be kept in mind. First, there
is a cluster of skills necessary to the process-oriented person. These
skills are considered in terms of their qualities and also in terms of what
the schools can do to provide opportunities for their learning. The skills
discussed in this work are *decision making, involvement,* and *peopling.*

A second cluster of concepts involve overlays on the first concepts.
This second cluster is critical to, but separate from, the skills of deciding,
involving, and peopling and is treated as it relates to these skills. These
concepts are *knowledge, communication,* and *social system.*

A third group of terms is useful in understanding the procedures and
setting of the book. These terms are *curriculum, feedback, context,* and
classroom setting.

Decision making

In this work, the concept of decision might be considered to parallel the question, "*What* shall I do?" Decision is defined as a purposeful act which takes place after the consideration of alternative courses of action and culminates in a cut from a previous course of action and the inception of new or altered actions. Decision is considered a basic skill of the process-oriented person because inherent in it is the concept that the individual can act upon his environment rather than only be acted upon by it.

Involvement

The concept of involvement as used in this book ordinarily parallels the question, "*How* does the person carry out what he decides to do?" In looking for answers to the question of *how,* the authors propose that involvement can be seen in such factors as the degree of intensity a person brings to the task, the amount of time he spends at it, and the number of times he returns to it. Involvement is seen as related to commitment which represents the long-term and ultimate purposes of the person. Involvement is the path by which commitments are achieved.

Peopling

Peopling is a term coined by the authors to answer the question, "*Why* should persons exist?" Peopling also answers the why question of the curriculum prototype being proposed. Basically, a person is peopling when he is fully "with it" in his relations with others—when he utilizes all his faculties in responding to or initiating communication with another, and when his full awareness of himself enables the other person to attain a heightened self-awareness. Peopling is interaction among persons resulting in new truths, new insights, new positive feelings, or constructive and possibly collaborative action for the persons involved in the act.

Knowledge

In the plan of the book, knowledge is an overlay of the skills just listed. Knowledge consists of schemes for interpreting information. These schemes may be ones which have been codified by scholars in a given field or they may be individual maps developed by individuals in order to obtain meaning for their own lives. Knowledge is a broad term which can have a range of meanings from information in a narrow sense to the application of clusters of information or wisdom.

Communication

In this work, communication is the vehicle through which information and feedback about persons are obtained. Communication is also an overlay on the skills of decision making, involvement, and peopling. Thus, communication is critical in terms of procedure, methodology, and curricular outcomes. Communication is the sharing of meaning both verbally and nonverbally through gesture, facial expression, and silence. Close in definition to terms such as service and community, these aspects of communication are important in our use of the term.

Social system

Another overlay on the skills of decision making, involvement, and peopling, the term social system refers to bonds among persons brought on by formal obligations, legal contracts, mores, customs, or traditions. Social system differs from peopling in that peopling deals more with informal relations. In addition, peopling has the potential for boundary-breaking behavior whereas social system applies primarily to what assists a society in achieving stability and cohesiveness. Inherent in the concept of social system as used by these writers is the aspect of humanity's common abode which necessitates attention to the systematizing of social policy.

Curriculum

Curriculum refers to the art of planning for, implementing, and gathering data on programs for children, youth, and adults. As used in this book, curriculum is an active word denoting a total process. Our view of curriculum is based on a view of the person as moving, dynamic—process-oriented. This concept of the person or the dynamic elements of people are frequently referred to as curricular priorities or simply priorities. Although curriculum frequently denotes the planned activities for learners, our view includes the planned activities or the planned environment, the view of the person from which the activities emanate, and the evaluation and research procedures. Feedback is an integral part of research and evaluation plans.

Curriculum also can be considered in terms of its time dimensions: (1) what happens prior to teaching or before the student becomes part of the classroom setting; (2) what happens when the student is engaging in the teaching-learning act; and (3) what the teacher does in evaluation and research as a result of the learner's encounter with his environment.

Context

Context refers to the interrelated aspects of the environment that an individual experiences. Context may be amorphous and undifferentiated or it may be smaller, less complex, and more structured for specific purposes. The concept of context, environment, or social setting is critical since the assumption is made that the individual is in constant interaction with persons, materials, and ideas within the setting. The individual both affects and is affected by the context.

Classroom setting

One type of context is the classroom setting. The classroom setting includes any context or environment in which the child or youth, in cooperation with those responsible for his schooling, considers and acts upon the following toward developing qualities of a process-oriented person: (1) engaging in activities; (2) achieving feedback; (3) reflecting upon the meaning of what transpired for the person's life in (1) and (2); and (4) designing new purposes, goals, and activities. A context can be specifically planned to teach a given quality, or it can be selected from existing contexts because it seems to possess the ingredients necessary to teaching a given quality.

Classroom setting includes (1) that arrangement of the environment designed for the child or youth to gain multiple and interrelated concepts, and (2) those contexts designed for more specific and specified learnings. In many instances the classroom setting includes spaces outside the immediate school or classroom, as when the youth engages in a work-study program outside the school or the child makes a trip to a doctor's office with the purpose of learning about the work of a physician.

Feedback

Feedback is the information gathered through observing and recording in diary-fashion or on previously developed observational instruments or guides. Feedback ordinarily refers to the information gathered at the moment a process is occurring, but the term can also be used to describe information which is gathered after reflective thought for the purpose of evaluating past actions and future direction. In this work feedback is viewed as information that facilitates broadening perspectives and opening new possibilities. It is *not* an element in a closed system.

Consideration is next given to the *what, how,* and *why* of human existence—decision making, involvement, and peopling. The three chapters of part two deal with theoretical analyses of these topics.

Suggestions for Further Reading

Argyris, Chris. "Alternative Schools: A Behavioral Analysis." *Teachers College Record* 75: 429–452, May 1974.

Association for Supervision and Curriculum Development, *The Way Teaching Is.* Washington, D.C.: The Association and the Center for the Study of Instruction, National Education Association, 1966.

Berman, Louise M. *New Priorities in the Curriculum.* Columbus: Charles E. Merrill, 1968.

————. "Not *Re*acting But *Trans*acting: One Approach to Early Childhood Education." *Young Children* 28: 275–82, June 1973.

Berman, Louise M. and Jessie A. Roderick. "The Relationship between Curriculum Development and Research Methodology," *Journal of Research and Development in Education* 6: 3–13, Spring 1973.

Borton, Terry. *Reach, Touch, and Feel: Student Concerns and Process Education.* New York: McGraw-Hill, 1970.

Bussis, Anne M. and Edward A. Chittenden. *Analysis of an Approach to Open Education Interim Report.* Princeton, New Jersey: Educational Testing Service, August 1970.

Carpenter, Edmund, and Ken Heyman, Photographer. *They Became What They Beheld.* New York: Ballantine Books, 1970.

Dubin, Robert. *Theory Building.* New York: Free Press, 1969.

Elliott, David L. *Beyond "Open" Education: Getting to the Heart of Curriculum Matters.* Urbana, Ill.: ERIC Clearinghouse on Early Childhood Education, 1971.

Ellul, Jacques. Trans. C. Edward Hopkin. *Hope in Time of Abandonment.* New York: Seabury Press, 1973.

Fauré, Edgar and others. *Learning to Be: The World of Education Today and Tomorrow.* Paris: United Nations Educational, Scientific, and Cultural Organization, 1972.

Hawkins, David. "What It Means to Teach." *Teachers College Record* 75: 7–16, September 1973.

Hyman, Ronald T., ed. *Approaches in Curriculum.* Englewood Cliffs, New Jersey: Prentice-Hall, 1973.

McClure, Robert. *The Curriculum: Retrospect and Prospect.* Seventeenth Yearbook of the National Society for the Study of Education. Chicago: University of Chicago Press, 1971.

Rathbone, Charles H., ed. *Open Education: The Informal Classroom.* New York: Citation Press, 1971.

Rubin, Louis J., ed. *Life Skills in School and Society.* 1969 Yearbook. Washington, D.C.: The Association for Supervision and Curriculum Development, 1969.

Schrag, Francis. "Teaching/Healing: The Medical Analogy." *Teachers College Record* 72: 594–604, May 1971.

Squire, James R., ed. *A New Look at Progressive Education.* 1972 Yearbook. Washington, D.C., Association for Supervision and Curriculum Development, 1972.

Suppes, Patrick. "The Place of Theory in Educational Research." *Educational Researcher.* 3: 3–10, June 1974.

Travers, Robert M. W., ed. *Second Handbook of Research on Teaching.* A Project of the American Educational Research Association. Chicago: Rand McNally, 1973.

Verhoeven, Cornelis. Translated by Mary Foran. *The Philosophy of Wonder: An Introduction and Incitement to Philosophy.* New York: Macmillan, 1972.

Yamamoto, Kaoru, ed. *The Child and His Image: Self Concept in the Early Years.* Boston: Houghton Mifflin, 1972.

part two

Deciding,
Becoming Involved,
and Peopling

Deciding, becoming involved, and dealing with persons—these are the *what, how,* and *why* of living. Yet how little we know about these processes and how inadequate is our attention to them in schooling. Because of our convictions that these processes need more explicit attention in the schools, we suggest why the skills are important, point out the need for an emphasis on each of these skills, define them, and explicate behaviors a person might exhibit who possesses skill in these areas. In addition, we deal with each of these three processes as it relates to other basic process skills of communicating, knowing, and dealing with social systems.

The three chapters which follow contain insights derived from a variety of fields in addition to education. In essence, they are written in order to provide the schools with background in certain concepts which need highlighting. The chapters are primarily philosophical and substantive in their orientation. For application of the concepts, readers should see the chapters with the some foci in part four. For example, the theoretical chapter on Decision is chapter 3. Application of the principles discussed can be found in chapter 11.

3

Decision:
The What of
Living

Theme: A person's decisions to a large extent determine who he is and what he will become.

Selected major points: (1) This chapter presents a philosophical framework for viewing the decision-making process. (2) Decision is closely linked to processes of communicating, knowing, and dealing with social systems. (3) Decision-making skills can be taught in the classroom. See chapter 9 for specific examples of application.

As you read: (1) This chapter presents a number of critical points about decision. With which ones do you agree? Disagree? (2) At what ages do you think each of the concepts about decision should be highlighted? (3) Do you agree that decision should be a major focus in school programs?

The power to make decisions is one of the person's most human qualities. If humanity has the ability to decide, then what it has been, what it currently is, and what it will ultimately become is to a large degree determined by its decisions. Indeed, so powerful is the concept of decision that the prominence given in educational circles to such qualities as abilities, learning, or intelligence may lessen as those concerned about persons become aware that it is primarily a person's decisions that determine what he is.[1]

A person can intervene in the course of events because of his ability to pinpoint, play with, and evaluate alternative courses of action. The nature of decision is of such significance in the course of affairs that Dubos has commented, "Trend is not destiny."[2]

Despite the fact that human decision is a major factor in life, students of human behavior have paid relatively little attention to it. For years persons with an existential turn of mind have extolled the concept of decision, but few have probed it systematically and in detail. For example, in describing the work of Kierkegaard, Kaufmann says, "Ethics is for him not a matter of seeing the good but of making a decision."[3] In other words, studying decision is more important than studying the ethical.

Even though the significance of decisions has been stressed, students at any level seldom find planned experiences to help them make more effective decisions. They seldom have the chance to consider the impact of the concept that a person ultimately, at least partially, determines his own present and future.

Obviously, no man is an island, and decisions are affected by circumstances outside one's self. But one always has a certain degree of control over his attitudes. Although the person may not be able to control floods, wars, pestilences, food shortages, and moral weakness in high places, he can determine his stance when these circumstances prevail. For example, consider the attitude of Frankl, who survived not only with life, but also with new insights that would be a boon to many, the experiences of a concentration camp.[4] Consider the stance of the millions of Africans facing severe food shortages, or the many inhabitants forced by disease, death, or a major move to build a new life. These persons face the options of falling into despair or shaping and creating attitudes and values which enable them to find new meanings in life. Both of these options involve the decision process.

Although the person can at least choose his attitudes and values in

1. For a discussion of the necessity of considering decision when dealing with children, see Rudolf Dreikurs, Bernice Bronia Grunwald, and Floy C. Pepper, "Never Underestimate the Power of Children," *Intellectual Digest* 2:54–56, June 1972.

2. René Dubos, *A God Within: A Positive Philosophy for a More Complete Fulfillment of Human Potentials,* (New York: Charles Scribner's, 1972), p. 291.

3. Walter Kaufmann, ed., *Existentialism from Dostoevsky to Sartre* (New York: Meridian Books, 1956), p. 17.

4. See Viktor E. Frankl, *Man's Search for Meaning: An Introduction to Logotherapy* (New York: Simon and Schuster, 1959).

a universe in which there is much chance or contingency, the person needs to learn to deal with the problem of choice, or he makes himself less than fully human. According to Bugental, "Where there is no uncertainty, there is no choice."[5] The person does not live unto himself, either in terms of forces of the universe or in terms of his relationships with his fellows. Decision, therefore, is coupled with a sense of interdependence which makes the person simultaneously humble because he cannot control all, and proud because he can have some voice in decisions affecting himself and others.[6]

Decision in Schooling

Basically persons must learn to live with themselves. The focus of schooling must be, therefore, to assist persons in understanding themselves in relation to their world. From that self-understanding might evolve self-generated activity based upon the values, attitudes, and manner of decision making one comes to see in oneself and the changes one wishes to make in the decision process.

Two assumptions need to be highlighted when decision becomes an integral part of schooling: (1) persons must learn to make decisions with integrity, and (2) persons must learn to make decisions with kindness realizing the basic worth of all persons. If consideration is not given to the development of persons who possess a basic honesty toward themselves and others, then qualities of maneuvering, role playing, and a lack of internal consistency may be fostered. If concern is not shown for the development of kindness, then we may encourage youth to possess a sturdy sense of individualism which may exclude concern for others.[7] Our position is that a sense of integrity must be coupled with an inner sense of kindness, of feeling that everyone is worth doing things for.[8]

Thus, a major purpose in discussing decision is to open up the area to those who have given little attention to this fundamental human process and to attempt to right current erroneous conceptions. A second reason is that a person makes himself through his decisions. He not only must understand his own decision-making process, but he also must realize the vitality that the process gives to the ongoingness of life. The

5. J. F. T. Bugental, *The Search for Authenticity: An Existential-Analytic Approach to Psychotherapy* (New York: Holt, Rinehart and Winston, 1965), p. 196.

6. For a discussion of the need for interdependence, see Madeleine L'Engle, "The One-Winged Chinese Bird," *Childhood Education* 50:266–73, March 1974.

7. For a discussion of integrity and kindness as "intrinsic goods," see Barrows Dunham, *Ethics Dead and Alive* (New York: Alfred A. Knopf, 1971), pp. 138–51.

8. *Ibid.*, p. 10.

quality of one's living is contingent upon the manner in which one makes both the major and minor decisions of life. What one decides not only has meaning for the behaver, but also for the world. It is the reflection that one gets of himself through the decisions he makes that reinforces certain behaviors and has a bearing upon future decisions. A third reason for the attention to decision making is to help persons establish a setting where decisions are not avoided, but made. Kaufmann talks about "decidophobia" or the fear of autonomy.[9]

The purpose of understanding and teaching decision, then, is to assist the person, with a context of integrity and kindness, to move from inept decisions to those which he prizes. The remainder of this chapter deals with specific concepts related to decision that invite further development and exploration.

The Nature of Decision

Thus far we have talked about the need for understanding the decision-making process. Now attention is directed to the nature of decision— some of its components and characteristics.

Defining decision

Decision comes from the Latin *decidere*, meaning literally to cut off. In the French the derivation is from *de* (down) and *cidere (caedere)* (to cut). According to Kaufmann, the root is the same as deciduous, meaning "to fall off."[10] Basically, the concept of "taking a plunge," cutting off, breaking, characterizes the meaning of decision making. Our assumption is that the process is one which has its inception in the birth of an idea or the initiation of an action and terminates in a cut or break which has the potential to change or actually changes the idea or the course of action.

If decision is a cut or a plunge, it is a purposeful, deliberate act. It is a mode of interacting with one's environment in which the individual assumes the responsibility as to whether he will act or be acted upon.

Not all decisions are observable nor are they communicated in words. This is true especially with mature and sophisticated persons who have learned to share only partially what is transpiring in their own thinking and feeling. If so much of the process of decision is felt but not spoken,

---

9. Walter Kaufmann, *Without Guilt and Justice: From Decidophobia to Autonomy* (New York: Peter H. Wyden, 1973), pp. 2–34.
   10. *Ibid.*, p. 3.

one of the tasks of the educator is to learn to gather information both through observations and inference about a person's decision processes in order to help him plan adequate contexts for learning.

Defining choice

Choice has been derived from words meaning to examine or test. According to Webster, choice is "the voluntary and purposive or deliberate action of picking, singling out, or selecting from two or more that which is favored or superior." It demands considering and acting upon alternatives.

Alternatives are paired or contrasted things, the selection of one resulting in the rejection of the other. Frequently, in common parlance, more than two things are in the situation. The concept of rejection, disallowance, and lack of pursuit must be possible among the alternatives, or else they are not truly alternatives.

Assuming that disallowance or rejection is inherent in the concept of decision, choosing takes place among alternatives. The root word of choose also means to taste or enjoy. Choosing, therefore, has an element of enjoyment accompanied by the exercise of free will and judgment. Choosing relieves the person of the tension that may be evident when equally attractive alternatives present themselves.

Decision could be a process which would have a high degree of rationality and predictability if it were not for the matter of contingency or chance. When complex alternatives are presented, a person can never possess all the information he needs to make an adequate decision—thus, contingency becomes a factor with which he must cope. Decision demands the highest of man's mental functioning, the sturdiest components of his emotional make-up, and the wisdom to know that much of life is a series of calculated guesses. We show this process in Figure 3–1. Obviously all decisions cannot be so neatly diagrammed. Usually the alternatives are not clear and therefore rejected alternatives may be only faintly visible to the person. Free will, choice, and alternatives usually characterize decision. These concepts, among others, are examined in the next section.

Decision and the Person

The qualities of the decision maker discussed here are derived from both research and theory related to decision and from insights gained from a number of studies related to decision in which the authors have been involved.

FIGURE 3–1. *The Process of Decision*

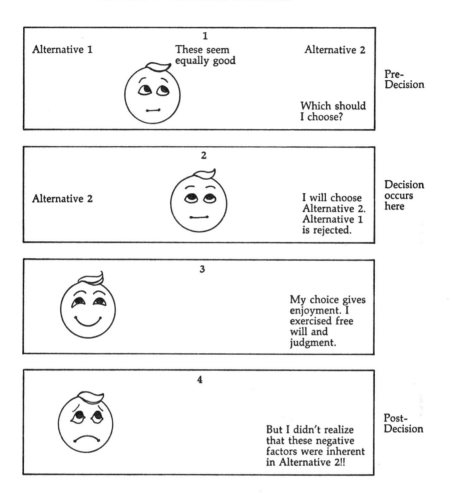

At the present time inadequate developmental literature on decision is available. Because of the gaps in our knowledge about decision, the qualities of the decision maker which are briefly discussed are goals toward which we might move but simultaneously test out in teaching the decision process. Each of the qualities probably can be placed on a continuum which suggests that the behaviors or qualities are such that the educational enterprise can begin considering them early in planning for children, yet they are also goals a mature adult might want to consider setting for himself.

The qualities discussed in this chapter and developed further in chapter 9 on suggestions for classroom practice are as follows:

1. The person is aware that he possesses free will within a context which is simultaneously freeing and yet binding, thus making decision an imperative of life.
2. The person is aware that as a decision maker he needs skill in identifying and dealing with alternatives.
3. The person learns to bring his total self to the decision-making process.
4. The person knowingly considers the context in his decision making.
5. The person utilizes pause as a means of refreshing and sustaining quality in his decision making.
6. The person assumes responsibility for the consequences of his decisions.

Free will

The person is aware that he possesses free will within a context which is simultaneously freeing and yet binding, thus making decision an imperative of life. The person has the unique quality of rational thought. Whatever the consequences of his thoughts, he has the ability to exercise a degree of freedom in his thinking. The results of his thoughts may or may not be acted upon, but he does have internal freedom which to some degree affects his outward behavior.

The Self as Locus. If the person possesses free will, then he is the locus for decision making. No matter how many factors are taken into account in making a decision, no matter what influence other persons have in the decision, no matter how great or how small the decision, the individual ultimately makes the decision and thus is bound by the consequences. The person can decide to be responsible or irresponsible. He decides whether his commitments will be to an idea, to a person or group of persons, or to an unfinished larger work.[11] The person decides whether to spend his life on each minute opportunity which comes along or to concentrate his efforts on some larger purpose which serves as a meaning-giver to his life.

Using the self as the locus of the decision is a learned process. Interestingly enough, the young child ordinarily sees himself as the locus of decision, but as he begins to become aware of the power of significant others to give and to withhold rewards, the child may lose some of his stalwart desire to maintain himself as the center of his world. Therefore, learnings which must accompany the concept of self as locus of decision are: (1) that the individual is a worthwhile person capable of increasing

---

11. Frankl, *Man's Search for Meaning*, p. 127.

skill in decision making; (2) that other persons are also worthwhile; and (3) that an individual's decisions should take into account the wishes and well-being of others in addition to his own well-being.

Contingency and Tragedy. One has only to observe persons around them to be aware that many are not rich decision makers because they feel that outward forces are the prime movers of their lives and that they have little control over their destinies. Contingency means that life has at any one point an abundance of possibilities and man at that point can "recognize only some finite part of this infinite array."[12] If we could know all the ramifications of every choice or every move we make in life, we would not have to face anxiety or discontent. What was predicted for a given course of action would be the outcome. However, since man can never know enough to foresee all contingencies, his choices become *a* determinant of consequences but not *the* determinant.[13] This is a critical point because responsibility is then seen as *a* determiner of what happens. Contingency, coupled with responsible planning and evaluation, becomes a fact of life resulting in an attitude which suggests, "These are decisions which I can make within this context; however, circumstances may change both my choices and the results of my choices."

Contingency is a powerful force in a person's life. Illness may wipe out plans for a trip. A person may serendipitously find a new bit of information which is useful to a project on which he is working. A second's look away from an active child can result in his death by a motor vehicle. A chance meeting in an airport can enrich the lives of two acquaintances. The factors which disrupt or enhance the most carefully designed plans are well known to all of us. Yet the concept that, "I can assume responsibility for much of my life and I can at least help shape my feelings, attitudes and values in the event of pleasurable or extenuating circumstances," gives the courage and joy necessary to live a responsive and responsible life.

The possibility always exists that the choice one makes at any moment in time results in consequences which are difficult rather than joyous to bear. When this occurs one feels the peculiarly human quality of tragedy. "The fully aware person can no more deny tragedy than he can deny gravitation."[14] Persons do not have the power to exclude tragedy totally from their lives. They do have the power, however, to determine how they will handle this phenomenon whether it occurs

---

12. Bugental, *The Search for Authenticity,* p. 153.
13. *Ibid.,* p. 23.
14. *Ibid.,* p. 151.

through some poorly made decision or through some act over which they have had no control.

Tragedy and joy—these emotions may accompany living up to the potential of one's humanness. To place oneself in a position where contingency is limited lessens the opportunities for basic human feelings.

Courage. "Decision making is a consideration of all possible alternatives and consequences. Otherwise it is secession from a thoughtful, courageous life," according to the Dodders.[15] The courageous life is one which examines the situation in which it finds itself and takes action which will bring the greatest good to the individual and the world for which he selects to be responsible.

According to Bugental, "Courage consists in the exercising of our choice and the taking of our responsibility while recognizing that contingency can overthrow our decision and reverse our best efforts."[16] If creative decision making is an aim in life, then one must develop courage to live in such a manner that one does not always select the easy choices and those with the less far-flung consequences.

Because man can be courageous and can take a stand when the context seems to so demand, "the real future is likely to be very different from any of the predictable futures. Men are never passive witnesses of events, because they are endowed with free will. Once motivated, they take a strong position against trends and change the course of events," according to Dubos.[17] A person can and will transcend himself in his decisions if he has the courage to make something of himself and the setting of which he is part.[18] Self-transcendence rather than self-actualization is a critical factor for making decisions which reach outward as well as inward.

Despite the contingencies in life and the resulting ambivalences as to the stance the person should take in his own deciding, he has far more freedom than he ordinarily utilizes. The courageous person looks at all possible alternatives and then acts in the best possible manner on the one he has freely selected.

Dealing with alternatives

The person is aware that as a decision maker he needs skill in identifying and dealing with alternatives. The turning point in the decision process is that

---

15. Clyde and Barbara Dodder, *Decision Making* (Boston: Beacon Press, 1968), p. 20.
16. Bugental, *The Search for Authenticity*, p. 26.
17. Dubos, *A God Within*, p. 288.
18. For a further discussion of this and related points see Frankl, *Man's Search for Meaning*, p. 175.

juncture at which a person decides to pursue one or more viable alternatives. The person therefore needs to develop increased skill in identifying alternatives, in committing himself to carry out or implement the selected alternatives, and in coping with the problem of the rejected alternative.

Identifying Alternatives.   As indicated in our definition, a critical aspect of decision is the identification of alternatives. Identification involves moral and ethical behavior on the part of the person. The person who is developing increased skill in decision has identified the values to which he gives high priority and which color both the identification and the execution of alternatives. He not only sees options but he sees the qualitative bases for the options. The decision maker develops predictive power in order to be able, at least partially, to ascertain the results of his selected alternative upon himself and others.

As a result of attention to the qualitative bases upon which decisions are made and the ability to predict the outcomes of decision, the person establishes modes of making routine decisions in order to devote more time and energy to critical decisions. What are routine decisions for a person will vary depending upon age, personal priorities and responsibilities, and the demands made upon his time. For example, selecting clothes to wear to work each day can be a routine decision to the adult. To a child learning the relationship between temperature, the kind of activity, and how one dresses, selecting clothes may be more than a routine. To a teacher the placement of certain materials in the classroom can be a routine decision. To a child, being included in decisions about where materials are located can be important to his development.

Adults can develop the capacity to predict long-term consequences of a given alternative. The child may need the opportunity to think through what will be the outcomes of the next hour if he pursues a given alternative. Dealing with alternatives is a learned process. Early experiences in this process followed by attention to identifying alternatives with increasing sophistication can aid the person in making routine decisions easily and critical decisions intelligently.

Commitment to the Selected Alternative.   The alternatives one sees in life are based on the openness of an individual's perceptual process, his values, and the mental act by which perceptions are processed. One of the factors meriting attention in the decision process is the concept of "playing for keeps."[19]

To decide not to pursue an opportunity may be the death of the possibility. To feel that he has caused this death may be more than the

---

19. Insight from Bugental, *The Search for Authenticity*, p. 45.

person can bear; therefore, several starving possibilities are allowed to be kept alive at a minimal level but none gets enough nourishment to thrive. Possibilities are frequently like flowers and weeds in an overgrown garden. All the flowers are allowed to crowd each other, but under the circumstances, none reaches its full beauty.

"Playing for keeps" means not only excluding certain alternatives in order to pursue others but also integrating one's knowing and acting upon the principles which are selected out from examined alternatives. Principle has no regulative effect until it is accepted.[20]

Rejected Alternatives. Until a person takes a stand and is willing to reject certain alternatives, he is not a sturdy decision maker. Dangling alternatives manage to keep a person from participating fully in executing the alternative he has selected. In turning one's back on rejected alternatives one contributes to his own well being and that of others.

Over a period of time the person begins to establish patterns of what he selects and rejects in life. The pattern may reflect a life of beauty, truth, wisdom, and love—these concepts taking many forms. Or the pattern may reflect a life of anger, distrust, dislike, and shoddy knowledge—these variables also taking many forms. Expression and rejection go hand in hand.

Total self

The person learns to bring his total self to the decision-making process. How difficult a task this is! The psychologically healthy person ordinarily has a myriad of opportunities and tasks competing for his time. How can one continue to care? to become involved? to make significant choices when so many good things are competing for time and energy? Perhaps the answer lies in acknowledging our ambivalent feelings, dealing with them as best we can, and then selecting the choices most appropriate for the particular time and carrying them out as wholeheartedly as possible.

Such an attitude might mean that the working parent gives to her children unstintingly of her time, energy, lovingness, and creativity, in the few hours a day she spends with them; that the writer becomes totally immersed in the thoughtful expression of his ideas during the time he carves out to give outward expression to his inward thoughts; that the student in an open-space classroom learns to tune out distractions as he concentrates with a friend on completion of an assignment.

Few of us have the opportunity to devote 100 percent of our time to one project—nor would we probably want it! A concern is, however, to

20. Dunham, *Ethics Dead and Alive*, p. 19.

insure that what one has selected to devote energies to at a given time receives the full complement of the person's energies and power. A second concern is that the individual continuously deals with the problem of ambiguity as it relates to the decision process and finds increasingly workable solutions for himself.[21]

The Complexity of the Process. Understanding the complexity of the decision process is necessary to the implementation of constructive decisions. Decision ordinarily is a culmination of a number of subprocesses operating simultaneously. Early literature on administrative practice attempted to define decision in terms of a series of steps ranging from identifying a problem, through considering the alternatives, to evaluating the outcome. As neat as some of the earlier statements were, observations of and discussions with persons in the process of decision indicate that many factors operate simultaneously. Basically, complex decision is a judgmental process, the cues for decision making being based upon nonverbal as well as verbal communications, multiple and simultaneous communication as well as singular communication, garbled as well as clear messages. How to assist persons in accepting the complexity of the process is one of the major problems in dealing with decision.

A related problem, therefore, is establishing with persons the development of autonomy of judgment as opposed to slavish dependence upon a series of logical steps. Although attention to the rational, step-by-step procedures of some descriptions of decision may be useful in introducing the process as a field of study, ultimately the student of decision needs to see the complexity of the process and the ramifications of considering decision only in unidimensional ways.

"Decision to . . .". How a person makes his decisions determines to a major extent the kind of life the person leads. As mentioned earlier, no life is so circumscribed by extenuating circumstances that the person does not have freedom at least to determine to a degree the attitudes and values which will govern his life.

The degree to which a person makes decisions to create something fresh, to participate in something new, or to integrate old understandings into a new framework partially determines the openness, the vitality, and the excitement he brings to his decision making. Persons

---

21. For a useful discussion of the problem of ambivalence as it relates to choice, see Kijo Morimoto with Judith Gregory and Penelope Butler, "Notes on the Context for Learning," *Harvard Educational Review* 43: 245–57, May 1973, esp. pp. 249, 250, 257.

need constantly to search for ways to make unique "decisions to . . ." as opposed to searching only for "freedom from. . . ."[22]

The "decision to . . ." concept is one which ordinarily opens new doors. Inherent in the concept is the notion that the person has searched for and considered alternative courses of action. As a result of his search, he decides to . . . and enters into that decision with all the eagerness and earnestness of which he is capable.

Evidences of "decision to . . ." behavior can be found in the person who culls the possibilities within his job and confines his major energies to those aspects of it which he feels he can carry out well. "Decision to . . ." behavior can be seen in the person who communicates in such a way that he builds upon the strengths of another person rather than elaborates upon his weaknesses. In person-building, "decision to . . ." behavior has a multiplying effect in that the decision to help release another person has the potential to increase the strength of the two persons involved in the encounter.

"Freedom from . . ." behavior does not necessarily have inherent in it the opening kinds of qualities found in "decision to . . ." behavior. The teenager may want freedom from his parents. The adult may wish freedom from his childhood fears. The older person may wish freedom from physical disturbances. To wish these and other "freedom froms . . ." can be productive if there is a "decision to . . ." inherent in one's desires. Lacking the "decision to . . . ," behavior can be closed and at best random.

The decision maker also faces the problem that it is easier "to make a talking decision than a doing decision."[23] A person can talk about quitting smoking, giving more time to his children, or learning a new skill. It is critical, however, that such verbalizations become reality or the person's integrity begins to wane and his own view of himself as an adequate decision maker is dissipated. The integrated person evidences congruency between his stated decisions and his actions.

Context

The person knowingly considers the context in his decision making. What a person is depends to a large extent upon his decisions and not on his conditions. A person knowingly can make at least a partial decision

22. For a discussion of this point, see Viktor Frankl, *The Doctor and the Soul: From Psychotherapy to Logotherapy,* 2d expanded edition, trans. Richard and Dora Winston (New York: Bantam Books, 1965), p. 142.

23. William Glasser, M.D., *The Identity Society* (New York: Harper & Row, 1972), p. 124.

about the degree to which he will allow the intertwining elements of time, space, persons, and ideas to influence his decisions.

Persons can have basically three outlooks relative to the influence of context upon decision making: (1) the person has relatively little decision-making power since the context largely influences his decisions; (2) the person is only minimally influenced by context and basically can make most major decisions; or (3) the person can knowingly consider factors in the context and determine the degree to which he will seek to accommodate to conditions or to change conditions.

In the first instance, persons are very conscious of rules, mores, principles, and customs that operate in the society and seek to make their decisions in accordance with what they see to be the stated or unstated expectations at the time.

In the second instance, persons see autonomy and individual freedom untempered by concern for others. Persons, then, make their decisions in line with what they see will bring them the greatest good. The needs and concerns of others are given low priority.

In the third instance, persons are aware of their individual autonomy but also of the rights and welfare of others. Persons then engage in more complex decision making, for consideration of conditions becomes part of the decision-making process. For example, some persons work better at various times of the day. Whether a person decides to follow his "body time" and work during his more productive periods may be partially contingent on other factors within the setting or context—the other demands of the job, family commitments, travel arrangements, regulations of the company for which he works, the number of other obligations, and so on. A person's decision may be to follow the dictates of his physical self as they relate to his work, or he may decide that the price of listening only to one's inner self is incompatible with other values. He then decides to accommodate to his "body time" on occasion and to accommodate to other demands at other times.

Pause

The person utilizes pause as a means of refreshing and sustaining quality in decision making. Pause may take many forms—engaging in the playful, exploring a new environment, practicing meditation, or participating in a diversion.

Decision making is ordinarily serious business. Unless one has learned to circumscribe his life so that few perceptions can enter, one has the problem of choosing the alternatives which appear worth an investment of energy. As soon as the matter of choice enters, one has the discomfort and feeling of ambiguity which frequently accompanies decision. To ease the discomfort, the decision maker can do a number of things. He can wear blinders so that he does not see the alternatives available to him; he can seek to negate his sense of caring; he can stifle the significance and worthwhileness of what appear to be the critical aspects of the decisions; or he can select what appear to be the best alternatives at the time and carry them out.

Once the decision has been made, playfulness assists the person in accepting it. The person cannot be a significant decision maker and not allow his own emotions to vent or he mutilates himself as a person. Pause allows for the purging and airing of the emotions without harming self or others. Pause can take the form of humor, or physical exercise, or utilization of mental processes unrelated to the points of decision. In any event it is a change of pace that gives pleasure and thus self-renewal to the decider.

Responsibility for consequences

The person assumes responsibility for the consequences of his decisions. Persons may make such small decisions that the consequences of them have little meaning for themselves or little bearing upon the lives of others. For example, a person can become so involved in the questions of, "What shall I wear?" or "Where shall I place this chair?" that questions such as "To whom shall I render service?" or "For what purposes shall I obtain a college education?" remain unanswered—and sometimes unasked. Thus, persons who wish to lead a productive, worthwhile life must see the need of making decisions of consequence. The consequential decision is one which has within it the seeds of responsibility.

Service and Decision. If one has chosen to be responsible to and for others, he probably has selected a life of service. One needs, then to decide on the balance of creative intake and the outreach which results in service. One needs to decide to whom he will render service. Life becomes a journey in which an individual's decisions may at times be to enrich himself and at other times to enrich others because of the overflowing nature of his own existence. Giving and receiving, creating and assisting others in their creativity, being involved and working with others on their involvements—a rhythmical pattern of inwardness and outwardness develops for the person who couples the decision-making process with an intent to be concerned about persons and to become deeply involved within the world that he finds himself. The person realizes values in "creative activity," or in giving; and in "experiential values"[24]

---

24. Frankl, *The Doctor and the Soul,* pp. 34, 35.

or in experiencing or receiving beauty, fullness, and higher meanings from life around him.

Accountability. In life a person must decide to whom he will be accountable—self, other persons, God or gods, family. Accountability serves to assist the person in seeing that his vision is becoming reality. Deciding to whom one will be accountable keeps the door open for constant consideration, evaluation, and revision of one's purposes. Such constant review assists the person in keeping living worthwhile and decisions in line with the vision he has established.

In addition to deciding to whom he will be accountable, the person needs to establish criteria for accountability and the modes of gathering information related to the criteria established. Basically, establishing adequate accountability procedures necessitates designating to whom one will be accountable, the intent of accountability, and data-gathering procedures.

Summary of qualities

What follows is a summary of some of the qualities of the person who is gaining decision-making skills as defined in the previous pages. These qualities are the ones from which characteristics of context are derived in chapter 9. The qualities or behaviors are also the bases for the suggestions for obtaining and recording feedback in the same chapter.

1. The person is aware that he possesses free will within a context which is simultaneously freeing and yet binding, thus making decision an imperative of life.
   a. The person realizes that he is the locus for decision making.
   b. The person takes into account in his decision-making problems of contingency and realization of possible tragedy.
   c. The person shows courage in taking action which brings the greatest good both to himself and the situation for which he selects to be responsible.
2. The person is aware that as a decision maker he needs skill in identifying and dealing with alternatives.
   a. The person identifies alternatives which reflect consideration of moral and ethical consequences.
   b. The person demonstrates a commitment to carry out the selected alternative.
   c. The person is willing to reject some alternatives in order to concentrate on others.

3. The person learns to bring his total self to the decision-making process.
   a. The person deals with the complexity of the decision process.
   b. The person makes decisions to . . . rather than only seeking freedom from. . . .
4. The person knowingly considers the context in his decision making.
5. The person utilizes pause as a means of refreshing and sustaining quality in decision making.
6. The person assumes responsibility for the consequences of his decisions.
   a. The person sees the consequences of his decisions as the reason for his existence.
   b. The person gives high priority to service in his decision making.
   c. The person determines to whom he will be responsible and the criteria for determining accountability.

Decision and Communicating, Knowing, and Social Systems

Integral to the processes of decision, involvement, and peopling are communicating, knowing, and dealing with social systems. The latter processes are not treated separately because of the interrelationships among them. Attention is therefore given to interrelationships, implications, and insights of decision to communicating, knowing, and dealing with social systems.

Communicating

Decision and communication are in a sense closely intertwined. Certain relationships among the two processes are next highlighted.

Communication as a Total Process. Communication is often seen as transmission of verbal messages. In this work, however, communication includes the total way in which persons relate to one another; therefore, communication is the verbal and nonverbal means of relating that exists among persons. Persons may feel that because they understand the language of another land, they can understand persons who communicate with them from that land. This is not often the case. The tilt of the head, the gestures of the hands, the rhythm of speech, the glances of the eyes—these and other factors all contribute to one's communication pattern. One needs to understand more than spoken language in terms of effecting good relations among persons.[25]

One of the obvious linkages between communication and decision is that if persons wish to understand others in terms of relating to them, then a decision must be made to consider the total person when communicating. It is not enough to work at communication only through the traditional channels of sender, receiver, and message. The decision maker must be acutely aware of the multiple strands of communication emitted both by himself and the person with whom he is communicating.

As the decision maker heightens his awareness of the process of communication he may become increasingly aware of the many facets of a person and the culture from which he comes. Decisions, therefore, must take into account the verbal and nonverbal behavior of other persons in light of their cultures.

If a person wishes to become skilled in communication, he should become involved with other persons.[26] One cannot learn six rules to relate to another person. Rather, the concept of participation followed by an analytical look at the communicative process may result in finer communication and ultimately greater decision-making skill.

Seen and Unseen.   If communication is a process that includes the total selves of two or more persons, it follows that the decision maker must include what is and what is not seen or heard. The visible and the invisible, the inward and the outward, the perceptions of persons representing various perspectives—all must be taken into account by the astute decision maker.[27] A person has a relationship to other persons, to himself, to his maker, to the total universe. His faith, rationality, and love influence his perceptions and thus his decisions. The person rich in his inner life may also be rich in his decision making.

Language.   Although we have indicated that communication is a total process which includes more than language, language *per se* contributes to the communication process. Persons see words on the printed page; they hear words on the radio; they see words on a billboard; they may

25. An anthropological view of the communication process is critical to the understanding of communication as used in this book. For further development of this view see Paul Byers and Happie Byers, "Nonverbal Communication and the Education of Children," in *Functions of Language in the Classroom,* ed. Courtney B. Cazden, Vera P. John, Dell Hymes (New York: Teachers College Press, Columbia University, 1972), pp. 3–31.

26. For a discussion of this point, ibid., p. 28.

27. For an elaboration of this point, see Gardner Murphy and Lois B. Murphy, *Asian Psychology* (New York: Basic Books, 1968), p. 75.

hear the words of a person without an awareness of the total being of the other person. Thus, a need exists to consider the significance of language in communication.

Language enables a person to transmit ideas or to hide or protect his thoughts.[28] In sharing with others, a person gives until meanings are adequate but communication ceases when no new meanings are required.[29]

Knowing

Among the critical processes having a bearing upon deciding is that of knowing. Knowing takes many forms. Brief consideration is given to knowing as it relates to deciding.

Forms of Knowing.   Knowing and knowledge production can be viewed from a variety of stances, many of them overlapping. We can deal with knowledge from the perspective of public and personal knowledge so ably discussed by Polanyi.[30] Public knowledge is what is found in the book, in public documents. Personal knowledge is derived from one's private logic and intuitive thinking.

Another way of viewing the problem of knowledge is through the framework established by Craig Wilson.[31] According to Wilson, we can view knowledge from the perspectives of "fact," "contested truth," and "open exploration."[32] The implications for decision of what Wilson says are that persons probably need to know the basis of knowledge for their decisions—which of the bases is predominant, and which is appropriate for different kinds of decisions.

Although the schools have traditionally given precedence to the teaching of public knowledge or to the study of the separate disciplines, currently many persons responsible for the education of youth are aware that emphasis solely on the exclusiveness of the various domains of knowledge is inadequate for the solution of many of life's problems. Consequently, there is a tendency to look at the overlap of the domains of knowledge and to show greater concern for the private logic and domain of knowing each individual brings to living.

---

28. Dean C. Barnlund, *Interpersonal Communication: Survey and Studies* (Boston: Houghton Mifflin, 1968), p. 2.

29. *Ibid.,* p. 3.

30. See Michael Polanyi, *Personal Knowledge: Towards a Post-Critical Philosophy* (Chicago: The University of Chicago Press, 1958). Also see Polanyi, *The Tacit Dimension* (Garden City, N. Y.: Doubleday, 1966).

31. L. Craig Wilson, *The Open Access Curriculum* (Boston: Allyn and Bacon, 1971), chapter 1.

32. *Ibid.,* p. 16.

For example, Rathbone, in discussing assumptions about knowledge held by open education advocates, includes the following:

> Knowledge is idiosyncratically formed, individually conceived, fundamentally individualistic. . . .
>
> Knowledge does not exist outside of individual knowers; it is not a thing apart. . . .
>
> Verbalization is not the only proof of the existence of knowledge. . . .
>
> Knowledge is not inherently ordered or structured, nor does it automatically subdivide into academic "disciplines." . . .[33]

For years Anshen, while realizing that there is a need for exclusive domains of knowledge, has also advocated the necessity of the unity of knowledge, of bringing cross-disciplinary concepts to bear upon problems. On this topic, she writes,

> The differences in the disciplines, their epistemological exclusiveness, the variety of historical experiences, the differences of traditions, of cultures, of languages, of the arts, should be protected and presented. But the interrelationship and unity of the whole should at the same time be accepted.[34]

Knowing and Uncertainty.   The point was made earlier that a person allows himself to be circumscribed by his environment when his decisions are determined by his knowledge. If a person needs full knowledge of a subject before he takes a leap, he fails to realize that the person is finite but participates in infiniteness. To the degree that the person goes beyond his finiteness with his faith, love, and rationality, he makes decisions which are filled with uncertainty but also decisions which are more human.

A person has to decide for himself how much uncertainty he can tolerate in his decision making. Learning to live with the consequences of decisions which do not turn out as intended is necessary if persons are to make leaps beyond the known in the decision process.

Wonder as a Key Factor.   The decision maker must simultaneously be earthy and heavenly in his orientation. To wonder about one's knowing allows one to penetrate more deeply into the core of what makes the

---

33. Charles H. Rathbone, *Open Education: The Informal Classroom* (New York: Citation, 1971), p. 102.
34. Ruth Nanda Anshen, "Introduction" in Ivan Illich, *Deschooling Society, World Perspectives* (New York: Harper & Row, 1970), p. xiii.

world and life. The decision maker who fails to give attention to wondering about his knowing may find himself groveling in the mundane and failing to give credence to the interrelationships in life. To wonder about the structure or possible structures of knowledge, to inquire why some knowledge seems to be discrete, isolated facts while other knowledge seems to fall into frameworks, to consider how one can move knowledge which appears to be shaky and uncertain to knowledge which begins to grow roots of certainty, to look at the modes of inquiry that appear appropriate for what one wants to know are the questions of the wondering person. We might consider: is the wondering person the more creative decision maker?

Deciding and social systems

The concept of decision is extremely critical to social systems. Based upon the assumption that it is possible to achieve some commonality of purpose, thinking, and action, social systems may succeed or fail depending upon how decisions are made, who makes them, how they are made visible, and how they are implemented. Although many kinds of societies can be found, implicit in what we are saying is a commitment to an open society, realizing that such a society is more difficult to operate effectively than a closed one.[35] An open society, despite its imperfections, is more in line with the personal characteristics deemed important than societies in which persons dwell together in unthinking and uncritical apathy.

Deciding What to Give to the Social System. Human social systems are dependent upon a rhythm of giving and taking. Maintaining existing institutions, wiping out obsolete institutions, and creating ones appropriate to the demands of the time are contingent upon citizens who are concerned about the common welfare as well as their own. Constant examination of institutions in light of the aims of one's society is necessary. The person needs to decide when to seek to change the purposes of society and when to seek to modify, eradicate, or create institutions.

At the present time many thoughtful persons are concerned about what the emphasis upon industrialization has done to the United States and to the world. Countries are beginning to reap both the benefits and

---

35. For a discussion of being open to the possibilities in a society, see Christopher Mooney, "Man and His Future," in *Projections: Shaping an American Theology for the Future,* ed. Thomas F. O'Meara and Donald M. Weisser (New York: Doubleday, 1970), pp. 27–48, p. 72. Also see Delmo Della-Dora and James E. House, eds., *Education for an Open Society,* 1974 Yearbook (Washington, D.C.: Association for Supervision and Curriculum Development, 1974).

the problems of the results of over- or under-industrialization. Humanity becomes a slave to its tools rather than tools becoming the handmaidens of humanity.[36] Persons concerned primarily about an industrialized society tend to allow others to make many critical decisions for them. Illich says, "Overconfidence in better decision making just hampers people's ability to decide for themselves and then undermines their belief that they can decide."[37]

There appears to be a need to reorganize certain human institutions so that persons have the opportunity to give. Assembly line factories are reorganizing so that persons operate in teams rather than singly. In this way the team can decide the quality of the product it wants to give. When a person merely works on an assembly line with little control over the product he creates, his capacity to give of himself to his work is stifled.

In the society in which there is some emphasis upon giving, it is necessary to be concerned about the diversity of gifts. Dubos writes:

> Diversity, not efficiency, is the *sine qua non* of a rich and creative human life.
>
> Since persons differ in their endowments and aspirations, they need different kinds of opportunities and surroundings for self-expression and creation. ... Diversity may cause the world to become somewhat inefficient and even inconvenient, but in the long run it is more important than efficiency and convenience because it provides the variety of materials from which persons and civilizations emerge and continue to evolve ... men are not completely free if they do not have options from which to select in order to create out of their potentialities the kinds of lives they desire and the achievements by which they would like to be remembered.[38]

In addition to diversity of gifts, it is necessary that the decision maker see alternatives. It has been said that without alternatives from which to choose there can be no altruism.[39]

In establishing what he can give to an institution the person must make use of his gifts and of his own unique forms of expression. At the same time he must be aware that collective activity is also necessary to creation.[40] To decide what is an appropriate balance of individual and

---

36. See Ivan Illich, *Tools for Conviviality,* World Perspectives, ed. Ruth Nanda Anshen (New York: Harper & Row, 1973).

37. *Ibid.,* p. 86.

38. Dubos, *A God Within,* p. 287.

39. Theodosius Dobzhansky, *The Biology of Ultimate Concern,* Perspectives in Humanism, ed. Ruth Nanda Anshen (New York: World, 1967), p. 88.

40. Edgar Fauré and others, *Learning to Be: The World of Education Today and Tomorrow* (Paris: United Nations Educational, Scientific and Cultural Organization, 1972), p. 150.

collective activity within human institutions is a concern of the individual interested in contributing to his society.

Deciding What to Take from the Social System. The concept that man is an unusual being, that he can have a part in shaping and changing his institutions must characterize the person if the society is to be healthy. When institutions are denigrated or the person sees institutions only as adding to his wealth or possessions, the institutions and eventually the larger society stand to lose.

In understanding the concept of the social system as it relates to one's decision about it, we might think about Verhoeven's concept of dwelling. Dwelling is an "attempt to establish and confirm identity."[41] Dwelling is an ethical term derived from the word *ethos* meaning "common abode" or "custom." "Ethics is the task of inhabiting the earth, giving and allowing oneself to be given a provisional identity. No one can, by his own efforts alone, give himself the identity, and nobody dwells alone."[42] Ethical obligation emanates from within as one contemplates, participates in, and seeks to encompass more of the outside in his dwelling.

Persons in what they take seek to create the ideal. Therefore, a person takes from institutions that which makes his abode more comfortable and enables him to establish himself as an individual with something to give to the world. What a person takes performs a dual function: (1) it helps the individual confirm himself, and (2) it helps institutions move in directions that seem fruitful to the individual.

At times this may mean the individual decides to reconsider the institutions in which he is involved to see whether major changes are in order. Current writers often advocate a totally new look at the problem of institutions because of their failure.[43] Not only must single existing institutions be renovated, but possibly a new conceptualization of institutions will emerge based upon a view of man as a deciding, involved, and peopling individual. For example, if the notion is accepted that each person is different, that he learns in different ways, that he responds to different kinds of stimuli, that he seeks different ends in life, that he responds to different types of persons, then a conceptualization of institutions will build upon these human qualities.

Limiting Circumstances. No matter how sophisticated the individual seeks to become in dealing with institutional development and change, be-

---

41. Cornelis Verhoeven, *The Philosophy of Wonder: An Introduction and Incitement to Philosophy* (New York: Macmillan, 1972), p. 137.

42. *Ibid.*, p. 140.

43. For example, see Dubos, *A God Within;* Illich, *Tools for Conviviality;* Marcus G. Raskin, *Being and Doing* (New York: Random House, 1971); Charles A. Reich, *The Greening of America* (New York: Random House, 1970).

cause of his very humanness, institutions will never be a perfect embodiment of the ideal. Limiting circumstances always hamper the realization and implementation of what appears to be the ideal. A person must learn to deal with these limiting factors. Dubos says, "... the logic of events must always yield to the arbitrariness of human choices. The willed future is always different from the logical future."[44]

In Retrospect

In this chapter attention has been directed to decision as a primary human quality which, because of its potential to help persons make more intentional leaps in their lives, should be given attention in school programs. It was pointed out that decision involves exercise of free will, treatment of alternatives, bringing to bear of the total person on the decisive act, need for flexibility in thinking and acting, necessity of pause, and responsibility for consequences. Decision was also discussed as it relates to communicating, knowing, and the social system.

In the next chapter, the *how* of human existence is considered. The nature of involvement is examined from the perspective of its need for study in school programs.

Suggestions for Further Reading

Bailey, Carol and Eleanor Haney. *Ventures in Decision.* Minneapolis: Augsburg, 1970.

Berman, Louise M. *New Priorities in the Curriculum.* Columbus: Charles E. Merrill, 1968.

Buber, Martin. Translated by Maurice Freedman. *A Believing Humanism: My Testament 1902–1965.* New York: Simon and Schuster, 1967.

Bugental, J. F. T. *The Search for Authenticity: An Existential-Analytic Approach to Psychotherapy.* New York: Holt, Rinehart and Winston, 1965.

Dodder, Clyde and Barbara Dodder. *Decision Making.* Boston: Beacon Press, 1968.

Della-Dora, Delmo, and James E. House, eds. *Education for an Open Society,* 1974 Yearbook. Washington, D.C.: Association for Supervision and Curriculum Development, 1974.

Dobzhansky, Theodosius. *The Biology of Ultimate Concern.* Perspectives in Humanism, ed. Ruth Nanda Anshen. New York: World, 1969.

Dreikurs, Rudolf, Bernice Bronia Greenwald, and Floy C. Pepper. "Never Underestimate the Power of Children." *Intellectual Digest* 2: 54–56, June 1972.

---

44. Dubos, *A God Within,* p. 218.

Drews, Elizabeth Monroe and Leslie Lipson. *Values and Humanity.* New York: St. Martin's Press, 1971.

Dubos, René. *A God Within: A Positive Philosophy for a More Complete Fulfillment of Human Potentials.* New York: Charles Scribner's, 1972.

Dunham, Barrows. *Ethics Dead and Alive.* New York: Alfred A. Knopf, 1971.

Engle, Shirley H. and Wilma S. Longstreet. *A Design for Social Education in the Open Curriculum.* New York: Harper & Row, 1972.

Fauré, Edgar and others. *Learning to Be: The World of Education Today and Tomorrow.* Paris: United Nations Educational, Scientific, and Cultural Organization, 1972.

Frankl, Viktor E. Translated by Ilse Lasch. *Man's Search for Meaning: An Introduction to Logotherapy.* New York: Alfred A. Knopf, 1955.

————. *Psychotherapy and Existentialism: Selected Papers on Logotherapy.* New York: Simon and Schuster, 1967.

————. Translated by Richard and Clara Winston. *The Doctor and the Soul: From Psychotherapy to Logotherapy.* New York: Simon and Schuster, 1959.

Fried, Charles. *An Anatomy of Values: Problems of Personal and Social Choice.* Cambridge: Harvard University Press, 1970.

Horowitz, Sandra and Louise M. Berman, ed. *Decision Making in Young Children: A Report of Research Findings. Part 1.* University Nursery-Kindergarten Monograph 2. College Park: University of Maryland, 1971.

Kaufmann, Walter, ed. *Existentialism from Dostoevsky to Sartre.* New York: Meridian, 1956.

Kaufmann, Walter. *Without Guilt and Justice: From Decidophobia to Autonomy.* New York: Peter H. Wyden, 1973.

Morimoto, Kiyo with Judith Gregory and Penelope Butler. "Notes on the Context for Learning." *Harvard Educational Review* 43:245–57, May 1973.

Poultney, Joan, Project Director and Others. *Decision Making in Young Children: A Report of Research Findings, Part 2.* University Nursery-Kindergarten Monograph 3. College Park: University of Maryland, 1970.

Rathbone, Charles H., ed. *Open Education: The Informal Classroom.* New York: Citation, 1971.

Shavelson, Richard J. "What Is the Basic Teaching Skill?" *The Journal of Teacher Education* 24:144–51, Summer 1973.

Sieber, Joan E. "Overcoming Secondary Ignorance: Learning to Be Uncertain." Research Memorandum No. 17, Stanford Center for Research and Development in Teaching, 1968. Mimeographed.

Stevenson, Carol A. *The Development of an Instrument to Examine Teacher Influence on Decision Making Behaviors of Children Ages Three to Five.* Center for Young Children Occasional Paper Thirteen. College Park: University of Maryland, 1973.

Terkel, Studs. *Working: People Talk About What They Do All Day and How They Feel About What They Do.* New York: Pantheon, 1974.

4

Involvement:
The How of
Living

Perspective on Chapter 4

Theme: The involved person has first-hand meaningful encounters with life.

Selected major points: (1) The person becomes involved because he desires meaningfulness, wishes to negate alienation, and tries to combat a surfeit of choice. (2) Since learners have a natural curiosity and can and should be active participants, schools should give attention to involvement. (3) Involvement is linked to communicating, knowing, and dealing with social systems.

As you read: (1) To what degree do you think involvement should be highlighted in the schools? (2) Read chapter 10, the companion chapter to this one. Which suggestions seem feasible in your setting?

The Need to Study Involvement

An individual faces many questions in the process of living, but the most basic questions he has to deal with are: What is my purpose in life?

and, How and to what degree shall I invest my energies in that purpose?[1] Each person must determine what he wants to do, what he needs
to do, and what he is capable of doing. Each person must also determine
how he will carry out that which he decides to do. As persons search
for answers to these questions, they need to become aware of and
develop their interests and desires in such a way that they derive a sense
of satisfaction for themselves and achieve a mode of interaction that
enables them to be " . . . creative, contributing members of society."[2]

Individuals who have identified a purpose in life and who have taken
steps toward its implementation are better prepared to become involved
or determine *how* they will pursue what they deem worthy of their
interests and efforts. In addition, these persons are more apt to interact
with others and the environment in such a way that the wholeness or
interrelatedness of elements is highlighted and fragmentation decreased.

Even though a person's tendency to find purpose in life is as natural
as is his tendency to become an involved and active participant in life,
the ability to determine focus for involvement and to identify those
aspects of the environment that help achieve a focus are not necessarily
natural. Cogent reasons for examining involvement are twofold: (1)
most persons require guidance in establishing involvement foci, and (2)
factors exist in the larger environment that tend to thwart and discourage individuals from becoming involved. Additional support for exploring involvement as a life process is found in current educational
concerns. A discussion of societal factors and educational concerns that
reinforce the need to study involvement follows.

Social Factors of Involvement

Meaningfulness in life, negating alienation, and combatting surfeit of
choice are among the social factors which influence a person's involvement. A brief discussion of each of these factors follows.

Desire for Meaningfulness. In their day-to-day experiences, some persons
feel that life is meaningless. They question whether opportunities for
interacting with the ideas, people, and materials of the environment are
worth their energies. If persons exert themselves in particular directions,
it is important to determine whether they derive meaning from and also
bring meaning to the endeavor.

---

1. Ideas in this discussion of man's need to determine purpose in his life were sparked
by Jonas Salk, *Man Unfolding,* World Perspectives, ed. Ruth Nanda Anshen, Vol. 46 (New
York: Harper & Row, 1972).
2. Ibid., pp. 51, 52.

Meaningfulness as used in this context derives from diverse experiences resulting in knowledge and feelings that enable a person to exercise some control over his destiny. Meaningfulness also emanates from in-depth interactions with others resulting in a better understanding of self and of the other as a unique person.[3] Meaning implies a sense of personal power resulting from interactions which contribute in various degrees to one's knowing and understanding himself and others. A mother who assumes leadership for a Girl Scout troop can experience meaningfulness so defined. An older child who regularly reads with younger children can also bring and find meaning in this experience.

Need for Negating Alienation. When life appears meaningless to persons, they sometimes become alienated from those persons with whom they formerly interacted and from those procedures and institutions in which they formerly engaged. Alienation in the sense of changing direction does not have to be considered negative or undesirable unless no attempt is made to become engaged in a new direction or a new purpose destructive to the self is selected. For example, consider the person who involves himself in a new field of study because he feels he has conquered the challenges of a prior career.

Combatting Surfeit of Choice. In addition to the chance of becoming alienated, the person in today's society faces the possibility of becoming involved in many endeavors at a surface and somewhat impersonal level. The surfeit of choice that multitudinous offerings present to a person might cause him to adopt a life-style devoid of intense feelings and depth experiences. Attempting simultaneously to watch a television program, listen to a conversation, and do a puzzle exemplifies behavior which, if encouraged and expanded upon, could result in a life of superficial interactions. The possibility of such behavior occurring further reinforces the need to explore how persons can be helped to live deeply, selectively, and purposefully.

If we support the assumptions that man desires to become involved by interacting with deep feeling and intent and that such involvement helps satisfy his need for fulfillment in life, it behooves us to consider certain predictions relative to the future. As elements of society become less permanent, personal life-styles will be characterized by less commitment and therefore fewer intense and enduring involvements.[4] How will a person function in the face of these conditions? What skills,

---

3. For a discussion of these and other dimensions or bases of meaning see Henry Nelson Wieman, *Man's Ultimate Commitment* (Carbondale: Southern Illinois University Press, 1958), pp. 298–99.

4. Alvin Toffler discusses this and other points related to it in *Future Shock* (New York: Bantam, 1971).

knowledge, and attitudes will he require in order to function creatively and fully in a context which already exists to some degree? We have suggested that societal factors can influence a person's involvement, but also that the larger context of society does not always encourage the kind of involvement that brings meaningfulness to life. These conditions imply that more thorough study of the concepts of involvement and commitment are necessary to help individuals who feel a sense of meaninglessness and alienation and who are faced with an ever-increasing rate of change in life to become involved to the degree they wish.

Educational concerns and involvement

Current literature on education lacks adequate evidence that involvement as it relates to curricular concerns has been carefully examined. Furthermore, the term involvement is widely used but often with little or no specification as to the implications for curriculum development. Other educational concerns which highlight the necessity for such study are presented next.

The Learner as Active Participant. Educators are urged to view education as a process in which the learner is an active participant and not a passive recipient. We are cautioned that learning is minimal where involvement is minimal. The drop-out is often viewed as one who withdraws because he sees neither reason nor opportunities for his becoming involved in school-related and school-sponsored activities. Exhortations or slogans are valuable for arousing interest and possibly even support for the importance of involvement in the learning process, but we must take the next step and discover and build the specifics which make these slogans operable in the learning situation.

Encouragement of Individual Curiosity. Advocates of the various forms of open education, however they define it, encourage those responsible for the education of others to provide learning experiences that not only encourage the learner's innate curiosity and his desire to see newness and become involved, but also to make it possible for him to pursue his interests in depth.[5] Suggestions are made on how to provide a setting in which learners want to explore and pursue their interests. Providing conditions for involvement which include opportunities for learners to

---

5. More complete discussion of the need to develop activities which meet these criteria is found in Herbert J. Walberg and Susan Christie Thomas, *Characteristics of Open Education: Toward an Operational Definition* (Newton, Mass.: TDR Associates, Inc., 1971).

choose from among alternatives and to participate in making decisions which affect their lives are concrete examples of these suggestions. Although such techniques are of prime importance, we feel that hand in hand with attempts to provide conditions the learner perceives as facilitating becoming involved must be attempts to answer some specific questions about involvement:

What does it mean to be involved?

How does a learner who is involved behave?

How does he interact with other persons, with materials, or with ideas?

What is minimal involvement?

When is a person highly involved?

What individual patterns of involvement are evident in a group of learners?

How does a learner's pattern of involvement change over time?

What kinds of settings or learning experiences cause some learners to become more involved or less involved?

These are some of the questions that must be answered if the concept of involvement is to become more than a slogan or rallying point and if teachers are going to be able to describe what happens in a stipulated setting.

Attempts to Find Answers. Persons interested in answering the preceding questions have been engaged in devising techniques which facilitate obtaining the answers. One approach explored is observing involvement in different settings. Observational systems often include categories related to involvement,[6] and in some instances whole systems are designed to describe involvement behavior.[7] However, a need still exists for more specificity in describing involvement and for establishing relationships between the concept of involvement and the implications for curriculum development.

A description of learners' involvement in the classroom setting would make it possible for educators to be more precise in differentiating between active participants and passive recipients, in identifying behavioral characteristics of minimal and maximum involvement, and in

6. See Alan R. Coller, *Systems for the Observation of Classroom Behavior in Early Childhood Education* for systems which include categories related to involvement. This publication is #1300–28 in the ERIC Clearing House on Early Childhood Education (Urbana: University of Illinois, April 1972).

7. An example of this is B. McCandless and W. C. Hodges, *Intensity of Involvement Scale.* This instrument is available from Boyd McCandless, Emory University, Atlanta, Georgia 30322. Mimeographed. Also ibid., p. 22.

building learning experiences that encourage learners to become involved in depth. Descriptions of personal involvement would also provide insight into the problems an individual faces in his search for meaningfulness and in his attempts to negate alienation and combat a surfeit of choice.

Having identified some educational concerns and societal factors which draw attention to the need to study involvement, we next focus on the nature of involvement and attempts to clarify its relationship to commitment.

The Nature of Involvement and Commitment

In order to make wise decisions about involvement, educators need to define both involvement and commitment and to obtain information about the factors which contribute to the nature of them. This information aids in differentiating between the terms and in establishing ground rules for using them in curricular matters. It also facilitates a person's describing the behavior of individuals who appear to be involved. In this section we propose an approach to clarifying involvement and commitment for use in a classroom setting.

Explicating terms

Involvement, commitment, and related terms are used widely in a variety of contexts and with many implied meanings. Individuals generally bring personal meanings to these terms and take equally personal meanings from exchanges involving them. However advantageous this broad usage appears to be in so-called everyday interaction, it can become a source of confusion and subjective conjecture when attempts are made to apply these terms to a specific field or situation. Becker provides us with an example of how a sociologist might attempt to reduce the confusion arising from the broad use of the term commitment. He proposes that in attempting to explicate the concept of commitment, attention be given to defining and describing the acts and states of commitment, the context or conditions under which commitment occurs and flourishes, the factors which effect a change in it, and the results of acts and states of commitment.[8]

---

8. For a more detailed discussion of specifying a commonly used term and developing a theory of commitment, see Howard S. Becker, "Notes on the Concept of Commitment," *The American Journal of Sociology* 66:32–40, July 1960.

The next sections deal with definitions of involvement and commitment, ways in which the two might be related, and ground rules for using these terms in this volume. The working definitions and related discussions are offered as a basis for and stimulus to further questioning into the nature of involvement and commitment. Out of such questioning and exploring can emerge guidelines and techniques for describing involvement, for designing contexts which facilitate a person's becoming involved, and for determining what happens when persons interact with these contexts.

Definitions

The definitions which follow are working definitions applied to the ideas on curriculum discussed in this volume. *Commitment* is an internalized process or state of mind which motivates a person in his search for meaning and is continuous over a period of time. *Involvement* is how and to what degree an individual engages in an interaction with persons, materials, or ideas. Stated another way, involvement refers to *how* an individual invests his energies in an interaction.

The proposed working definition suggests that commitment constitutes the driving force behind an individual's interactions, and that this force is guided by a set of values which defines the parameters for meaning a person brings to or takes from an interaction. The driving force behind commitment is a generative power that sustains a condition over a period of time. The person's search for meaning implies a seeking posture fed by an air of expectancy which focuses on beginnings and openings from which can emanate temporary or small closures.

The definition of involvement implies the existence of evidence that a person is engaged with other persons or with ideas, materials, or tasks. The evidence might be in the form of observable behaviors, artifacts made or utilized, or self-reports about the person's involvement. The person committed to alleviating the food shortage might write to government officials, think about how to communicate his ideas about the shortage, make kits to give to children to arouse interest in the problem. Commitment to a larger idea is evidenced in involvement in tasks related to the commitment. Evidence of mental interaction with ideas may be delayed, difficult to identify, or appear nonexistent without the aid of technical devices which measure bodily changes that can be read as indicators of mental activity. The definition also implies that overt evidence can reveal something about the degree of involvement or engagement.

To summarize, commitment, as defined and used in the context of this book, is an internalized process or state of mind which appears to motivate and guide a search for meaning over a period of time. Involvement is viewed more in terms of overt acts and behaviors or evidences of them which might indicate the nature and degree of an individual's interaction or engagement with people, ideas, or things.

Distinguishing between commitment and involvement advances certain information for those questioning what an individual's overt or visible behavior suggests about his involvement in an interaction. However, in order to give meaning to this information, involvement must be placed within the larger context of commitment. In order to facilitate a person's accomplishing this, the possible relationships between involvement and commitment must be clarified and explored in some detail.

Relationship of involvement and commitment

Defining involvement and commitment separately in no way denies the existence of possible relationships between them. On the contrary, stating these definitions and using them in describing what appear to be involvement behaviors further establishes and clarifies the relationship.

One attempt to distinguish between commitment and involvement is to speak of commitment *to* and involvement *with*. Although this mode of referring to the concepts seems to distinguish them in certain contexts, we feel the distinction is not precise enough for application to our curricular concerns.

Our ideas on the relationship between involvement and commitment are based on the following assumptions about the process of becoming involved:

1. The degree to which an individual engages in an interaction or the forcefulness of an interaction varies with individuals.
2. Personal, material, and ideational factors determine what an individual becomes involved in and the degree to which he does so.
3. It is possible to obtain information about the nature of an individual's behavior as he interacts with other individuals, materials, or ideas.
4. Rendering the identifiable aspects of involvement meaningful and functional requires placing them within a broader context that fleshes out the concept and adds a qualitative dimension to it.
5. The concept of involvement void of a larger contextual meaning is limited in its value to those faced with problems of curriculum development and implementation.

Motivated by the belief that these assumptions are valid ones and having taken into account the aspects of the working definitions of commitment and involvement, we propose that involvement and commitment are related and that the relationship can be discussed in terms of (1) process and input; (2) motivating force; (3) comprehensiveness; and (4) duration. However, at this point, we cannot definitively state that for each of the aspects listed the relationship between involvement and commitment has been determined and is predictable. For instance, at times the relationship might be described as an undulating or flowing one in which it is difficult to determine whether involvement or commitment is the motivating force. Or, if the distinction between involvement and commitment can be determined for one individual's interaction at one time, will it hold true for the same individual at another time in another interaction?

Admittedly there are still many unanswered questions, but a comparison and contrast of the definitional elements of involvement and commitment suggest the following:

1. The interactions or engagements associated with the *process* of involvement are often readily identified and can be viewed as overt manifestations of commitment. Furthermore, these interactions or engagements might be looked upon as *input* for commitment or the locus for the generation of the raw materials utilized in the internalized process or state of commitment. They may also be viewed as factors contributing to understanding which prompts or makes commitment possible.

2. Although commitment has been described as a *motivating force* which facilitates the individual's search for meaning, the point in time or the order in which the motivating force becomes operative does not appear to be fixed. The primary motivating force is most likely a function of commitment, but the direction of motivation may not always be from commitment to involvement. Initial motivation may be engendered by the involvement, and as involvement moves toward commitment the motivation may heighten and become more intense. This aspect of the involvement-commitment relationship might be diagrammed as follows:

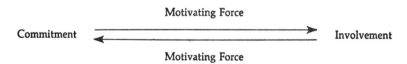

Motivating Force

Commitment ————————————————→ Involvement

Motivating Force

3. Commitment appears to be more *comprehensive* and more elusive than involvement. The definitional aspects referring to a state of

mind and a search for meaning in life suggest this comprehensive and elusive character of commitment. Implied in comprehensiveness is an ordering or establishing of relationships as well as a postulation of implications and future directions. This difference appears to be one which can be expressed more in terms of degree than quantity. A diagram of the relationship between involvement and commitment in terms of comprehensiveness might look like this:

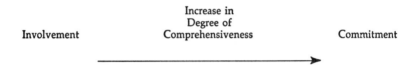

Increase in
Degree of
Involvement   Comprehensiveness   Commitment

4. Involvement and commitment appear to vary according to *duration* or *time*. Commitment is more enduring and continues over a longer period of time.

Each of the above relationships is open to scrutiny and review. Further examination of these aspects may uncover more specific elements of the relationship and their implications for learning experiences. A factor which has not been discussed, but which may be inherent in the relationship between commitment and involvement, is responsibility. Perhaps involvement moves toward commitment as an individual progresses toward assuming responsibility for his interactions. Responsibility might be evidenced by a personal involvement that endures.

Ground rules

Since the relationship of involvement to commitment as far as curriculum questions are concerned is still in the process of being explored and established, it is necessary to state some ground rules for using the terms in the context of this book.

The following guidelines should help the reader understand the separate uses of the terms and also why they are often used interchangeably.

1. In general, when the context does not dictate the specific use of either involvement or commitment as defined, the terms are used interchangeably. Cases in point might include general discussion of involvement or commitment as they relate to an individual's lifestyle, to a learner's understanding his interactions, or to selected facets of learning and living such as communicating and knowing.
2. When curriculum questions are explored and analyzed and when the specifics of feedback on these questions are examined, the term

involvement is likely to be employed. An example would be evidence of a person's going beyond what might normally be done with a set of ideas or materials.

3. When the broader issues related to implications are examined, and when judgments about these issues are made, the term commitment is usually used. Consider many evidences of a child's involvement with different children in the neighborhood, school, and larger community. Might this evidence indicate a broader commitment to interacting with a variety of persons?

FIGURE 4–1. *Diagram of Ground Rules for Involvement and Commitment*

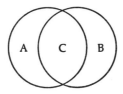

A represents situations in which the working definition of involvement is employed in a specific context.

B represents situations in which the working definition of commitment is employed in a specific context.

C represents those situations in which the working definitions are used interchangeably.

These ground rules are shown in figure 4–1. That portion of A that does not intersect B is where curriculum questions are explored and analyzed and the specifics of feedback on these questions examined. For instance, a teacher observes and describes a child's nonverbal behavior while he works in the block corner. The term involvement is employed here. That portion of B that does not intersect A is where the broader issues related to implications are examined and where judgments about these issues are made. Consider the teacher who has observed a child over a year's time and has described how long he spends painting, how often and when he returns to it, the number of times he refers to his work and also brings in books about painting. The teacher's decisions about long-range art experiences for this child are related to commitment. C, or the intersection of A and B, is where the context of the discussion does not dictate the use of one term and therefore either is acceptable and used interchangeably.

In summary, the need for defining involvement and commitment was established and working definitions of each were stipulated. How involvement and commitment might be related was explored by comparing them in terms of process and input, motivating force, comprehensiveness, and duration. Finally, ground rules were established for using the terms involvement and commitment in this volume. In the next section, qualities or characteristics of the involved person are discussed.

Involvement and the Person

The involved person perceives his interactions with ideas, materials, and other persons as opportunities for satisfying his need for engagement,[9] for fulfillment,[10] and for simultaneity.[11] As a result, he can progress toward satisfying his inner drive to explore, achieve, accomplish, and to discover meaning and newness in life.

The involved person approaches life with the expectation that he can accomplish and that, indeed, he will. In other words, he acts with intent and purpose believing that his goal will be achieved. He is not involved for involvement's sake, but rather because he sees his interactions as means to achieve fulfillment and purpose in ways that add meaning and perspective to his life.

The posture of the involved person can be likened to that of the curious person. It is a seeking out and reacting positively to the new and the mysterious.[12] He can identify those experiences or the factors within them that have the potential to excite and to motivate a continuous search for challenge and complexity. The possibilities for newness and for change do not constitute a threat to the involved person's lifestyle, but rather a motivating force that initiates and guides.

Another quality of the involved person is his personal and vivid approach to life's experiences. He does not lead a life of imitation or a borrowed life,[13] but instead lives to the fullest with every fiber of his being. The involved person experiences life first-hand, feels deeply, acts with intensity, and is not reluctant to show his feelings in ways that are unique to him.

The involved person looks beneath the surface and pushes his sights beyond his own personal concerns to the concerns of others. He sees

9. Philip Slater, *The Pursuit of Loneliness: American Culture at the Breaking Point* (Boston: Beacon Press, 1970), p. 5.

10. Hans Selye, *The Stress of Life* (New York: McGraw-Hill, 1956), p. 297.

11. Anthony Schillaci, "Celebrating Change: Communications and Theology," in *Projections: Shaping an American Theology for the Future,* ed. Thomas F. O'Meara and Donald M. Weisser (Garden City, N.Y.: Image Books, 1970), p. 183.

12. Hy Day and Florence Maynes, "Curiosity and Willingness to Become Involved," *Psychological Reports* 30:807–14, June 1972.

13. Contributors' Discussion, "The Self in Early Years: Discussion," in *The Child and His Image: Self Concept in the Early Years,* ed. Kaoru Yamamoto (Boston: Houghton Mifflin, 1972), pp. 209–10.

relationships and experiences the wholeness that exists beyond the fragmentation of limited and shallow experiences.

Another quality of a highly involved person is his tendency to take a stand or stance, thus forsaking the role of a straddler who consistently occupies the middle road of neutrality.[14] Along with taking a stand he is willing to endure the privation or loneliness that might accompany his position.

Recognizing that stress is a normal and necessary part of life, the involved person does not necessarily try to alleviate it.[15] He is also aware that man's essential freedom consists of his capacity to " . . . feel strongly or weakly for a moment or for all his life, about anything under the sun and to govern himself by such motives. . . ."[16] As a result, the involved person is able to temper his desire for highly intense interaction and to recognize the need for a balance of involvement and noninvolvement or detachment. L'Engle proposes that it is the ability to achieve this balance " . . . which makes us creatively useful. . . ."[17] Temporary, apparent detachment or disengagement need not be negative, but can result in positive change or growth. Frenzied commitment resulting from indiscriminate involvement in many unrelated experiences can be as unproductive as no involvement at all.

Finally, the involved person sees life as being in process and seeks to facilitate this process in a creative manner. As one who participates wholeheartedly in shaping the nature and direction of his life experiences, the involved person utilizes his skills, abilities, and knowledge to facilitate interacting with his personal and material environment. He also develops new knowledge, skills, and attitudes. In so doing, he is better able to discover, utilize, and channel the power he possesses. He learns more about himself, his strengths and weaknesses, and achieves a sense of identity.

The person who perceives his interactions with persons, ideas, and materials as opportunities to contribute in a fresh manner to the ongoingness of life needs to determine to whom or to what he will commit his energies. He also needs to determine the channels for his commit-

14. For further discussion of commitment requiring taking a definite stand on the part of the person see Elizabeth O'Connor, *Eighth Day of Creation: Gifts and Creativity* (Waco, Texas: Word Books, 1971), and Rolf Schulze, "An Exploration of Alienation and Commitment Among Indian College Students," *International Journal of Contemporary Sociology* 8:143–59, April 1971.

15. For a discussion of stress as a basic energy source, see Samuel Klausner, ed., *Why Man Takes Chances: Studies in Stress-seeking* (New York: Anchor Books, 1968).

16. Silvan S. Tomkins, "The Psychology of Commitment, Part I: The Constructive Role of Violence and Suffering for the Individual and for His Society," in *Affect, Cognition, and Personality: Empirical Studies*, ed. Silvan S. Tomkins and Carroll E. Izard (New York: Springer, 1965), pp. 148, 149.

17. Madeline L'Engle, *A Circle of Quiet* (New York: Farrar, Straus and Giroux, 1972), pp. 118–19.

ments. How will his involvement be of service or contribute to creating and unfolding social systems and new knowledge? In addition, the involved person needs to assess his motives and the forces in life which contribute to and strengthen his commitments as well as those which deter them.

The qualities of the involved person can be summarized as follows:

1. The person sees his interactions with the personal, ideational, and material environment as opportunities for engaging whole-heartedly in life and taking a definite stand instead of just tolerating life or being satisfied with a neutral, middle-of-the-road stance.
   a. The person realizes his own sense of power in terms of what he can do and how much control he has in a situation.
   b. The person enters into an interaction with the expectation that his purpose will be achieved because he has the capacity to accomplish it.
   c. The person can assess his capacities for contributing to life recognizing those areas where he can change and those where he feels he cannot yet risk change or revision.
   d. The person is more willing to make sacrifices, take risks, and set aside temporarily that which earlier seemed indispensable.
2. The person seeks out and engages in experiences that have holding and leading-on power and that are characterized by a flow or ongoingness.
   a. The person moves beyond the givens of a situation, searching for more complexity and challenge.
   b. The person invents newness and can project over time and space.
   c. The person is capable of bringing closure when appropriate, but he also is aware of new openings and beginnings which can emerge as a result of closure.
   d. The person is self-propelling and self-generating, initiating without constant external motivation.
3. The person engages in interactions that result in new knowledge in ways unique to his learning style.
   a. The person creates knowledge in a variety of ways that are unique to him.
   b. The person goes beneath surface issues and creates knowledge that reflects his personal interests, thinking, and concern for others.
   c. The person is able to generate knowledge about himself and how he interacts with the various facets of his environment.
4. The person interacts with his environment in such a way that he develops not only agreed-upon meanings, but also meanings

emerging from his interactions with individuals, ideas, and materials.

  a. The person brings to interactions his own personal meanings, and as a result his actions and thoughts are not always dictated by predetermined structure and meanings.
  b. The person realizes that meanings can emerge as a result of personal interaction and that in this process participants interact *with* another and do not act *upon* or do things *to* another.

5. The person utilizes as many facets of his life and the environment as is possible or appropriate in accomplishing a goal.

  a. The person approaches interactions from many different perspectives, applying his senses and personal meanings in the process.
  b. The person moves his thinking and actions from the simple to the complex and from himself to the larger world.

Individuals who possess personal qualities related to involvement will most likely become engaged in interactions that can be described as enduring, meaningful, and personal. Enduring interactions are those that extend over time, are returned to after having been withdrawn from, and have leading-on and opening-up possibilities.

Meaningful interactions afford the person opportunities for in-depth explorations which encourage wholeness and completeness and reduce fragmentation in experiencing. Meaningful interactions also make it possible for the person to act with intent and purpose.

Interactions that are characterized as personal help the individual see the significance of input, see what he can do, and learn how much control he has in a situation. They also encourage the person to believe he can accomplish something and provide opportunities for him to be self-propelling and self-generating.

Having derived personal qualities of the involved person from an examination of involvement and commitment, we turn in the next sections to a discussion of achieving additional insight into commitment and the process of involvement. By examining the relationship of involvement and the processes of communicating, knowing, and dealing with social systems we propose to learn more about involvement.

Involvement and Communication

The interplay between involvement and communication may be viewed from three related perspectives: (1) the nature of a communicative context that encourages a life style of involvement; (2) uses of language during involvement; and (3) the communication style of individuals who have had opportunities for involvement.

Contexts that encourage involvement

Key words describing the nature, characteristics, and quality of communicative contexts encouraging involvement are participatory, open, and complete. A participatory context is one in which individuals engaged in interpersonal communication are not talked at, ordered, or directed, but rather are encouraged to give and take—to participate in direct human involvement. "Human encounters are creative involvements in which two people put their personalities together."[18] Individuals are encouraged to initiate as well as respond, and all contributions to an interaction are valued. The spirit of sharing is evident in a communicative context that is participatory in nature. In this context, sharing is not division into parts, but rather it is joint participation for the mutual benefit of all.

Communicative contexts that encourage involvement have also been described as open. In this sense, open refers to a generous outpouring of ideas, thoughts, and feelings and a welcoming consideration of them. Predetermined barriers or closures are not set. On the contrary, participants are encouraged to push ideas as far as possible and to tease out, as it were, all possible ramifications and implications. There is time for ideas and thoughts to germinate and to ripen; and there is time to return and pick up strands at an appropriate place. This kind of openness provides the freedom to dream, to expand, to extrapolate, and also provides the necessary structure for following through and building upon. It is this kind of openness that encourages communication that is not fleeting but that endures and makes an impression.

Complete communicative contexts are ones in which verbal and non-verbal expressions of meanings are encouraged and evident. In attempts to analyze the components of communication, often the verbal aspects are emphasized and the nonverbal neglected. Speaking, gesturing, and moving bodily are closely intertwined and together comprise the process of communicating.

What is the target of the communication? What is the point of concentration—the point from which other ideas or feelings might emerge? It is possible that a consistently singular focus may be too narrow to facilitate involvement or commitment. Often the focus needs to be

---

18. Paul Byers and Happie Byers, "Nonverbal Communication and the Education of Children," in *Functions of Language in the Classroom,* ed., Courtney B. Cazden, Vera P. John, and Dell Hymes (New York: Teachers College Press, 1972), p. 29.

expanded to include the process in which persons become participants in society at increasingly higher and more complex levels.[19] A broader view of the communication context is suggested in which the focus is expanded to embody the communication of care, concern, interest, and warmth. There is a moving beyond individuals' personal concerns.

A communicative situation that aids in a person's search for meaning must lift the person beyond the content of the message to the larger realm of who is communicating and the purpose of the interaction. These higher level concerns seem to be implied in Gerbner's discussion of communication as " . . . interaction through messages bearing man's notions of existence, priorities, values and relations."[20] It is interesting to note that frequently schools which label themselves as open do not give adequate attention to the open, frank communication necessary to evoke involvement and commitment. A school might examine itself in terms of opportunities for truly communicative situations.

Uses of language

Although it is often difficult to determine the specific point or moment of involvement, it is possible to identify instances in which individuals appear to be deeply engaged in an interaction. Consider the learner who is not distracted from his reading by persons moving in and out of the room and groups working in close proximity to him. However one captures instances of involvement, we propose that an analysis of communication that occurs during obvious involvement provides some insight into how persons engaged in an interaction utilize language to facilitate their becoming involved and what that language communicates to others about the involvement.

Verbal, both spoken and written, and nonverbal language might facilitate an individual's involvement by providing the means to discuss with another person what one is engaged in. This exchange might include checking hunches, getting direction, or helping another see a point. Possibilities and problems related to the interaction can be disclosed through this process. A verbal interchange might be particularly pertinent to an interaction or engagement that deals predominantly with ideas, whereas nonverbal interchanges might be more pertinent to situations calling for manipulation of materials. Although separate examples of each are given, both verbal and nonverbal parts of the stream of communicative behavior function together in conveying messages.

19. Ibid., p. 7.
20. George Gerbner, "Communication and Social Environment," *Scientific American* 227:152–60, September 1972, esp. p. 156.

The examples cited above refer to specific situations where one aspect of the communicative stream appears to predominate but does not necessarily exclude the other.

Implicit in the help an individual gives another in interpersonal communication during involvement is the benefit one receives himself in this exchange. Ideas can be clarified, speculations verified, and directions obtained. Nonverbal behaviors can facilitate trying out ideas and procedures. It is assumed that the use of language in checking out hypotheses and generating new ones related to the task at hand expedites the process of becoming more deeply and purposively involved.

In addition to generating knowledge about involvement by using communication during an interaction, persons can learn about involvement by analyzing the communication that occurs during the interaction. What clues does an individual give about his involvement? When and how are aspects of involvement communicated? Does there appear to be a moment or definable point or points of involvement? What might verbal and nonverbal expressions reveal about involvement? Are certain feelings, attitudes, or skills revealed more readily than others? These and other questions might be answered by examining communicative acts that occur during an interaction or engagement.

Since involvement or the degree to which an individual invests his energies in a task suggests the intensity with which he applies himself, it is assumed that accompanying this intense application are deep feelings. It is also assumed that an individual's communication can be an overt manifestation of these feelings. Feelings are more apt to be expressed nonverbally than verbally. Consequently, observation of the nonverbal behaviors of an individual engaged in an interaction can reveal something about the intensity with which he is involved. Eye contact, body movements, body orientation, and proximity are some observable nonverbal signals which have the potential for revealing something of the nature of involvements. Talking with an individual about his involvement can provide information relative to the intensity of his interactions, but he may be somewhat hesitant to discuss his involvement and, as a result, not reveal as much verbally as he might nonverbally. In addition, the flow of his interaction is interrupted by attempting to gain information from him.

Communication style of involved persons

The last perspective from which we view the interplay between involvement and communication relates to the characteristics of the language employed by individuals who have taken advantage of opportunities to become engaged in an interaction. The nature of the language can be examined in terms of vocabulary *per se* and the kinds of thought processes that the language seems to reflect.

The vocabulary used by an individual who has been deeply engaged in an interaction with people, ideas, or things might be more action-oriented, more precise, and perhaps more expressive. One can expect that it would move beyond language learned from the dictionary and from the teacher to what Britton alludes to as the language employed in seeking and discovering.[21] It is also possible that the vocabulary is more personal and peculiar to the individual who employs it. Deep involvement decreases the use of so-called borrowed terms and increases the number and variety of words which have direct meaning for the individual.

The construction of language that a person employs after having been involved reveals the nature of the thought processes he has utilized and that have become part of his repertoire. In this context no attempt is made to establish which comes first, language or thought. Verbal and nonverbal language are viewed as indicators of the kinds of thinking a person engages in. One might expect that language which emanates from an interaction requiring deep introspection or concern about a person or issue would reflect this depth of thinking. It is also possible that much has been learned about the self in the process and much about the interests and cares of another.

Analytic and synthetic thinking skills can be reflected in the constructions a person uses as he organizes, categorizes, and attempts to see the whole picture. Plans stated in terms of alternatives for time and duration of projects are indications of thinking which is projective, tentative, and open to revision. "What if" questions and "Suppose" statements reflect thinking on the many facets of an idea or activity. Reflective language may indicate rethinking or a period of overt noninvolvement.

Although at this point we cannot establish a direct relationship between involvement and language that appears to tell something about the thinking processes, we are suggesting that an examination of language may reveal something about the nature of the involvement.

Involvement and Knowing

Most interactions with persons, ideas, or materials result in some change in the knowledge an individual already possesses, has produced, or is in the process of producing. These changes in knowledge and knowl-

---

21. For a discussion of different forms of language see James Britton, *Language and Learning* (Coral Gables, Fla.: University of Miami Press, 1970), p. 127.

edge production can also affect the nature of the interaction or involvement. However, in this discussion our primary focus is on the influence that involvement in an interaction can have on an individual's knowing. We examine this relationship from two perspectives: (1) how an individual who has been deeply involved might view approaches to knowing, and (2) what might characterize his knowing behavior.

Approaches to knowing

A basic premise underlying an examination of the relationship of involvement to knowing is that in the process of becoming and being involved, an individual creates new knowledge and tests his own prior knowledge as well as that of others. We also assume that as a result of intense involvement, an individual's view of the knowledge-producing process is expanded. In the discussion which follows, knowledge production is considered in terms of the variety of approaches possible, the attitudinal set toward producing knowledge, and the role of the person in the process.

Variety. An experience which has led a person to examine and test many notions has the potential for revealing to the individual the variety of ways in which knowledge is produced. Selye speaks of man's advancing from observation to wisdom through instinct as well as through science. Faith, art, and intuition as well as science, where what is observed must be defined and measured, can be used to span the distances between observation and wisdom.[22] Modes of knowing that Sutton-Smith identifies are imitation, exploration, testing, and construction.[23]

A procedure for knowing which can supplement some of the approaches mentioned earlier consists of monitoring one's own behavior during an interaction. Techniques for obtaining information on how an individual acts in a situation need to be carefully devised to fit the purpose and to provide relevant information. A simple questionnaire in which an individual is asked to recall the approach to knowing he employed, what new insights he gained, and how the new meshed or did not mesh with the old can provide knowledge about his approach to and use of knowledge in a specified situation.

In summary, a person who has been deeply involved probably becomes aware of and utilizes a variety of modes of knowing.

---

22. Selye, *The Stress of Life,* p. 255.
23. Brian Sutton-Smith, "Child's Play: Very Serious Business," *Psychology Today* 5:66–69, December 1971, p. 87.

Attitude toward Knowledge Production.   In proposing growth or changes in knowledge production that would probably result from involvement, it seems appropriate to consider one's attitude toward producing knowledge. What is an individual's mind set or attitudinal set as he approaches and becomes involved in deep exploration of an idea or interchange? What motivates him to pursue and sustain his initial efforts?

A person who approaches a task with the expectation that he as an individual will generate new knowledge, most likely has faith in his ability to produce valuable knowledge which can be fruitfully used. A person who has this mind set or attitude about knowledge production is apt to become involved more deeply in an interaction and to see more readily the implications of involvement for the process of knowing.

Personal Participation.   Closely interwoven with the attitudinal set discussed above is the personal participation of the knower in the process of knowing. The person is an active participant in knowing when he makes objects in the external world a part of or an extension of his own thinking and feeling. Because objects of the outside world become inextricably intertwined with the person, he can utilize them wisely in dealing with life's dilemmas.

Personal participation in knowing might also imply that one can think by feeling. This appears to be particularly appropriate in situations of deep personal involvement. Struggling through a problem with another person sometimes calls for sharing which goes beyond a reasoned, carefully planned thinking. Yet the feeling element contributes to a personal knowing that transcends a superficial cooperative search for objective answers.

Knowing behavior of involved persons

The effect that a deep involvement might have on the knowing behavior of an individual is explored in terms of the characteristics of knowledge those individuals create and possess and the use they make of it.

Characteristics.   If the person enters into the knowing process to the degree we described previously, the knowledge he produces is apt to be more in-depth and subjective in nature although not to the exclusion of the general and objective.

We might also expect that an individual who had engaged rather intensely in an interaction would probably develop more "intensional" meanings as opposed to "extensional" ones. Intensional meanings are more personal; extensional are agreed upon, or dictionary meanings. In a discussion of children and materials, Kallet differentiates between "intensional" and "extensional" meanings, and discusses the application of them to communication and to materials and children's manipulation of them.[24] Intensely involved persons most likely readily identify and use materials with the potential for developing intensional meanings. Their language style reflects the intensional meanings developed and the resulting knowledge is in-depth and personalized. We might also expect a decrease in the dependence on predigested material in developing new knowledge.

Knowledge resulting from personal involvement is also more individualized. It can be employed to help a person feel a sense of control over his destiny.

One characteristic of knowledge resulting from involvement is openness. Open knowledge is still in the process of being developed, changed, and revised. It allows for much personal participation as well as much testing and rigorous evaluation against objective and subjective standards.

Use. We might expect individuals who have been engrossed in an interaction to employ knowledge to reinforce, change, revise, or alter their commitment. We might also expect them to act in accordance with the knowledge that has resulted from their interactions. In either case, we can expect carry-over into everyday life experiences.

Individuals who have been deeply involved in experiences that have provided some feedback on personal knowledge gained should be better able to ask themselves what areas of knowing they wish or need to explore. Which knowledge is most pertinent to the issues facing the individual and society? How might this knowledge best be achieved and applied?

In addition to raising questions relative to the kind of knowledge needed and how to utilize it, we hope that individuals will invent more personal ways of producing knowledge and more creative ways of wondering about, verifying, and evaluating it.

Involvement and
Social Systems

Since man is disposed to living in companionship with others or in a community rather than in isolation, it is appropriate to explore some of

---

24. Tony Kallet, "Some Thoughts on Children and Materials," *Outlook* 6:21, Autumn 1972.

the implications that the search for purpose or commitment has for social systems. We recognize that the nature of social systems has implications for involvement as well, but our major focus is on the impact that involvement can have on the way people live with others.

Certain questions related to purpose or seeking and achieving meaning in life inevitably face individuals and social systems. These questions pertain to a person's ability to assess the characteristics or qualities of a social system that encourage or discourage involvement, the possibilities for individual involvement in a social setting, and the conceivable effects of involvement on the social system.

Assessing social systems

The following are some questions a person with a purposive life style might ask about a social system:

What ideas, problems, or issues which require attention and action are paramount to a society's survival and functioning?

Which of these concerns provide opportunities for persons to extend, to mold, and to reshape; and which by their nature require individuals to fit a mold?

What is the range of questions or issues facing a system and, concomitantly, what are the opportunities for involvement of varying degrees?

In a more specific vein, an individual can identify those whose actions are purposive, and he can determine the effect of being part of a social system that contains many persons seeking involvement. It has been suggested that individuals seek the company of those with values similar to their own, and that personal interests are reinforced by the expectations of these individuals.[25]

Potential for individual involvement

A person who is highly motivated in searching for meaning in life is not only capable of assessing social systems as a whole but also the potential for individual involvement within the context of them. Once the nature of a system at large has been identified, the individual must address himself to questions such as the following:

---

25. For further discussion of this theory see Ralph M. Stodgill, *Individual Behavior and Group Achievement: A Theory* (New York: Oxford University Press, 1959).

Is the social milieu characterized by variety or opportunities for differing degrees of involvement?

If so, on what basis does one decide where he will expend his energies?

Which of the many cultural bombardments does one select for emphasis?

Which does he cast aside and which postpone?

Decisions on these matters depend on the strength of the commitment and the manner in which the individual sees both internal and external forces relating to his purpose. How an individual answers these questions is important, but equally important is his ability to continually raise questions which help him see the relationship of his involvement to social systems.

The social context for involvement can be viewed on a continuum from those involvements related predominantly to the individual alone, to those in which the individual interacts with a small or immediate group, to those in which the individual interacts with persons in the broader or world community. Involvements at the second and third points are desirable if the impact of individuals and groups is to be realized in a social setting.

Not all individuals and groups have to be encouraged to extend their involvements beyond the immediate and personal level, but for those who do there is a need to look at how the progression might be brought about. Ellul asserts that total involvement in prayer leads individuals and their actions " ... to take on a value which far surpasses our personal concerns."[26] Perhaps other kinds of intense involvements which engage every facet of an individual's life move a person beyond the confines of himself to the place where he can see himself in light of those outside himself.

If actions of involved persons benefit social systems by reaching beyond the self, then it is important to look at how this movement might be accomplished. According to Ellul, the reach beyond self is a natural outgrowth of deep earnest commitment. One cannot help but see the implications of the person's concerns for others in his immediate as well as more distant environment.

Insight into moving from self to others can be gained by carefully scrutinizing the risks and unknowns that emerge when one considers moving from involvements related predominantly to himself to those related to social systems. Raising and answering questions about the

---

26. Jacques Ellul, *Prayer and Modern Man,* trans. Edward Hopkin (New York: Seabury, 1970), p. 178.

opening and closing potential of a person's actions also contribute to an understanding of how one moves from self to others. Selected sample questions are:

How might involvement with others help me better understand them and myself?

How do I move from self to others?

What factors influence my choice of purpose and how I proceed in achieving it?

When is it appropriate to move from others to self?

What are the possibilities that commitment might hinder or encourage extending involvement to a larger group?

What do I stand to gain by moving from self to others or others to self?

When is opening or pushing out appropriate and beneficial to an interaction?

When is closure appropriate and beneficial?

How do I determine?

No answers are provided since each person after assessing his own situation finds answers which are unique to his interaction in social systems. Based on the premise that in a social setting an involved person must move beyond the limits of engagements which are related predominantly to the self, we propose that a careful analysis of the situation might aid an individual in that move.

Effect of involvement

It is possible to hypothesize what might occur as a result of carefully scrutinizing one's involvement process. An individual who cares and experiences deeply would most likely have a better understanding of others' search for meaning after having gone through the process himself. This would include sharing in the struggles as well as the joys which accompany the pursuit. He would probably be more willing and skillful in encouraging others in the search for purpose that not only affects their lives but the lives of those around them.

It is possible that a true sense of community would develop as depth of living on the part of individuals and groups is increased. This sense of community encourages diversity and a sense of unity motivated by sharing in the process of a search for meaning. Implicit in the search for meaning is progression along the path from what *is* to what *might* be or *could* be. Platt suggests, "A creative and evolving society will be continually driven by the gap and tension between what is and the ever-changing realization of what might be."[27]

Summary

The importance of studying involvement or the *how* of living and the nature of involvement and commitment preceded a presentation of the qualities of the involved person. In the remainder of the chapter the relationship of involvement to communication, knowing, and social systems was explored. Having examined the *how* of living in these terms we move in the next chapter on peopling to the *why* of living.

Suggestions for Further Reading

Becker, Howard S. "Notes on the Concept of Commitment." *American Journal of Sociology* 66: 32–40, July 1960.

Etzioni, Amitai. *Power, Involvement and Their Correlates.* New York: Free Press, 1961.

Frankl, Viktor E. Translated by Ilse Lasch. *Man's Search for Meaning: An Introduction to Logotherapy.* New York: Alfred A. Knopf, 1955.

Illich, Ivan. *Tools for Conviviality.* World Perspectives, Vol. 47, edited by Ruth Nanda Anshen. New York: Harper & Row, 1973.

Klausner, Samuel, ed. *Why Man Takes Chances: Studies in Stress-seeking.* Garden City, N.Y.: Anchor Books, 1968.

L'Engle, Madeleine. *A Circle of Quiet.* New York: Farrar, Straus and Giroux, 1972.

O'Connor, Elizabeth. *Eighth Day of Creation: Gifts and Creativity.* Waco, Texas: Word Books, 1971.

Platt, John R. *Perception and Change: Projections for Survival.* Ann Arbor: University of Michigan Press, 1970.

Polanyi, Michael. *Personal Knowledge: Towards a Post Critical Philosophy.* Chicago: University of Chicago Press, 1958.

————. *The Tacit Dimension.* Garden City, N. Y.: Doubleday, 1966.

Raskin, Marcus G. *Being and Doing.* New York: Random House, 1971.

Roderick, Jessie A. (Principal Investigator) and Barbara Littlefield (Associate Investigator and Author) and Others. *The Project on Involvement: An Interim Report.* Center for Young Children, Occasional Paper Number Four. College Park: University of Maryland, 1972.

---

27. John R. Platt, *Perception and Change: Projections for Survival* (Ann Arbor: University of Michigan Press, 1970), p. 155.

Salk, Jonas. *Man Unfolding.* World Perspectives, Vol. 46, edited by Ruth Nanda Anshen. New York: Harper & Row, 1972.

Selye, Hans. *The Stress of Life.* New York: McGraw Hill, 1956.

Slater, Philip. *The Pursuit of Loneliness: American Culture at the Breaking Point.* Boston: Beacon Press, 1970.

Tomkins, Silvan S. and Carroll E. Izard, eds. *Affect, Cognition, and Personality: Empirical Studies.* New York: Springer, 1965.

Wees, W. R. *Nobody Can Teach Anyone Anything.* Ontario: Doubleday Canada Limited and New York: Doubleday, 1971.

Wieman, Nelson. *Man's Ultimate Commitment.* Carbondale: Southern Illinois University, 1958.

Yamamoto, Kaoru, ed. *The Child and His Image: Self Concept in the Early Years.* Boston: Houghton-Mifflin, 1972.

5

Peopling:
The Why of
Living

Perspective on Chapter 5

Theme: Peopling is the process by which a person can enjoy, obtain comfort from and give comfort to, and live fully with others.

Selected major points: (1) The school is a gathering place and hence provides a setting in which persons can learn new truths, gain fresh insights, and engage in constructive action with others like and unlike themselves. (2) The person can learn to solve problems related to living with and caring about other persons. (3) Learning the concepts relative to peopling discussed in this chapter can be facilitated by engaging in classroom activities found in chapter 11.

As you read: (1) Has this chapter highlighted critical points relative to a person's relations with others? (2) What points would you add to or subtract from this chapter? (3) Would you assign the high priority to person-person relations that the authors have?

How stark, lonely, boring, and depressing the world would be for most persons if they did not share companionship with other persons! How bleak our own sense of awareness would be if we did not see ourselves reflected in the universality of human desires, strivings, anxieties, truths, trepidations. If we could not draw up ledgers on which we recorded our commonnesses and uncommonnesses in relationship to other persons, we would fail to see the phenomenal range of sometimes overlapping and sometimes diverse characteristics ascribed to *homo sapiens*. The person is indeed central to life and its meaning and is the reason for existence. And yet, how neglected in the life of the average citizen and child is the study of the person and the impact of person upon person. Our lives are cluttered up with trivia both in terms of material things and inert facts so that little time and energy are left to dwell in the intensity of relationships offered by contact with our fellow human beings.

In this work, the informal interactive process between persons that results in heightened awareness and feeling for others is called *peopling*. Peopling deals with the *why* of human existence. It is a process by which a person can enjoy, obtain comfort from, and live fully with his fellows.

It will be recalled that two other concepts are integral to this work: deciding and becoming involved. Deciding has to do with the *what* of human existence. Deciding means designing alternatives and carrying out the appropriate one.[1] In talking about peopling, one must be concerned about the act of deciding, for Ferkiss indicates:

> ... there are no individual decisions any more than there are actually geometric points in the empirical world. Decision making is part of a seamless process. Man cannot become free by being outside or apart from the process. He is affected by what others do—that is, he is the subject of power—and he exercises power because his actions affect others.[2]

Involvement has to do with the intensity of man's interactions or behaviors. It answers the question: *How* does a person engage in an activity? How committed is the individual to what he sets out to do? Does the person involve himself primarily with other persons, ideas, things, or a combination of these? If the notion is accepted that persons' acts affect the larger whole, then the concept of peopling becomes the central focus, and the other process-related skills, such as deciding or involving, become vehicles through which persons become more adept at peopling.

---

1. Ernest Becker, *The Structure of Evil: An Essay on Unification of the Science of Man* (New York: George Braziller, 1968), p. 259.
2. Victor C. Ferkiss, *Technological Man: The Myth and the Reality* (New York: George Braziller, 1969), pp. 252–53.

The concept of social system is also critical to peopling. Peopling involves *informal* interrelationships and collaborative efforts that persons engage in throughout life. Social system refers to more *formal* relationships, such as those found in organizations or institutions. Frequently, informal relations or peopling are formalized, in which case one may move from primarily peopling to a more major emphasis on social system. In this chapter, however, our thrust is upon peopling—the why of man's existence, the potential within persons which enables them to throw aside apartness and loneliness in order to enjoy other persons fully.

When persons improve their informal relations with others, it is our hunch that social systems will be better and more responsive to human needs. The vitality of persons is reflected in social systems which are viable and evolving.

Peopling in Schools

Although many persons who write about the schools, either in a critical or a supportive vein, see that many of the functions which the school now fulfills could be carried out in other places or by other organizations, few persons can dispute that the school is a "gathering place."[3] As a gathering place the school has the opportunity to arrange the environment in terms of persons, materials, utilization of time and space, so that the young have the opportunity to acquire systematic bodies of knowledge and processes to improve their own competence in acts of peopling.

In the gathering place children and youth can have the opportunity to fulfill secret longings of which they may be only dimly aware. It is in creatively designed meeting places with contexts established to foster mutual confirmation that children and youth can learn a highly critical dimension of life.

Lewis and Miel acknowledge the significance of persons in schooling and its curriculum when they define curriculum as:

> . . . a set of intentions about opportunities for engagement of persons-to-be-educated with other persons and with things (all bearers of information, processes, techniques, and values) in certain arrangements of time and space.[4]

3. Arthur J. Lewis and Alice Miel, *Supervision for Improved Instruction: New Challenges, New Responses* (Belmont, Cal.: Wadsworth, 1972), p. 131.
4. Ibid., p. 27.

Traditionally, the school has planned opportunities for engagement with things but has planned to a lesser degree for engagements with persons. The school has an opportunity to provide the setting in which persons can learn "information, processes, techniques, and values" as they relate to persons. If this is done, individuals can build personal knowledge of peopling and ultimately we might possess a body of public knowledge in this area. Such knowledge might cut across the disciplines and fields which now exist and purport to deal with various dimensions of man. If the school is concerned about the critical area of person-to-person relationships, it will seek to give high priority to the topic of peopling. Without a fuller awareness of person-to-person growth and caring, persons lose individually and collectively. Having stated that the school should show major concern for the concept of peopling, what are some supporting reasons for our position?

First, the school provides a place where children can relate to a variety of persons from *differing* backgrounds. The common school is indispensable to the purposes of our society since all kinds of individuals live in communities.

Second, much evidence exists to support the notion that children tend to go through developmental stages in their social awareness and growth. Since children spend a large percentage of time in school, it can assume partial responsibility for describing, assessing, and planning appropriate settings for further stages in the developmental process.

Third, the school is an institution in which social creativity can be fostered. The 1960s saw a heavy emphasis upon the creative process. The seventies and eighties need to ensure that our knowledge of creativity is applied to developing *social* creativity in our young—a form of creativity which manifests itself through the ability to perceive persons in their richness and diversity, to be flexible in one's approach to persons, to be original in solutions to problems involving persons, to be tentative in judgments relative to persons, and to be fluent in seeing alternative causes of behavior.

Lastly, a focus upon peopling within the schools gives the opportunity for the young to relate to one another in terms of mission and purpose. When persons work in concert, there is the chance for the continuous examination of the purpose of mission, the worthwhileness of it, and the degree to which it is being accomplished.

Attention has been given to the reasons why peopling is an important concept both for the society in general and more particularly for the schools. Next, attention is directed toward a fuller definition. The remainder of the chapter is then devoted to an analysis of the concepts inherent in peopling.

The Nature of Peopling

A person is peopling when he possesses the quality of being fully "with it" in his relations with others—when he utilizes all his faculties in responding to or initiating communication with another, and when his full utilization of himself and all his faculties enables the other person to gain a heightened image of himself. Peopling is interaction among persons resulting in new truths, new insights, new positive feelings, or constructive action for the persons involved in the process.

Peopling is giving, but it is a caring and knowing kind of giving. Verhoeven makes two points about giving: (1) giving is tilting toward the other person, and (2) if the gift is appropriate, the other person will tilt also in order to receive it.[5] In elaborating upon these premises, Verhoeven further says, "The gesture of giving a gift is never a careless flinging but a careful accompaniment. The giver of the gift is present by the giving and in the gift, not outside it. He transfers himself to the other in and with the gift."[6]

If peopling, broadly defined, involves appropriate kinds of giving, of initiating contact with others for mutual enhancement, then one might look for several qualities which have the potential for development in school.

Peopling and the Person

The qualities of peopling which we have selected to examine are as follows:

1. The person sees other people in his world as co-equal but as possessing diverse gifts.
2. The person can reach toward people in different arrangements of time and space.
3. The person can establish a variety of kinds of contact in giving to others.
4. The person has criteria for determining when he will attempt to change another and when his giving will be primarily supportive.
5. The person indicates that he can solve problems relative to peopling.
6. The person is aware of the potential power of presence and consequently seeks to utilize his own self appropriately in the contexts in which he finds himself.

---

5. Cornelis Verhoeven, *The Philosophy of Wonder: An Introduction and Incitement to Philosophy*, trans. Mary Foran (New York: Macmillan, 1972), pp. 166, 167.
6. Ibid., p. 167.

Co-equal persons

The person sees other people in his world as co-equal but as possessing diverse gifts. Ross says, "We are participating in the celebration of a return to a people-to-people world."[7] The gifts persons bring to others may be interests, attitudes, values, manners, strivings, desires, or any peculiarly human quality, as well as material things.

If we accept the assumption of co-equal persons but diverse gifts, then certain other concepts bear examination.

Man as Piece of Art.   Basic to any consideration of person-to-person relationships is the notion that the person is an exquisitely complex being. We may try to analyze the person in order to understand him better but simultaneously we must accept the uniqueness of the individual. Each person's gifts, then, are particular to himself even though universal and national attributes are part of his personality. Salk says, "Many of man's attributes still need to be explained, such as his aesthetic sense and its expressions and those transcendental qualities which might be referred to as the art in him—the essence of his character and personality that distinguishes each individual from all others."[8] If the mystery, the transcendental nature, and the artistry of each person are accepted, persons are less apt to subject him to that type of analysis which might examine the pieces without giving adequate attention to the interplay of the parts.

A valuable piece of art is handled carefully and sensitively. With no less finesse should persons be treated if their personal qualities are to have the opportunity to develop and flourish.

Reciprocity.   Assuming persons are co-equal and possess gifts worth sharing, the possibility exists that each person may tilt toward the other so that gifts can be given and received. When a person tilts toward another but the other turns away, a problem exists. But when a person initiates turning toward another and the other person responds by tilting toward the person, the potential for a healthy relationship exists.

At least three types of relationships are possible. In the first situation, one person gives and the other receives but the second person gives little (figure 5-1).

---

7. Ramon Ross, *Story Teller* (Columbus, Ohio: Charles E. Merrill, 1972), p. 4.
8. Jonas Salk, *Man Unfolding,* World Perspectives, Vol. 46, ed. Ruth Nanda Anshen (New York: Harper & Row, 1972), p. 8.

FIGURE 5–1

A second type of relationship is one in which neither person is willing to give much, thus creating little potential for communication and interaction (figure 5–2).

FIGURE 5–2

In the third instance, both persons are willing to tilt and to give, thus creating the opportunity for mutuality among persons (figure 5–3). In this latter interchange man finds reciprocity and a sense of mutual concern.

FIGURE 5–3

Giving Appropriately.   It is not enough to give or even to give without any strings attached. The giver should also give appropriately. Bambara, in the short story "The Lesson," aptly describes a situation in which attempts toward giving are made by Miss Moore but the intended gifts are inappropriate. On a hot day when a group of children would rather go swimming, Miss Moore thinks she is doing them a favor by taking them downtown. One of the children says,

> I'd much rather go to the pool or to the show where it is cool. ... And finally I say we oughta get to the subway cause it's cooler and beside's we might meet some boys. ...
> So we heading down the street and she's boring us silly about what things cost and what our parents make and how much goes for rent and how money ain't divided up right in the country. And then she gets to the part about we all poor and live in the slums, which I don't feature.[9]

In addition to finding a gift which makes sense to the receiver, the person who gives appropriately allows others to contribute to him. Although one should not attach strings to his giving, one needs to realize that at times to accept from another is to give. The person who gives appropriately lets others know that he is open to their gifts, that he will utilize them but that the relationship is not dependent upon a checker-game type of giving and receiving.

Differing Purposes and Gifts. Each individual has his own gifts which may be combined and recombined in a variety of ways, and it behooves persons to acknowledge and take into account the gifts of others in their own thinking and planning. Those responsible for the education of the young have been notorious in failing to account for the distinctive gifts of Mexican-Americans, blacks, and other minority groups.

O'Connor says that ". . . a person is in his very being a gift."[10] When we learn to prize the person as a gift, we can better learn to prize the gifts he bears.

Reaching toward others

The person can reach toward people in different arrangements of time and space. The many changes which have accompanied the development of a technological society mean that persons must develop new ways to see, relate to, and contribute to the welfare of people. In many situations the task is so complex that persons may become remote and distant from

---

9. Toni Cade Bambara, "The Lesson" from *Gorilla, My Love* (New York: Random House, 1973). Taken from Stephanie Spinner, ed., *Live and Learn: Stories about Students and Their Teachers* (New York: Macmillan, 1973), p. 3.

10. Elizabeth O'Connor, *Eighth Day of Creation: Gifts and Creativity* (Waco, Texas: Word Books, 1971), p. 27.

their fellows rather than engage in the difficult task of trying to create a person-to-person world. So much seems to militate against the development of strong and meaningful relationships. Frequently in today's hurried world, persons see each other as playing some role or performing a specified task rather than as total human beings. Persons should view their fellows as bringing longings, aspirations, values, and heartaches to their day-to-day ventures if peopling is considered important.

Entanglements. For persons in a family group or close friends to form warm, intimate relations is ordinarily not difficult. The frequency of meeting and the close space in the worlds of the individuals involved provide a setting where peopling can flourish if the persons involved have the psychological bent to be open with and caring for each other. Problems may arise when persons attempt to formulate relationships of a meaningful type where meeting is infrequent due to distance in space and living. If a person is concerned about peopling, he needs to develop a plan to insure that within his world are persons representing a variety of locations in space and a diversity of points of meeting. This person may include in his plan means of describing and assessing his own sense of responsiveness and responsibility to persons on different points of a space-time continuum.

Spaces that Facilitate Diversity. A characteristic of many twentieth century communities is the tendency toward homogeneity. Families tend to group themselves in communities where persons from similar socioeconomic standings reside. The placement of children in classrooms is frequently based upon similarities rather than differences. Members of an occupational group frequently develop a sense of comaraderie with other members of the same occupation and denigrate or ignore persons with unlike vocations. Families tend to be concerned only about the immediate family, leaving aunts, uncles, cousins, and grandparents to fend for themselves psychologically if not financially. States and nations tend to care for their own and provide little incentive and often deterrents to an exchange of persons across boundaries. In brief, we live in a world where little is done to assist persons in shaping their attitudes towards persons representing diversity and heterogeneity.

Occasionally one does come across uses of space where every attempt is made to provide for diversity. For example, consider the school in which criteria necessitating diversity of population are established for entrance.[11] Or, consider the sidewalks of a city street where children are

---

11. An example of such a setting was the Center for Young Children, University of Maryland, College Park.

allowed to play. Nearby shopowners, parents, and older persons all assume a modicum of responsibility for each other and for the youth growing up in the neighborhood.[12] Consider the community school where parents and children together engage in worthwhile activities. If persons are concerned about peopling, they need to look at who occupies various spaces in the course of a day, week, month, or year.

Reaching Out in Time and Space.   Basically, each person needs to work through for himself the numbers and kinds of relationships he enjoys in time and space. He needs to consider the nature and kind of community in which he feels most comfortable and points at which he wishes to change either his sense of community or actual community.

If persons are to remain alive, alert, and responsive to other persons, then peopling must provide for a variety of contacts in time and space. How each person achieves this must be worked out by each person with himself—his attitudes, values, and feelings toward his fellows.

Establishing degree of giving

The person can establish a variety of kinds of contact in giving to others. In an analysis of giving which does not necessarily involve material things, but rather gifts of the person, there are many stances from which we can view the concept of giving or tilting.

Relating to the Few and the Many.   One of the problems of human encounter is that many persons, in order to survive the bombardment of people-stimuli, must learn to cope with the problem of selecting the degree of intensity with which they will relate to the various persons with whom they have contact. For example, persons have to make choices relative to the individuals with whom they will become intimately involved, the circumstances under which they will become involved, and the numbers with which any intense involvement is possible. When the person allows a degree of involvement with another, peopling takes place. The point we are making is diagrammed in figure 5–4.

Most persons in a given period of time probably have opportunities in each of the four quadrants of the diagram. The person concerned about peopling has some awareness of when and how frequently he falls into each of the four quadrants. For example, the person who is extremely concerned about his work and is a contributor to his occupation falls into quadrant II; however, he might want to consider whether

12. For a discussion of the advantages of city sidewalks, see Jane Jacobs, *The Death and Life of Great American Cities* (New York: Random House, 1961), chapter 4, "The Uses of Sidewalks: Assimilating Children," pp. 74–88.

FIGURE 5–4

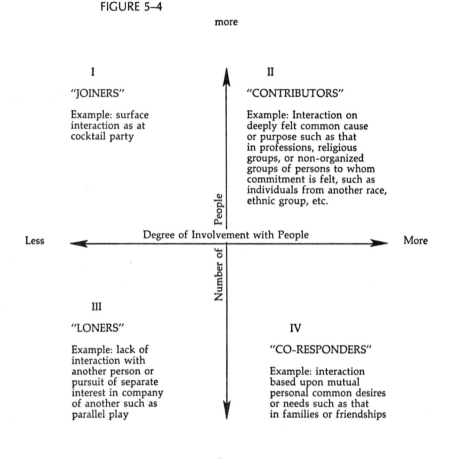

more

I

"JOINERS"

Example: surface
interaction as at
cocktail party

II

"CONTRIBUTORS"

Example: Interaction on
deeply felt common cause
or purpose such as that
in professions, religious
groups, or non-organized
groups of persons to whom
commitment is felt, such as
individuals from another race,
ethnic group, etc.

People

Less ←——— Degree of Involvement with People ———→ More

Number of

III

"LONERS"

Example: lack of
interaction with
another person or
pursuit of separate
interest in company
of another such as
parallel play

IV

"CO-RESPONDERS"

Example: interaction
based upon mutual
personal common desires
or needs such as that
in families or friendships

less

at times it would be worthwhile to participate in activities of quadrant
I so that he can enlarge his potential circle of persons with whom to
people. Again, a person might consider the advantages and disadvantages of excessive activity in each of the quadrants. For example, if a
person spends most of his time in quadrant III "Loners," or quadrant I
"Joiners," what might be the consequences? What are the consequences
of being primarily engaged in solitary activity or in activity with one's
family and intimate friends? Basically, persons periodically should examine their adventures in peopling.

Indifference vs. Love.   Another stance from which one can consider giving
is from the perspective of indifference versus love. Few persons actually
hate others although hate is frequently seen to be the antithesis of love.

Many persons are indifferent to other persons, however, and consequently may tilt toward them only infrequently. Frequent tilting may accompany a loving relationship. Sutherland says we can be in union with someone, or we may abandon him. When we move toward union we are moving toward love.[13] When we are moving toward abandonment we are moving toward indifference. Neglectful attitudes, uncaring gestures, and thoughtless words are instances of little attention to peopling and consequently to loving. Such instances indicate a minimal concern for giving. Tilting strongly toward others indicates maximal giving. When individuals cross barriers which seem almost unsurmountable, when they have an interest in diversity among persons, when they seek to find common interests with others, then loving, giving, or tilting exists.

Individualistic vs. Cooperative Giving. Another way of considering the concept of giving is through an analysis of cooperative as opposed to individualistic giving. According to Sawyer, if a person is cooperative, he will try to maximize his own welfare and that of the other person. If the person is individualistic, he will maximize his own welfare without regard for that of the other person. Altruism ordinarily exists in the cooperative person but not in the highly individualistic one.[14]

In a day when humanity's problems are of such magnitude that the refined sensibilities of persons with diverse gifts should be brought to bear upon them, it is critical that certain forms of giving be of a cooperative nature so that the gifts contain the workmanship of many and thereby assist in the solution of problems not solved by one person alone.

Giving Comfort. In our giving to others we can give coldly and mechanically, or we can tilt or give with grace and warmth. A study of the words *comfort, consolation,* and *solace* indicates that there are fine but significant discriminating differences in these words. Within the concept of *comfort* are the notions of imparting strength, of soothing, of encouraging, cheering, and extending sympathetic kindness. Comfort denotes an intimate relationship in which the alleviation of distress is accompanied by cheering and encouragement. *Consolation* is a less intimate word. Although it connotes the alleviating of grief or discomfort,

13. Richard Sutherland, "An Anatomy of Loving," *Journal of Religion and Health* 11:167–74, April 1972.

14. Jack Sawyer "Altruism Scale," in *Measuring Human Behavior,* ed. Dale G. Lake, Matthew B. Miles and Ralph B. Earle, Jr. (New York: Teachers College Press, 1973), pp. 10–13.

it does not contain within it the notion of cheering or encouraging. *Solace* is even a less intimate concept and applies more to a planned giving of aid by an agency or organization. The concept of solace also lacks the joyous note of cheer and encouragement. Providing solace may not be a person-to-person act, but rather an agency-to-person kind of behavior. In our giving, and therefore our peopling, the concept of bringing encouragement and pleasure to those in sorrow and grief should be inherent.

Giving and changing

The person has criteria for determining when he will attempt to change another and when his giving will be primarily supportive. Any book about teaching must be concerned about the concept of change, for inherent in the teaching act is the notion that behavior can and should be changed. Teaching or changing may contradict the concept of loving, for Sutherland has defined loving as "the attentive assent without the desire for change."[15] We, therefore, need to raise questions such as the following: By what criteria do persons simultaneously love and yet want to change another? Since teaching is concerned with changing behavior, is it possible to love a student in the same sense that one loves a friend? What is the form of love most appropriate to those who deal with the young?

Answers to these questions can only be found if those who dare to work with the young are willing to lay out for examination their own gifts and to the young the option to appropriate some of these gifts and to reject others.

Adults who work with the young need skills in finding points of entry to their concerns—whether through sports, music, cooking, or simply acting as concerned listeners. Another gift useful in working with the young is the ability to listen nonjudgmentally. If adults can lay out their own gifts and possess the gift of establishing a common bond with another person, then points of coercion between the young and their mentors may be minimal.

No responsible and responsive adult would be expected to take the position that education does not have inherent in it the concept of change. The issue is: Under what conditions shall change take place? It is our position that only the person can decide whether or not to change himself. The most that his mentors can do is to provide creative and varied opportunities which possess the potential for encouraging change.

15. Sutherland, "An Anatomy of Loving," p. 171.

Solving problems

The person indicates that he can solve problems relative to peopling. Working with and enjoying people demands two sets of competences. The first set has to do with the inner resources of persons—modes of thinking and deciding, characteristic ways of feeling, means of achieving and utilizing feedback about one's own behavior and vehicles for creating and demonstrating attitudes and values. These kinds of internalized competences of persons should be brought to the level of awareness so that persons who are concerned about others can utilize their inner resources in the service of others. Since these inner qualities are given much attention throughout the book, they are only acknowledged here.

A second set of competences is related to outer conditions—being able to identify and deal with problems or considerations related to peopling.

Creating Readiness. If a person is concerned about peopling, he needs to know when it is appropriate to contribute to the life of another person and when another person wishes to receive what he has to give. As the teacher considers the readiness of pupils in the teaching of mathematics or reading, so in the commitment to peopling one has to determine readiness to receive. If a person rejects what one has to give, the individual needs to have criteria to ascertain whether to try to reach the person in another way, whether to delay, or whether to withdraw.

For example, a group of teachers from a pre-school wished to establish contact with the teachers who would receive their children in an elementary school. Rather than make direct contact with the elementary school, the teachers first conducted an inventory of the gifts they might bring, such as knowledge of community resources, knowledge of families. They then conducted an inventory of their own attitudes. Such a procedure was necessary to insure that they were not coming with the idea that they had the answers, but rather with a willingness to explore possibilities. Moving slowly, making sure that the initiating school was willing to accept as well as give, and planning carefully for points of entry resulted in more favorable kinds of peopling than if the readiness factor had not been considered.

Crossing Barriers. Another problem meriting major attention if a person wishes to people is that of finding means to cross barriers. Crossing barriers involves moving into areas different from the norm. For example, in the movie "Sounder," Mrs. Boatright (a white person) seeks information about David's father (a black person) who is in jail. Since seeking and giving such information is against the law, she is crossing barriers when she attempts to gain it.

Again, one is crossing barriers when one supports a person in a group who takes a position which is uncommon or unpopular. The one who supports the person must find ways to deal with the unpopular stand which he has assumed for himself.

A person also crosses barriers when he stands in the shoes of another. How does a teacher feel when he tries to stand in the shoes of a student? A poor person in the shoes of the rich and vice versa? A farmer in the shoes of a businessman? A daughter in the shoes of a mother? A North American in the shoes of an African? A sorrowing person in the shoes of a joyful person? The person who peoples practices standing in the shoes of others so that when the need arises he can cross the necessary barriers easily.

The power of presence

The person is aware of the potential power of presence and consequently seeks to utilize his own self appropriately in the contexts within which he finds himself. Unfortunately, persons frequently do not stop to think about the power of presence. In a highly active and verbal culture, unless a person is doing something or speaking something, it appears that he is inactive and consequently of little use to the persons or groups around him. Such may not be the case. The parent who is with a child, whether in active or inactive interaction, may do more for the child psychologically than a series of parent substitutes.[16] The teacher who is merely available to the child without necessarily talking at him may be more critical to the child than the teacher who feels his function is to impart knowledge.

Presence or being there—listening, responding, assuming responsibility, doing what seems appropriate at a given moment in time—is critical. Being willing to watch and wait, to respond appropriately are the qualities of the person willing to utilize presence in the act of peopling.

Summary of Qualities
of Persons Who People

The qualities or behaviors of persons concerned about peopling are next listed. This summary fairly closely parallels the behaviors discussed in chapter 11. In that chapter opportunities are also developed as a means

---

16. See John Bowlby, *Attachment and Loss,* 2 Vols. (New York: Basic Books, 1969 and 1973), for theory and research relative to the significance of the mother in the life of the child.

for observing and recording feedback in settings designed to provide chances for increased skill in these areas.

1. The person sees other people in his world as co-equal but as possessing diverse gifts.
   a. The person is seen as a piece of art, possessing unique qualities, yet having universal qualities.
   b. The person is aware that reciprocity results in more healthy relationships than if giving or receiving is done primarily by one party.
   c. The person seeks to give appropriate gifts.
   d. The person realizes that purposes and gifts differ.
2. The person can reach toward people in different arrangements of time and space.
   a. The person can form entanglements in larger and smaller worlds.
   b. The person can deal with persons representing diverse backgrounds found in common meeting places.
   c. The person reaches out to others in time and space.
3. The person can establish a variety of contacts in his giving to others.
   a. The person can relate to the few and the many.
   b. The person seeks to be indifferent to few, loving to many.
   c. The person is willing to engage in cooperative as well as individualistic giving.
   d. The person can give comfort appropriately.
4. The person has criteria for determining when he will attempt to change another and when his giving will be supportive.
5. The person indicates that he can solve problems relative to peopling.
   a. The person can create readiness to receive a gift.
   b. The person can cross barriers or move into areas which are different from the norm.
6. The person is aware of the potential power of presence and consequently seeks to utilize his own self appropriately in the contexts within which he finds himself.

The remainder of this chapter deals with the relationship of peopling to other major skills—communicating, knowing, and dealing with the social systems.

Peopling and Communicating

Through communicating we can help identify the gifts each person brings to peopling. Looking at others, listening to them, clarifying with them all aspects of communication are critical if persons are to understand their gifts. O'Connor says, "Very few of us have had a listening, seeing person in our lives. We do not hear what others—not even our children—are saying because we, ourselves, have had no one to hear us.[17]

If individuals are to live as persons capable of giving and receiving affection then they need to see beyond themselves in order to facilitate the contributions of others. Seeing beyond one's self means communicating with others. And when communication takes place within the context of mutual tilting and exchange, we have peopling.

Language as a vehicle

One of the greatest gifts man has for establishing person-to-person contacts for mutual cooperation is language. Through language the person attempts to insure that a symbol such as cat is a stimulus and a response and that the same symbol has similar meanings for different persons. Through the use of symbols, a person is able to derive meanings which are similar to those of his neighbors. In addition to understanding symbols, the person who wishes to insure that his messages are honest and reality-oriented is also aware that words can have many representations; hence, he realizes he must be a close observer to make certain that words convey what is seen. Action *is,* but when it is interpreted through words there are problems of differentiated meanings among persons. By clarifying, qualifying, apologizing for mistaken interpretation, amplifying, and reconsidering an individual becomes truly human. Returning to what is being observed and refining language to see that the real is represented by the symbolic as accurately as possible is a human function demanding skill, patience, and wisdom.

Language is a vehicle for peopling also in that it provides a means for making the context personal. Persons who are in familiar contexts have common meanings. Change of context invites the development of new sets of meanings. The reverse is also true. Language can invite changes in context. If it were not for language, contexts might not change when newness seems necessary.

Integrating meanings among persons

Through the use of language and creative interchange each person can appreciate individuality and transform his own personality through

---

17. O'Connor, *Eighth Day of Creation,* p. 19.

integrating what he receives from others.[18] The creative interchange enables a person to appreciate the "other's joys, sorrows, hates, loves, pieties, and other features of that vast complexity which makes up the total experience of every human being."[19]

One of the excitements of human interaction is the unpredictability of persons. Platt says, ". . . we cannot predict other people's behavior because we are interacting with them all the time."[20] Thus, although persons try to find common meanings with others, at the same time they must be prepared to deal with the ambiguity which results from the variability of human nature.

Basically, a person uses language as a vehicle for integrating himself with others. This is done when he sees and communicates his commonalities, his own uniqueness, and his predictable and unpredictable nature. Since he simultaneously sees the uniqueness and predictability and unpredictability of his fellows, he is able to develop a feeling of comaraderie with them.

Mass media and peopling

One cannot talk about communication and peopling without some attention to mass media. The mass media have opened doors to all kinds of interchange among persons but at the present time the moral and humane use of our new technological tools has been inadequately conceptualized. Lowenthal says, ". . . despite telephones, radios, television, increased literacy, expanded circulation of books, newspapers, and periodicals we are lonelier than ever before. . . ."[21] Recent developments in American political life have drawn attention to the potential of the mass media to distort reality in order to highlight a point. Teachers are frequently concerned about children's reliance on second-hand rather than direct experience because of the long hours they spend in front of television out-of-classroom.

On the other hand, we are aware that the mass media enable rapid communication from one point on the globe to the others. Basically, however, we are concerned in this book with face-to-face communication, with the potential of persons to enhance themselves and others

18. For a fuller discussion of this point, see Henry Nelson Wieman, *Man's Ultimate Commitment* (Carbondale: Southern Illinois University Press, 1958), pp. 22 and 305.

19. Ibid., p. 23.

20. John R. Platt, *Perception and Change: Projections for Survival* (Ann Arbor: University of Michigan Press, 1970), p. 115.

21. Leo Lowenthal, "Communication and Humanities," in *The Human Dialogue: Perspectives on Communication*, ed. Floyd W. Matson and Ashley Montagu (New York: Free Press, 1967), pp. 335–45, esp. p. 335.

through direct confrontation and encounter. Yet, we are aware that the media can be used to enhance man's sense of community, his brotherhood with his fellows, and his sense of tilting toward others in order to give and to receive.

Peopling and Knowing

Peopling requires careful attention to knowing. One needs to know one's self, others, contexts and/or situations, and how one can best contribute to society.

A basic question is: What knowledge do we need in order to people? A second question is: What knowledge is generated by persons who people?

Gaining necessary knowledge

Self-knowledge. A major kind of knowledge for the person concerned about reaching out to others is a basic understanding of self—one's strengths and weaknesses. As a person becomes aware of his gifts, he can see what he has to offer to others and what he does not. For example, one person might have the gift of being able to listen to another person while another has the gift of clarifying what is being said in a group. A third person might have a gift of a body of information useful to some project.

The peopling person is a wise person. The wise person operates with charity and humility, for he is aware of the diverse and multitudinous gifts necessary to living in today's world. Although he recognizes the significance of his own gifts, he is also aware that others have gifts. Part of the discipline of living is the ability to help another improve his gifts as well as to enhance one's own. As one comes to understand himself, he prizes wisdom as well as information and knowledge. Wisdom implies that a person can apply his learning and knowledge, that he sees essential and inner relationships, and that he has the insight to see the relationships between the knowledge of his fellows and his own knowledge. The wise person operates on the premise that it is through the integration of knowledge of many persons that new learnings can be achieved. Although the wise person has a degree of idiosyncrasy and individuality, he uses these qualities to involve his fellows for causes more significant than could be achieved by any one person alone.

Persons concerned about self-knowledge are also concerned about the problem of how they make attributions to other persons. They are aware that unless their skill in seeing others is accurate, sympathetic, and loving, they are not apt to help others enhance their own gifts and hence the common good. The following is a discussion by the authors on making attributions.

L.: Let's talk about a very significant area in peopling—that of making attributions about people. Attributions are made on the basis of what we think we are seeing in another person and what we are hearing from him. What seems to influence our judgments about others?

How do I decide that another person is attractive? Honest? Creative? How do we learn to keep our ideas about other people open and fluid? If somebody has done something dishonest, how do I determine the degree to which a single act is indicative of his character?

Once I have attributed some qualities to another person, do I communicate them to him? Do I keep them to myself? Do I ask the other person to communicate to me the attributions he is making about me? We are dealing with the problem of building knowledge about other persons or building knowledge relative to peopling.

One area which we can study in our attempt to understand the nature of making attributions is the influence of context. For example, recently a group of persons were analyzing an instrument to use with young children. One of the questions dealt with how teachers see the attractiveness of a child. What conception of the child is appropriate? White Anglo-Saxon? Black? Oriental? Are we talking about the nature of attractiveness within subgroups of the larger categories? The problem of the relation of context to attribution is one that we need to look at very critically and assist our young with if we are going to build toward a knowledge of peopling. Do you agree?

J.: Yes, I do. Peopling is an individual matter. If we could generalize about the qualities of persons, we could negate the whole idea of peopling. I would like to respond to some of your points.

First, how do we arrive at attributions of people? Stated another way, we might ask what influences what we see in other persons and what we hear them saying? One factor that enters into this process is the closeness of the relationship between the two persons. If I am very close to a person, I might have a greater concern for the qualities I would like to see in that individual and I might make attributions which fit my expectations or preconceived notions. These attributions might not be in line with the perceptions of others or how the individual perceives himself. We try so hard to see those qualities which will deepen and strengthen the relationship. We also tend to make many attributions, whereas in a less meaningful relationship we might make fewer.

Another factor which seems to have an impact on the attributions I make about others is my concern about what others see in me and hear

me say. I generally would like the responses from others to indicate that
the relationship is a good one. How I arrive at my attributions about
others might well be determined to a large degree by the attributions
I think others are making about me and by what I hope they would
attribute to me. In short, our perceptions of the feedback we are receiving determine the kind of attributions that are made.

L.: You are pointing out the need of getting feedback on the attributions that we think we are making to others. We need to sit back at times
and ask, "Is what I am attributing to the person really there?"

J.: Yes. I think this is particularly necessary in a close relationship
where viewing a person objectively might be quite difficult. However,
distance in a relationship might also cause one to be subjective. I might
not think it worth the time or effort it takes to achieve objectivity.

You also asked the question: Should we communicate our attributions to others and should we ask them to communicate theirs to us?
One would have to determine whether a discussion of attributions is
going to be harmful to the individuals involved. I think there can be
value in an open discussion of attributions because we can always err
in our perceptions of others. Giving objective feedback may be less
threatening to a relationship and may aid in correcting misconceptions.

L.: In other words, you are suggesting that whenever it seems appropriate, persons should try to give feedback on perceptions of attributions.

J.: Yes, as long as you use good judgment so that a person or a
relationship is not destroyed in the process. This last point is in line with
the question, "How do we build knowledge about people?" I think that
as we progress in building or generating knowledge in this area, we will
achieve more sophisticated and objective bases for seeing others. When
we become more aware of what occurs, then it will be easier to convey
what we see with grace and humility. Of course, persons must strive to
keep their minds open and to plan for obtaining a variety of kinds of
feedback which will lessen the number of erroneous and sometimes
harmful attributions. We also need to look for thoughtful ways of
communicating the information we gather.

Understanding Context.   Hartup discusses a person's ability or skill in
assessing "... the people present in a situation, his skills in adjusting
his behavior to these attributions, and his past history of exposure to
values about these attributions."[22] We have just discussed the problem
of making attributions to persons. One major factor that influences how

---

22. Willard W. Hartup, "The Needs of Young Children and Research: Psychosocial
Development Revisited," *Young Children* 12:129–135, April 1973, esp. p. 129.

we make attributions is how persons see and utilize context. Persons need knowledge relative to when they are behaving in ways which the context suggests and when they are deviating from the contextual norm and operating idiosyncratically. Persons concerned about the relationship of their behavior to the setting need to determine how best to achieve feedback relative to their own behavior within the context in which they are living and moving at the moment.

To live in one's setting successfully requires skill in self-knowledge, skill in making attributions about persons, and skill in understanding the total context or social milieu. Searching for and achieving feedback can be useful in the integration of these skills.

Knowing Others.   In addition to knowledge about self, how one makes attributions, and the relationship of context to peopling, one needs to know other persons. If I am concerned about another and care for him, there are many things I must know. Mayeroff says, "I must know, for example, who the other is, what his powers and limitations are, what his needs are, and what is conducive to his growth; I must know how to respond to his needs. . . . Such knowledge is both specific and general."[23]

Mayeroff goes on to explicate that what we know about caring for another we know in different ways. For example, we know both explicitly and implicitly. Explicit knowledge can be verbalized; implicit cannot. We know persons both directly and indirectly. When a person is known directly, he is known in his separateness and individuality. When a person is known indirectly, one has knowledge about him but does not necessarily experience him.[24] It is critical that in looking for ways of knowing persons we are aware that knowledge can be described in various ways and we must be open to these several modes if we are to know and care for others.

Generating knowledge

If persons are concerned about and care for others, certain qualities might characterize the knowledge generated.

Reflects Shared Ideas.   When a child learns something of importance to himself, he will have a desire to share it with others.[25] In addition, the

---

23. Milton Mayeroff, *On Caring* (New York: Harper & Row, 1971), p. 13.
24. Ibid., pp. 14, 15.
25. Roland S. Barth, "Open Education: Assumptions About Children's Learning," in *Open Education: The Informal Classroom,* ed. Charles Rathbone (New York: Citation, 1971), p. 127.

person who enjoys peopling also enjoys developing knowledge in collaboration with others. Thus, the knowledge generated by persons who people often comes through collaboration, cooperative probing and analysis, group synthesis, and discussion involving a variety of persons. The process is an exciting one, often full of conflict, but ordinarily resulting in knowledge which could not have been generated by one person working alone.

Reflects Interdisciplinary Approach, Social Focus, or Reworking of Personal Meanings. We often find knowledge generates interdisciplinary responses to critical social or human dilemmas. People-oriented persons may be interested in breaking barriers to help alleviate human need and suffering. Knowledge produced in peopling, therefore, probably is deduced from multiple sources and is utilized for problems which might be new, futuristic, or incapable of being categorized within the realms of existing disciplines.

In creating knowledge, Lee says that we should give thoughtful attention to the "social importance" of the phenomena to be studied rather than to "relative stability or relevance to existing theory."[26] When persons are involved in peopling, they realize that the knowledge of most worth is meaningful to the person or immediate group.

In reworking personal meanings, persons take into account the multiple contexts of their lives. Lee talks about "the many-mindedness of individuals."[27] Many-mindedness makes it necessary to insure that knowledge is constantly being formulated and reformulated. Although the reformulation of knowledge is primarily for the individual, some reformulations are useful to other persons. On this point, Becker indicates that "the genius is the one who has reworked personal meanings into a product the whole culture can share: that is to say, he has made a *personal* resolution which can be utilized by others."[28] Whether or not persons are endowed with the qualities of a genius is not critical. The point is that personal meanings appropriate to the context or situation are generated by persons who people.

Peopling and Social Systems

Social systems frequently refer to formal relationships among persons, whereas peopling refers to more informal relationships. Peopling takes place within social systems which foster or deter peopling in terms of their basic structure and operating principles.

26. Alfred McClung Lee, *Multivalent Man* (New York: George Braziller, 1966), p. 32.
27. Ibid., p. 19.
28. Becker, *The Structure of Evil,* p. 253.

According to Bugental, "Man has evolved many forms of relation-ships: acquaintance, friend, intimate, companion, opponent, bystander, family, social group, formal and informal groupings, cities and nations; loves, spouse, parent, and child; member officer, outsider."[29] Bugental goes on to say that in these various kinds of relationships we relate in varying degrees of personal involvement and intimacy. Social systems provide the arena for intimacy and involvement, but persons' attitudes toward each other determine the quality of life within the social system, particularly democratic ones or ones which purport to care about the person.[30] Let us briefly consider some distinctions between social systems and peopling.

Response-responsibility

Basically, a person responds to an act initiated by another. The response is individualized and personalized. Response does not imply obligation, external imposition, or public accountability. Basically, peopling is a responsive kind of interaction.

Responsibility implies external imposition of rules or standards, obli-gation, and public accountability developed by the social system.

Self-serving—other-serving

The concept of service is integral to good peopling and good social systems. The word institution, according to Dubos, "did not refer to buildings, administrative structure, and other mechanisms of the work-a-day world. Rather it expressed a commitment binding diverse activi-ties focused on a mutual concern; it denotes a concerted effort to create a coherent whole out of multiple efforts devoted to this concern.[31] Institutions are a form of social system, and social systems come about when the effort of the whole can make a greater impact than the effort of discrete units. We people when mutual care exists among persons in the immediate and larger communities.

Self-authority—institutional authority

A major problem of our times is related to the concept of who has control over individual lives. Schools have given inadequate attention

---

29. J. F. T. Bugental, *The Search for Authenticity: An Existential Analysis Approach to Psychotherapy* (New York: Holt, Rinehart, and Winston, 1965), p. 35.

30. Alice Miel and Peggy Brogan, *More than Social Studies: A View of Social Learning in the Elementary School* (Englewood Cliffs, N.J.: Prentice-Hall, 1957), chapter 1, "The Discipline of Democracy," pp. 3–24. In this chapter Miel and Brogan discuss the compe-tences an individual needs to maintain the discipline of democracy or the kind of social system in which simultaneous attention is given to individuation within a social order.

31. René Dubos, *A God Within* (New York: Charles Scribner's, 1972), p. 198.

to the problem of personal freedom and authority. We fail to recognize that different kinds of authorities exist in life—the authority of the law, the authority of expert knowledge, the authority of one's self, the authority of tradition. Becker says, "Neurosis is a problem of the authority over one's life."[32]

One of the reasons for the attention to decision in this work is that ultimately the individual must decide how he will respond to various authorities external to himself. If he does not respect the authority of the law, he is making decisions which negate the existence or validity of such a social system. The wise person has learned to incorporate into his self-authority a way of responding to various types of authority. To the degree that he is able to work out compatible arrangements among the various authorities competing for his allegiance, he will be able to live a life which is harmonious to himself.

Likewise social systems must recognize the various authorities competing for the attention of the individual and not place undue pressures upon the person to meet unnecessary demands. If a social system fails to recognize the problem of authority, it may find itself with confused persons and a sick institution or organization. The task is to free individuals to develop frameworks for dealing with the problem of authority and to set up within institutions mechanisms that deal realistically with conflicts of authority. Persons freed from internal constraints relative to authority may find themselves full of unexpected energies.

In Retrospect

In this part attention has been directed to central concepts necessary to the development of decision making, involvement, and peopling. In addition, consideration was given to the relationship of communication, knowledge, and social systems to these basic threads.

In the next part attention is directed to means of achieving feedback as a way of building curricula based upon the critical processes of deciding, becoming involved, and peopling.

Suggestions for Further Reading

Adams, Paul and others. *Children's Rights: Toward the Liberation of the Child.* Introduction by Paul Goodman. New York: Praeger, 1971.

Adkins, Winthrop R. "Life Coping Skills: A Fifth Curriculum." *Teachers College Record* 75: 507–26, May 1974.

---

32. Becker, *The Structure of Evil,* p. 258.

Ashbrook, James B. "Paul Tillich Converses with Psychotherapists." *The Journal of Religion and Health* 11: 60–72, January 1972.

Becker, Ernest. *The Structure of Evil: An Essay on Unification of the Science of Man.* New York: George Braziller, 1968.

Borgatta, Edgar F. and William W. Lambert, eds. *Handbook of Personality Theory and Research.* Chicago: Rand McNally, 1968.

Bowlby, John. *Attachment and Loss.* 2 vols. New York: Basic Books, 1969 and 1973.

Buber, Martin. Translated by Maurice Friedman. *A Believing Humanism: My Testament 1902–1965.* New York: Simon and Schuster, 1967.

Curran, Charles A. "What Can Man Believe In?" *Journal of Religion and Health* 11: 7–39, January 1972.

Drews, Elizabeth Monroe and Leslie Lysson. *Values and Humanity.* New York: St. Martin's Press, 1971.

Ferkiss, Victor C. *Technological Man: The Myth and the Reality.* New York: George Braziller, 1969.

Graubard, Stephen R. *Kissinger: Portrait of a Mind.* New York: W. W. Norton, 1973.

Hess, Robert D. and Judith V. Torney. *Development of Political Attitudes in Children.* Chicago: Aldine, 1967.

Jacobs, Jane. *The Death and Life of Great American Cities.* New York: Random House, 1961.

Keyes, Ralph. *We, the Lonely People: Searching for Community.* New York: Harper & Row, 1973.

Lake, Dale G., Matthew B. Miles, and Ralph B. Earle, Jr., eds. *Measuring Human Behavior.* New York: Teachers College Press, 1973.

Lewis, Arthur J. and Alice Miel. *Supervision for Improved Instruction: New Challenges, New Responses.* Belmont, Cal.: Wadsworth, 1972.

Martinello, Marian L. *Making Education Relevant.* Lafayette, Ind.: Kappa Delta Pi, 1973.

Matson, Floyd W. and Ashley Montagu, eds. *The Human Dialogue: Perspectives on Communication.* New York: Free Press, 1967.

Mayeroff, Milton. *On Caring.* New York: Harper & Row, 1971.

Metcalf, Lawrence E., ed. *Values Education: Rationale, Strategies, and Procedures.* National Council for the Social Studies, 41st Yearbook. Washington, D.C.: National Education Association, The Association, 1971.

Miel, Alice and Louise M. Berman, eds. *In the Minds of Men: Educating the Young People of the World.* Washington, D.C.: Association for Supervision and Curriculum Development, 1970.

Miel, Alice and Peggy Brogan. *More than Social Studies: A View of Social Learning in the Elementary School.* Englewood Cliffs, N.J.: Prentice-Hall, 1957.

Miel, Alice with Edwin Kiester, Jr. *The Shortchanged Children of Suburbia.* New York: The American Jewish Committee, 1967.

Perrone, Vito and Warren Strandberg. "A Perspective on Accountability." *Teachers College Record* 73: 347–55, February 1972.

Platt, John R. *Perception and Change: Projections for Survival.* Ann Arbor: University of Michigan Press, 1970.

Read, Paul Piers. *Alive: The Story of the Andes Survivors*. Philadelphia: J. B. Lippincott, 1974.

Salk, Jonas. *Man Unfolding*. World Perspectives, Vol. 46, edited by Ruth Nanda Anshen. New York: Harper & Row, 1972.

Spinner, Stephanie, ed. *Live and Learn: Stories about Students and Their Teachers*. New York: Macmillan, 1973.

Sutherland, Richard L. "An Anatomy of Loving." *Religion and Health* 11: 167–74, April 1972.

Verhoeven, Cornelis. Translated by Mary Foran. *The Philosophy of Wonder: An Introduction and Incitement to Philosophy*. New York: Macmillan, 1972.

Wieman, Nelson. *Man's Ultimate Commitment*. Carbondale: Southern Illinois University Press, 1958.

part three

Observing and Describing the *What, How,* and *Why* of Living

Deciding, becoming involved, peopling—these skills can be vaguely stated aims or goals or they can provide a dynamic structure for the curriculum. If the latter is to be realized, means must be found to: (1) translate broad philosophical ideas into classroom procedures, and (2) determine whether the recommended procedures do indeed provide opportunities for learners to acquire skills deemed significant.

The purposes of this part are three-fold: (1) to orient the reader to the need for and nature of achieving feedback; (2) to provide a basic understanding of the process of communication as it can facilitate persons achieving feedback; and (3) to suggest procedures for developing feedback techniques. One chapter is devoted to each of these purposes.

Describing or clarifying what transpires when persons interact with context provides an empirical base for making decisions about teaching process skills. Persons who achieve feedback by using observation or reflective techniques become more aware of the elements of context interacting. These individuals also become more skilled in anticipating behaviors apt to occur in settings designed to encourage selected skills.

Underlying our discussion of the rationale and techniques for obtaining information on process skills related to the what, how, and why of living are the following assumptions:

1. When persons are concerned about progress or growth in personal qualities, procedures for obtaining feedback must be directly related to the personal qualities in which opportunities for change are given.

2. Objective feedback gathered by teachers and others makes it possible to compare the information generated with expectations, and consequently to devise more realistic expectations and more satisfactory means of obtaining feedback.

3. Interactive situations are in constant flux, and any means of describing them must accommodate and reflect the flux.

The chapter which follows is a discussion of the need for and nature of describing progress within the curricular position we are assuming.

6

Why Observe
and Describe?

Perspective on Chapter 6

Theme: Observational procedures for recording changes in learner behavior are consistent with the curricular orientation of this work—highlighting the process-oriented person.

Selected major points: (1) Establishing contexts that encourage process-oriented behavior is critical. (2) Careful procedures for obtaining feedback must be devised if educators are to know what is transpiring in the classroom.

As you read: (1) Think about the definition and characteristics of context. In what way does the authors' view of context differ from your own view of it? (2) Do you agree with the significance accorded gathering on-the-spot feedback? Why?

The primary purpose of this chapter is to help persons who are responsible for the learning of children gain knowledge about the degree to which they acquire the personal qualities discussed in chapters 3, 4, and 5. Obtaining such knowledge is facilitated when procedures employed in curriculum development are interrelated and are viewed as a unified whole.

Developing a Process Curriculum

Curriculum development as defined in this work consists of establishing a view of man and ascertaining what the school can do to help persons achieve the qualities inherent in this view. Procedures directed at helping learners achieve the designated qualities consist of selecting or designing contexts that encourage the development of the qualities and obtaining feedback on the degree to which the qualities have been developed. Achieving a close fit between the view of the individual established and the procedures involved in helping persons progress in the personal qualities inherent in the view is central to our concerns.

The importance of unity

We propose that the value and relevance of decisions pertinent to developing curriculum are enhanced when priorities in terms of personal qualities, contexts for developing them, and methods for describing progress in these qualities are related. The starting point for developing curriculum can be any one of these three interrelated aspects of the curricular enterprise. However, all phases must be acted on at one time or another in order for wise decisions to be made.

In addition to the implications for decision making in developing curriculum, a unity among the aspects of curriculum development has implications for the responsibilities and expectations of all persons who participate in any aspect of planning, teaching, and achieving feedback. The kind and amount of personal involvement in curriculum development both influence and are influenced by the unity of purpose and action we propose.

Personal involvement

A close relationship or unity among the aspects of curriculum development identified above implies input on the part of all persons engaged in planning, implementing, and evaluating what transpires in the classroom. Teachers, learners, and others who share responsibility for classroom learning experiences can and should participate in explicating the nature of the person who contributes constructively and creatively to his and society's progress. As individuals identify the qualities of the person, they also gain direction for determining the nature of context which enables the learner to develop these qualities. When contexts are appropriate to the enhancement of the personal qualities, and when persons have opportunities to determine the nature of each, personal involvement in developing curriculum is promoted, and unity of purpose and action advanced.

The importance of continuous personal involvement in achieving the fit or unity among the phases of curriculum development is further highlighted when the process of obtaining feedback is considered. We assume that individuals who are responsible for making curricular decisions can and should participate in gathering information for such purposes, thus making the results more germane to the specific situation. In addition, knowing that one can participate in the process of generating the knowledge on which decisions are based motivates the decision maker to improve the quality of the feedback procedures and to clarify how the information influences the decisions he makes.

The impact of the researcher, evaluator, or data collector on the process of curriculum development is also evident in our assumptions about the knowledge generated while obtaining feedback. We assume that knowledge generated during the process of describing what is happening in the classroom reflects the concerns, values, attitudes, personal commitments, and priorities of the persons who have designed and implemented the information-finding procedures.

To acknowledge the impact of the person on knowledge production is not to negate the need for objectivity in describing what is happening in the classroom. Instead, it allows us freedom to examine more carefully factors that influence our approach to knowledge production and to come to grips with the characteristics of the knowledge we generate.[1]

In summary, we propose that one factor contributing to quality curricular decisions is knowledge generated by obtaining information about what transpires within the classroom setting. We also propose that in order for this to occur, there must be a unity or relatedness among identification of process-related priorities, designing the contexts in which they can be developed, and devising procedures for gathering information relative to the degree to which the qualities are developed. The importance of the teacher, learner, or curriculum worker in achieving unity among the phases in curriculum development is also stressed.

In the remainder of this chapter, we discuss contexts as facilitating the development of desired personal qualities, an overview of the process of obtaining feedback, additional support for emphasizing information-generating techniques, and implications for ways to obtain feedback.

---

1. See Center for New Schools, "Strengthening Alternative High Schools," *Harvard Educational Review* 42:313–50, August 1972, for a discussion of the role of the researcher or evaluator in generating knowledge about or describing a situation.

Contexts that Develop
Process-Related Qualities

In this work, we chose as our initial point of exploration in the curriculum development cycle our priorities in terms of skills of the process-oriented person. These personal qualities and skills related to decision, involvement, and peopling were discussed in part two of this volume. In this chapter we will first discuss the elements of context, and then move to the process of obtaining feedback.

An elaboration of context

Context, as used in this volume, is the learner's perception of the setting in which he decides to become a participant by interacting with materials, other persons, or ideas. In addition to materials, ideas, and other persons, the setting can consist of spatial or physical arrangements and time dimensions. These aspects of context may be considered singly or in any combination. Although teachers generally establish contexts designed to implement designated priorities, in the final analysis it is the learner's perception of these contexts which determines the nature of his interactions with them and whether or not he develops the anticipated or hoped-for personal qualities.

The nature of context that facilitates a learner's development of the qualities inherent in process-related curricular goals is discussed in terms of the components or elements of context, some general characteristics of context as the term is used in this book, and the anticipated nature of learners who interact with contexts designed to develop process-related skills.

Elements of context

In our definition of context we propose that elements of the context with which the learner may interact or which provide direction for his interacting include materials, other persons, knowledge or ideas, time, and space. Those who engage in planning for contexts that are designed to facilitate a learner's development of specified personal qualities need to consider what constitutes each element and the potential of each for helping the individual learner achieve his goal.

Materials are the realia placed within the learning context or brought to it during the interaction. The teacher may initially plan for placing realia in the context, but teachers and learners can add or remove materials at appropriate times. The nature of materials should be such that learners can bring to bear upon them their personal meanings and ideas for using them. In short, the structure provided by realia in the context should not preclude an individual's contributing to and revising the structures. The purpose of realia is to facilitate, not to dictate.

Other persons are the significant others in the learning context with whom the individual learner interacts. There may be many or few or only one at a given time. The teacher, classroom aides, peers, children from other classrooms, parents, and resource persons in the community are examples of the human resources that can be part of a reciprocal relationship which facilitates the development of designated personal qualities. Learners need guidance in discovering how other persons can contribute to and benefit by a mutual interaction that is satisfying and challenging to all concerned. Learning when and how to initiate an interaction with another person and when and how to respond are vital to learning how to learn from others.

Knowledge comprises the substantive or ideational aspect of an interaction. Persons interact with other persons and with materials, but underlying and emanating from these interactions are perceptions or content which help give direction to them. If it were not for knowledge, a person often would have little reason to interact. Knowledge also makes it possible to maintain an interaction over time, to build up prior interactions, and to project and plan for future ones.

Public knowledge that exists in books or in the many forms of audio and visual media can be utilized by the learner, but it is only when that knowledge has meaning for the person that significant learning takes place. Meaningful knowledge can be public knowledge that the learner has scrutinized, examined, revised and made part of his own thinking; or it can be knowledge that the learner himself has generated in the process of interacting with already established or public knowledge, materials, or significant others.

Time as an element of context is viewed from two perspectives. It can be duration or length of time available or needed for an interaction and the point in time of an interaction. This perspective represents clock time or attempts to establish points in time and to measure the passage of it.

Time can also be viewed from the perspective of individual psychological and biological clocks.[2] This is not the passage of time in terms of the clock, but the time when an individual works best, the time when an individual feels he can commence a task, the pace at which he functions at optimal level, or the feeling of time as passing rapidly or slowly. Too often the time of human individuality is ignored or de-

---

2. For an examination of related ideas see Gay Gaer Luce, *Body Time* (New York: Bantam Books, 1971 and 1973).

emphasized in all types of contexts. The time of initiating and ending an interaction is often best determined by individual biological and psychological clocks rather than by the clock on the wall. On the surface, inner time tables appear easier to manipulate than the time table of the clock, but the personal price of *apparent* success at such manipulation is prohibitive.

With L'Engle we appreciate the fact that the Greeks had two words for time: *chronos* and *kairos*.[3] The teenager absorbed in fashioning a bowl on the pottery wheel and a group of youngsters listening to a reading of a favorite book for perhaps the third time are in *kairos*. Measured time is not and should not be the major consideration in these instances. In addition to being aware of and appreciating the two ways of viewing time, we need to make sure they are taken into account when establishing learning contexts.

Space can also be viewed from two perspectives: one concerns the objective requirements of the task; the other the psychological requirements of the person engaging in the task. Viewed from the first perspective, space is (1) the area of a floor, gathering place, or work space utilized in an interaction or (2) the distance between materials, groups of persons, or any focus in the learning setting. Space viewed from the second perspective relates to the individual—his personal need for physical space.

These two perspectives for viewing space can be clarified in the following illustration. A writer ordinarily needs a desk, chair, and writing equipment. However, some writers prefer the closeness of a carrel or booth, and others prefer the expansiveness that an unobstructed view of the ocean or mountains provides.

Space, in the first sense, is objective area or distance, and is often predetermined by the limits of architectural design or by the preplanning of a teacher. Space, in the second sense, involves the improvisations and revisions by learners and teachers based upon their psychological needs. Persons can move equipment, thereby changing spatial dimensions and adapting objective space to personal requirements.

When consideration is given to personal space, the individual is given opportunities to participate in determining the nature of spatial arrangements of elements within the context or setting, the chance to claim some area that he knows is his and in which he can plan and implement his work, and the opportunity to determine the context where he feels comfortable in interacting with others.

---

3. Madeline L'Engle, *A Circle of Quiet* (New York: Farrar, Straus and Giroux, 1972), p. 245.

Interaction of the elements of context must be considered in planning for teaching. In planning for the kind of context that facilitates the development of skills of the process-oriented person, teachers and learners should consider the interrelationships of the elements. Interaction is different in a setting in which all learners must read from the same set of basic readers than in a setting where learners can select their own reading materials and discuss them with others.

A *postscript?* Although the individuality of the learner and his role as interactor with contexts have been stressed in the discussion of each element, a statement that the person is a part of context is in order. The individual is a vital, active aspect of the context—one whose contributions to the setting are shaped by his past and present experiences as well as hopes for the future. The larger social group and the cultural context which surround the learner also contribute to shaping what he brings to an interaction or task and how he perceives and utilizes elements within the immediate learning context.[4] These aspects of the larger context, although not obvious at the time of the learning interaction, must be reckoned with as influential factors.

General characteristics

The elements of context just described are closely interrelated in terms of how they facilitate a learner's progress toward achieving his goals. At times one element such as knowledge may predominate or be the focal point while the other aspects provide support and perspective. Knowledge of how context elements are utilized either singly or in combination by the learner and how they facilitate his achievement of goals enables us to identify the more general characteristics of context.

Closeness to Real Life. A learning context or setting should approximate as closely as possible the real and natural in life. Questions, situations, and materials are not contrived or artificial, and interaction with them is not just a game. A natural context might include some incongruous or unexpected elements or even aspects that may produce some concern or even confusion on the part of the learner. Sometimes these elements appear during an interaction as a result of the interplay between the learner and the various aspects of context.

---

4. For a discussion of the major components of a learner's situation and the importance of examining a situation and its influence on behavior and cognitive development see, Willard W. Hartup, "The Needs of Young Children and Research: Psychosocial Development Revisited," *Theory into Practice* 12:129–35, April 1973.

Structure.   Closely related to the naturalness or reality of the context is the structure implicit in it. Elements of context should be planned so that the learner perceives a structure which enables him to give direction to his actions. Purpose and arrangement, evident in how the elements are made available to the learner, help him grasp the structure and utilize it to his advantage. Too much structure imposed by persons not directly involved in the interaction can result in a setting that is sterile, protected, and controlled. These conditions can discourage a learner from dealing honestly with valid concerns and issues. The appropriate degree of structure needs to be determined jointly by teachers and learners. Information relative to the desired kind and amount of structure can be more objectively and realistically ascertained when feedback on how persons interact with the context is obtained and examined.

Flexibility.   A flexible context not only allows for but encourages the unexpected and unanticipated. It makes possible the utilization of the range and complexity of human behaviors. Different behaviors are in evidence at different times. Flexibility allows for the individuality of the person by accounting for psychological and biological rhythms.

Flexibility also has an impact on the available alternatives and the ways in which knowledge is handled. Learners can reassess private and personal knowledge. Since learners do not necessarily behave in predictable patterns and since they vary in their perceptions, elements of a context must be flexible. The emerging individual learns not by adding on layers but by much fitting, reshaping, and integrating the new and the emerging.

Feedback.   In order to facilitate the individual learner's progress in developing skills related to the process-oriented person, contexts should include opportunities for the learner to gain feedback on his interactions either during the interaction or shortly thereafter. Teachers and peers can gain this knowledge by observing the learner in the process of his interactions with contexts. The individual learner can also obtain feedback by reflecting on an activity after it is completed or by making observations during the activity.

Responsible Behavior.   Finally, contexts should be designed to encourage responsible behavior on the part of the learner and to help him see the implications and effects his behavior has on himself and others. It is possible to arrange or structure the elements of context in such a way that the learner is aware of how his decision to select one alternative over another changes a series of future steps. In its simplest form this information may be gained by planning a procedure and projected out-

comes, changing the plan via a personal decision, and noting the outcome. The projected and observed outcomes can then be compared and
the implications of the difference between the two examined. Specific
examples of such procedures as they relate to designated processes are
found in chapters 9, 10, and 11.

Learners Who Interact
with Context

Learners who have opportunities to interact with contexts characterized
by immersion in the critical issues of life, flexible structures, and possibilities for learners to assess and see the implication of their actions can
be expected to approach life situations in a particular manner. These
persons do not view context as *doing* something *to* them but as opportunities for them to shape their direction, make choices, revise, and select
those elements pertinent to their concerns and to the task at hand. They
have power over context—they can at least partially shape it and adapt
it to themselves rather than be controlled by it. They see and are able
to deal with and benefit from the adverse or the incongruent in the
setting. They also see themselves as contributors to the setting.

A learner who interacts with contextual elements of the nature we
propose values his uniqueness and recognizes that genuine knowledge
is that which he internalizes as a result of his interactions with persons,
materials, and ideas. He not only actively participates but also sees how
the context helps shape his ideas, feelings, and experiences. It is not an
either-or, but a give-and-take relationship that brings both the learner
and the context together.[5] A learner who engages in interactions within
this setting also seeks out challenging contexts that enable him not only
to approach a problem from many perspectives but also to see himself
and how he relates to the social, material, and ideational environment.
He perceives connections between the immediate learning setting and
the larger social and cultural setting. In essence, if facilitating the development of process-related skills is prized, then the context should contribute to the learner's development of a unique life-style, a sense of
responsibility for developing common perceptions, and an ability to
relate this knowledge to that of others.

In summary, persons who assume responsibility for educational experiences must be able to select or design contexts that facilitate the
development of skills related to the process-oriented person. We have

5. For a discussion of the unity and interplay between learner and context, see Frances
Minor, "Cognitive Development: Some Pervasive Issues," *Theory into Practice* 12: 78–87,
April 1973.

attempted to equip educators for the task of designing contexts by presenting a discussion of the elements and characteristics of context and the anticipated characteristics of learners who interact with these contexts. As individuals interact in specifically prepared settings, feedback relative to the nature of the interaction can be obtained.

Feedback: An Overview

The purpose of this overview is to establish the need for obtaining feedback on what transpires in the classroom setting. A definition of feedback and reasons for obtaining it are presented. Factors which support the need for and provide impetus for obtaining feedback are also presented as is the need to emphasize a match between curriculum questions and feedback procedures. Specific guidelines for developing feedback techniques are described in chapter 8.

Definition

Feedback is defined in this volume as descriptive information about an individual's interaction with the elements of a designated context or setting. Although feedback is generally defined more narrowly than it is here, we use the term only to facilitate clear and succinct communication. For the most part, the learner's interactions with context are described while he is engaged in them. However, at times what transpires during an interaction is recorded after an observation or interview. What transpires may also be reflected on by the learner. In this definition of feedback, primary emphasis is placed on *describing* as objectively as possible interactions *in process.* We propose that the procedures used in obtaining feedback are as important as the kind of information sought in this process.

The feedback obtained by describing what is occurring when learners interact with the context can consist of descriptions of verbal and nonverbal behaviors which denote the learner's process-related qualities. These descriptions can also indicate how and to what degree the learner engages in processes such as making decisions, becoming involved, or relating to other persons.

Feedback can also include descriptive information about elements of the context such as materials, spatial conditions, time, and significant others. The way feedback is recorded varies with the nature of the context and the purpose for obtaining it. Guidelines and specific suggestions for recording observations and reflections are presented in chapters 8, 9, 10, and 11.

Outcomes

Earlier we stated that without specific information as to whether or not learners are acquiring the skills and qualities characteristic of the process-related person, individuals engaged in curriculum planning are forced to make decisions based on hunches, guesses, and opinions. Any effort which results in decreasing the number of curricular decisions based on opinion or conjecture constitutes a valid reason for obtaining feedback. However, there are additional and equally important reasons for obtaining it.

Personal Responsibility. When we gain knowledge about what happens as a result of our efforts, our sense of personal responsibility is heightened and we are made more aware of the moral dimension of our tasks. Persons who in any way participate in planning for conditions or situations that are meant to influence another's perception of and interaction with the environment are responsible to a degree for the outcome. Since learners and teachers can participate in this planning, both parties also share in a sense of responsibility for the outcome of these plans. Although the person engaged in planning cannot assume complete responsibility for the learner's response to contexts, his conscious sense of personal responsibility forces him to consider the consequences of his planning not only for the learner but for himself and any future planning he does.[6]

Search for Order and the Unexpected. In his attempt to understand and to enjoy the world in which he lives, the individual looks for things that go together and also things that do not fit. According to Platt, "Our highest mental organization is a continual search for patterns and surprises."[7] Teachers and learners are aware of patterns and surprises in their day-to-day interactions in the classroom setting, but how can they be helped to capitalize on the existence of these patterns and surprises and on the natural tendency of a person to seek them out? How can individuals be guided in discovering order and the unexpected in their lives and the lives of others and in understanding how the rhythm of order and surprise influences decisions they make?

A teacher's search for patterns and diversity in the classroom can be facilitated by the use of techniques for gathering information. Such techniques are characterized by a structure and an openness which make

6. A discussion of responsibility from a biologic perspective is found in Jonas Salk, *Man Unfolding* (New York: Harper & Row, 1972), pp. 53–59.
7. John R. Platt, *Perception and Change: Projections for Survival* (Ann Arbor: University of Michigan Press, 1970), p. 107.

it possible to heighten awareness of surprise and to utilize and build upon it. Knowledge gained in using these techniques facilitates planning which helps learners see the meaning of order and the unexpected in their lives.

Desire to Invent. The continuous and vigorous search for order and surprise in the flow of life and the knowledge gained in this search verifies what exists. However, the teacher does not stop at verification of the existing but utilizes this information to generate new ideas, thus becoming genuinely excited about exploring alternatives. Efforts on the part of individual teachers to achieve feedback about what happens in their classrooms can provide them with the stimulus to invent new ways of accomplishing their goals. What *is* can be used as a springboard to anticipate what *might* be.

In summary, information generated in the classroom setting can make students and teachers more aware of their responsibility for their actions; can contribute to satisfying their need to seek order and surprise in life; and can stimulate their desire to invent or inject newness.

Major purpose for obtaining feedback

The major purpose for obtaining feedback in the classroom is to determine whether or not learners are acquiring the skills deemed important at a given time by the teacher and the learner. In turn, this knowledge makes it possible to examine critically the priorities set and contexts designed to implement them.

Value of obtaining feedback

One way of ascertaining the value of feedback obtained in the classroom setting is to consider what the knowledge gained enables the teacher and the learner to do. At times feedback helps an individual see congruence or lack of it between the ideal or priorities that *should* be and what *is.* Congruence or agreement between what a person *thinks* is happening and what *is* happening can also be determined.

In addition to identifying areas of agreement, obtaining feedback can help an individual see relationships among the various kinds of knowledge gained in different ways. Knowledge gained through precise, organized observations and recordings can be used to verify hunches or casual observations. In addition, information derived from continuous record-keeping of a learner's interactions can be compared over time and in different settings.

Modes of gathering descriptive information about behavior in process also lead to generating information that reflects the realities of the context. For example, an observer may record information in addition to, but related to, the learner's behavior. The additional information might consist of a description of the larger context or social milieu in which the learner lives. Planning and using feedback procedures also aids in developing in-depth insights into the processes observed and the means employed in recording what is observed. In addition, needed questions are raised.

Factors Necessitating
Feedback Procedures

Earlier in this chapter we stated certain outcomes resulting from obtaining feedback in the classroom setting. We also delineated some values of generating information. Both the stated outcomes and value of feedback support the need to obtain it. However, additional support emerges from an examination of certain factors related to schooling and curriculum development.

Highlighting the person as seeker

Our present educational system is sometimes viewed as a mass production system in which the individual has difficulty finding opportunities for being recognized and for contributing as a person. In line with this view, Peck asserts that "... contemporary practice seems largely to treat students as passive, teacher-controlled units in an almost faceless mob."[8] In contrast to this perception of the situation are pronouncements advocating the development of learning opportunities that "... open possibilities and responsibilities to teachers and learners."[9] Often exhortations to move in this direction are accompanied by suggestions for procedures and descriptions of attempts already in motion. Those responsible for what happens in the classroom are encouraged to consider interaction with persons, materials, and ideas from the perspective of learning as transacting as opposed to reacting.[10]

Teachers and learners are asked to consider the views of knowledge that are appropriate to learning experiences which are more facilitative

---

8. Robert F. Peck, "Promoting Self-Disciplined Learning: A Researchable Revolution," in *Research in Teacher Education: A Symposium*, ed. B. Othanel Smith (Englewood Cliffs, N.J.: Prentice Hall, 1971), p. 84.

9. Anne M. Bussis and Edward A. Chittenden, *Analysis of an Approach to Open Education*, Interim Report (Princeton: Educational Testing Service, August 1970), PR–70–13, p. 12.

10. Louise Berman presents the values of learning as transacting in "Not *Reacting* but *Transacting:* One Approach to Early Childhood Education," *Young Children* 28:275–82, June 1973.

and open in nature. In this context knowledge and the knower are not separate, and the plurality of modes of cognition and evidences of knowledge are recognized.[11]

Literature which both encourages and describes the development and implementation of approaches to learning that might open up responsibilities and possibilities is replete with phrases, terms, and slogans descriptive of this approach. Among them are action, active modes of learning, purposeful involvement, opportunities to make decisions, education for diversity, learning experiences that give the learner control over what happens to him, personalized education, and the learner as an evolving individual.[12]

A composite view of the above exhortations and phrases reveals a set of primary emphases or thrusts. One emphasis is on encouraging diversity, the unexpected, and the unanticipated. Convergence or attempts to bring closure are not excluded, but the primary emphasis is on opportunities which encourage exploration.

A second emphasis relates to the development of desirable personal qualities. There is concern for the nature of the person in terms of how he creates and utilizes knowledge and how he interacts with others, ideas, and materials. In addition, how he handles available options is considered of prime importance. Does he recognize responsibilities and possibilities? If so, how does he act upon them? The concern for the person in the learning process is evident in goals which are stated in terms of what a person can become and in attempts to determine what happens in the process of his becoming. The person is seen as constantly in the process of growing and developing or becoming.

Two other points are emphasized in the literature. One is the need for experiences that make it possible for learners to become intensely involved if they wish. Another is the importance of a view of knowledge that recognizes the role of the person in generating knowledge.

If we believe in and support educational priorities that encompass active, transactive learning where persons become aware of and act upon their possibilities and responsibilities, we obviously need to address ourselves to how we can determine whether or not objectives related to these priorities are fulfilled. How can we ascertain what happens when learners interact with contexts designed to develop and

11. Charles H. Rathbone, "The Implicit Rationale of the Open Education Classroom," in *Open Education: The Informal Classroom*, ed. Charles H. Rathbone (New York: Citation Press, 1971), p. 102.

12. The idea of the evolving individual is elaborated on by Frances P. Hunkins and Patricia F. Spears in *Social Studies for the Evolving Individual* (Washington, D.C.: Association for Supervision and Curriculum Development, 1973).

fulfill the state priorities? A commitment to learning experiences in which the person can partially determine the qualities he wishes to develop and ascertain whether his practice is congruent with intent forces us to reexamine some basic ideas related to achieving feedback.

Matters requiring reexamination and rethinking

Selye proposes that in some instances what we know is more of a deterrent to furthering our investigations than what we do not know.[13] If we agree with Selye, the first matter that needs to be carefully scrutinized concerns the bases on which we presently operate in the classroom and those we might consider adopting.

We are cautioned that because something is happening or because we have a strong commitment to it, is not sufficient reason to encourage and cultivate it.[14] Neither is "doing one's thing" because the freedom to do it is there enough reason to justify its happening. There must be a clearer specification of purposes and how they can be implemented and evaluated.

As we reexamine the bases on which we make decisions about learning experiences, it is important to look at the sources of knowledge utilized. Knowledge about classroom behavior includes learners' interactions with peers and materials as well as teacher-learner interaction.

A second matter that needs reexamining or rethinking is how feedback is obtained and recorded. We deal with this process in detail later, but recent trends in education have strong implications for this function. Procedures employed must catch the individual in the process of learning or provide means for the learner to analyze and chart his own growth as he experiences it. Also, teachers and learners must realize that they are mutually responsible for not only achieving feedback but also for utilizing it. Persons engaged in this process are not totally objective, neutral entities, but rather active participants who bring themselves and their experiences to bear upon the situation.[15]

A third matter requiring careful consideration relates to the factors that might tend to discourage efforts to achieve feedback as proposed in this book. Often research is discussed in terms of pre-testing, treatment, and post-testing which measures changes in achievement. Also, teachers might tend to feel unprepared. As a result they give low pri-

13. Hans Selye, *The Stress of Life* (New York: McGraw-Hill, 1956), p. 35.
14. Center for New Schools, "Strengthening Alternative High Schools," p. 336.
15. Ibid.

ority to knowledge production in classroom settings. In addition, learning is often viewed as a process in which learners are trained to perform a skill which can be measured in a controlled manner as opposed to a process in which learners develop qualities that can have an impact on the totality of their lives and others.

The fact that an education characterized by diversity and surprise as well as by unity and structure is not widely valued in our society constitutes another force which can deter progress in initiating and carrying through knowledge-producing procedures. Recognizing the possible factors which can discourage efforts in this direction should not cause us to abandon our plans but instead strengthen them by knowing in advance the nature of possible obstacles.

A final factor, the examination of which reveals the importance of obtaining feedback in the classroom, relates to achieving a match or fit between curricular concerns and procedures for gathering information about these concerns.

Achieving a match

On the surface, emphasizing the importance of achieving a match between curriculum design and the procedures for ascertaining what happens when learners interact with context related to that design might appear to be a truism. Obviously, techniques for gathering information should match the questions asked or information sought. However, the development of procedures for generating knowledge about what transpires in classroom settings based on a curriculum design that assumes man is a creative force and not just a reactor is still in exploratory stages.

Achieving a fit between process-related curriculum priorities and procedures for obtaining feedback on the attainment of these priorities in the classroom becomes increasingly important if one considers the idea of "data-finding" as opposed to "data-accumulating."[16] If learning experiences are opportunities for learners to exercise their individuality and initiative within a structure that is flexible enough to accommodate and encourage these qualities, then procedures are needed which enable us to observe and describe learners' actions in flexible, flowing situations. "Data-finding" seems to imply an attitude toward obtaining feed-

16. David Guttman discusses shifting from a data-accumulating to a data-finding approach in the context of interviewing techniques in cross-cultural studies. The idea presented here was stimulated by the content of Guttman's chapter entitled, "Psychological Naturalism in Cross-Cultural Studies," in *Naturalistic Viewpoints in Psychological Research*, Edwin P. Willems and Harold L. Raush, eds. (New York: Holt, Rinehart and Winston, 1969), pp. 162–76.

back that is congruent with the view of the person inherent in a process-related curriculum. The person does not just respond to an interaction, but is an active contributor to it and a potential change agent.

Similarly, "data-finding" is an active process—one that does not just mirror the interaction in terms of predetermined criteria, but helps the person find information that results in his adding, deleting, or revising criteria as the situation suggests. In this way, the subtleties of human behavior and the unanticipated dynamic qualities of it are included in the feedback.

Another reason for emphasizing the need to achieve a match is to counter the notion that feedback procedures dictate curricular goals and methods for implementing them. The relationship between goals and feedback should be a reciprocal one in which each phase facilitates the development of the other. Curriculum priorities and practice should have as much impact on designing feedback procedures as knowledge gained in achieving feedback has on establishing curriculum priorities and designing ways of implementing them. When this occurs, the unity among the phases of curriculum development is achieved.

Implications for Ways
to Obtain Feedback

A commitment to designing learning experiences which facilitate the development of personal qualities and knowledge and to obtaining feedback on progress in this development has implications for how feedback is obtained. First, means of gathering data on the learner's interactions within designated contexts must reflect how time, space, materials, significant others, and ideas contribute to the learner's achievement of goals as he perceives them. A view of personal growth and knowledge generation as in process and not always defined as terminal points or as solutions requires ways of obtaining information that capture the person in action and are sensitive to knowledge as it is derived and utilized.

In proposing this broader view of generating information on the complexities of ongoing personal, material, and ideational interactions in the classroom setting, the need to conceptualize what goes on in the classroom is disclosed. Diagnostic and achievement tests administered at pre-determined times throughout the school year leave many gaps in the teacher's and learner's knowledge of how growth in personal qualities and knowledge production has taken place and of the impact the learning environment has had on this growth.

Second, seeing the larger picture as well as the complexities within it implies the need for many attempts to obtain feedback from a variety of perspectives and for varying durations of time. Although a learning context is designed or selected with the intent that the learner develop certain personal qualities as he interacts with it, the learner may perceive the setting in a different way. Consequently, his interactions would deviate from those anticipated.

Third, the emphases on personal responsibility and initiative evident in some recent efforts to facilitate learning strongly support the need to obtain feedback on progress within the classroom setting. When feedback is obtained in this manner, the information gathered reflects the wide range of human competences within a classroom that encourages the individual to see life and his interactions with it as nonlinear and dynamic. The person's interactions with space, time, human and material resources, and knowledge are always emerging, revealing their many-faceted nature.

The two chapters that follow contain specific recommendations and guidelines for feedback procedures. The first looks at communication as a vehicle for describing overt learner behaviors from which process-related personal qualities can be inferred. The last chapter in the section offers guidelines, with examples, for developing procedures for obtaining feedback in the classroom setting.

Suggestions for Further Reading

Barker, Roger G. and Paul V. Gump. *Big School, Small School: High School Size and Student Behavior.* Palo Alto, Calif.: Stanford University Press, 1964.

Barker, Roger G. *Ecological Psychology: Concepts and Methods for Studying the Environment of Human Behavior.* Palo Alto, Calif.: Stanford University Press, 1968.

Berman, Louise M. "Not *Re*acting But *Trans*acting: One Approach to Early Childhood Education." *Young Children* 28: 275–82, June 1973.

Berman, Louise M. and Jessie A. Roderick. "The Relationship between Curriculum Development and Research Methodology." *Journal of Research and Development in Education* 6: 3–13, Spring 1973.

Berman, Louise M., ed., and Staff. *Toward New Programs for Young Children: Program and Research Possibilities.* University Nursery-Kindergarten Monograph 1. College Park: University of Maryland, 1970.

Brandt, Richard M. *Studying Behavior in Natural Settings.* New York: Holt, Rinehart and Winston, 1972.

Broudy, Harry S., Robert H. Ennis, and Leonard I. Krimerman. *Philosophy of Educational Research.* New York: John Wiley, 1973.

Burger, Henry G. "Behavior Modification and Operant Psychology: An Anthropological Critique." *American Educational Research Journal* 9: 343–60, Summer 1972.

Bussis, Anne M. and Edward A. Chittenden. *Analysis of an Approach to Open Education: Interim Report,* Princeton: Educational Testing Service, August 1970.

Center for New Schools. "Strengthening Alternative High Schools." *Harvard Educational Review* 42: 313–50, August 1972.

Elliott, David L. *Beyond "Open" Education: Getting to the Heart of Curriculum Matters.* Urbana, Ill.: ERIC Clearinghouse on Early Childhood Education, 1971.

Glaser, Barney G. and Anselm L. Strauss. *Discovery of Grounded Theory.* Chicago: Aldine, 1967.

Guttman, David. "Psychological Naturalism in Cross-Cultural Studies." In *Naturalistic Viewpoints in Psychological Research,* edited by Edwin P. Willems and Harold L. Raush. New York: Holt, Rinehart and Winston, 1969.

Gordon, Ira J. *Studying the Child in School.* New York: John Wiley, 1966.

Hall, Elizabeth. "Ethology's Warning: A Conversation with Nobel Prize Winner Niko Tinbergen." *Psychology Today* 7: 65–80, March 1974.

Harman, Willis W. "The Coming Transformation in Our View of Knowledge." *The Futurist* 8: 126–28, June 1974.

Hartup, Willard W. "The Needs of Young Children and Research: Psychosocial Development Revisited." *Theory into Practice* 12: 129–35, April 1973.

Hunkins, Francis P. and Patricia F. Spears. *Social Studies for the Evolving Individual.* Washington, D.C.: Association for Supervision and Curriculum Development, 1973.

Hutt, S. J. and Corinne Hutt. *Direct Observation and Measurement of Behavior.* American Lecture Series. Springfield, Ill.: Charles C Thomas, 1970.

Jackson, Philip W. *Life in Classrooms.* New York: Holt, Rinehart and Winston, 1968.

Keen, Sam. *To a Dancing God.* New York: Harper & Row, 1970.

Labovitz, Sanford and Robert Hagedorn. *Introduction to Social Research.* New York: McGraw-Hill, 1971.

Lachenmeyer, Charles W. *The Essence of Social Research: A Copernican Revolution.* New York: Free Press, 1973.

L'Engle, Madeleine. *A Circle of Quiet.* New York: Farrar, Straus and Giroux, 1972.

McCall, George J. and J. L. Simmons. *Issues in Participant Observation.* Glencoe, Ill.: Free Press, 1969.

Minor, Frances. "Cognitive Development: Some Pervasive Issues." *Theory into Practice.* 12: 78–87, April 1973.

Peck, Robert F. "Promoting Self-Disciplined Learning: A Researchable Revolution." In *Research in Teacher Education: A Symposium,* ed. B. Othanel Smith. Englewood Cliffs, N.J.: Prentice Hall, 1971.

Phillips, Bernard S. *Social Research: Strategy and Tactics.* 2d edition. New York: Macmillan, 1971.

Platt, John R. *Perception and Change: Projections for Survival.* Ann Arbor: University of Michigan Press, 1970.

Polanyi, Michael. *The Tacit Dimension.* Garden City, N.Y.: Doubleday, 1966.

Rathbone, Charles H. "The Implicit Rationale of the Open Education Classroom." In *Open Education: The Informal Classroom,* edited by Charles H. Rathbone. New York: Citation Press, 1971.

Rowen, Betty. *The Children We See: An Observational Approach to Child Study.* New York: Holt, Rinehart and Winston, 1973.

Salk, Jonas. *Man Unfolding.* In World Perspectives. Vol. 46, edited by Ruth Nanda Anshen. New York: Harper & Row, 1972.

Sarason, Seymour B. *The Culture of the School and the Problem of Change.* Boston: Allyn and Bacon, 1971.

Sjoberg, Gideon and Roger Nett. *A Methodology for Social Research.* New York: Harper & Row, 1968.

Willems, Edwin and Harold L. Raush, eds. *Naturalistic Viewpoints in Psychological Research.* New York: Holt, Rinehart and Winston, 1969.

7

Communication:
Vehicle for Describing
Interactions

Perspective on Chapter 7

Theme: Communication is the means by which inferred meanings about skills of the process-oriented person can be made explicit.

Selected major points: (1) Personal qualities of the process-oriented person are revealed through the verbal and nonverbal behaviors a person exhibits during an interaction and during the communication of a person's reflections. (2) Person-to-person communication is a sharing of personal meanings, a participatory process, a creative process, and a rich complex process.

As you read: (1) After you have had an opportunity to reflect on the points of this chapter, what implications do you see for shifts in common school practices relative to communication skills? (2) How can educators become more attuned to the subtleties of the communication process?

~~~~~~~~~~~~~~~~~~~~

The importance of obtaining feedback in the classroom setting was established in the preceding chapter. We also emphasized the need to obtain this information while the learner is engaging in an interaction with the setting or while he is in the process of considering the meaning of an interaction. Generating knowledge in both these instances implies that interactions for which school personnel are responsible can take place in spaces outside the immediate school or classroom.

The major purpose of this chapter is to explore how knowledge of the components of communicative behavior and skill in applying such knowledge can facilitate obtaining feedback about interactions in the classroom setting. Since our priorities are in terms of process-related personal qualities, we need to develop ways to ascertain the nature of the person's decision-making behavior, his peopling behavior, and his involvement. However, a person's participation in these processes is not always obvious to another individual because inner thoughts are not always announced directly. Consequently, these processes must be inferred. We propose that a study of the communicative behavior of persons as they engage in or reflect upon an activity designed to develop process skills can facilitate making inferred meanings explicit.

Rationale for Selecting Communication

By focusing on communicative behaviors, astute observers can derive help in describing growth in process skills. Since process-related personal qualities frequently are internal processes which individuals do not generally verbalize or describe as they engage in them, they often must be inferred. One feasible way of explicating these internal processes is to infer them from nonverbal and verbal behaviors that are evident during an interaction or that are communicated when a person reflects on the meaning an experience has for his life. In proposing this approach we have made the following assumptions:

1. All nonverbal behaviors have the potential for being communicative in nature. (This is the basis for our calling nonverbal behaviors communicative.)
2. Whether or not a person wants to, he is always sending signals to others and receiving signals from them. In this process he communicates something about himself in addition to the content or substance he is trying to project.
3. Persons engaged in activities designed to develop certain personal qualities most likely utilize communicative behaviors that are appropriate to the context in which the interaction occurs.

Although we have said that the communicative behaviors exhibited by an individual engaged in an activity can be viewed as overt manifestations of mental processes, occasionally we do not have to infer from these behaviors. For example, an individual may state that he is making a decision or that he will make it as soon as he gets sufficient information. In other words, it is conceivable that individuals verbalize or describe what they are doing or thinking relative to the personal quality focused upon. However, unless the individual is asked to do so he is not likely to verbalize in this manner. The degree to which we can bridge the gap between what an individual intends to convey through his verbal and nonverbal behaviors and what we infer from these communicative behaviors depends on our knowledge of the person and his purposes, the context with which he is interacting, the process-related personal quality which is the focus of our efforts, and the procedures and techniques for observing and recording what happens during the interaction.

In the process of employing communication to infer internal processes such as making decisions, our knowledge about communication is increased. As a result, gaps in knowledge about communication as a process are narrowed and new thresholds in communication and communications are uncovered.

Clarifying a Person-to-Person View of Communication

In this work, communication is viewed and treated as a person-to-person process. The importance of clarifying this view of communication and the qualities inherent in it are explored in this section.

Importance of clarifying

Clarifying what is meant by the process of communicating can provide sharper insight into the relationship between communication and attempts to employ it in achieving knowledge about what transpires when persons interact with a setting. The nature or view of communication gives direction to and is reflected in not only the knowledge-building process related to obtaining feedback but also in establishing process-related priorities and designing contexts to facilitate accomplishing them.

Another reason for identifying and clarifying concepts related to a particular view of communication is that a person's knowledge and understanding of interpersonal communication can influence how he perceives the communicative behaviors of individuals interacting with each other, with materials, or with ideas. Such knowledge can also aid in providing direction for organizing these perceptions and for utilizing them to infer internal processes.

It is important to note that bringing to bear a view of interpersonal communication on the processes of describing, organizing, and examining what transpires when persons interact with a context does not necessarily decrease the objectivity with which perceptions are noted and recorded. Instead, decisions about such perceptions are made within a framework that is congruent with the reasons for efforts to gain knowledge and the nature of the knowledge sought. When this occurs, there is apt to be less guessing based on inadequate information and more of an objective fit between perceptions and the context of the interaction.

Nature and qualities

The following discussion of person-to-person communication includes a section on communication as: a mutual sharing of meanings, a participatory process, a creative process, an ever-present process, a process that can be enacted in different ways, and a rich complex process.

Mutual Sharing of Meanings. Viewing communication as a person-to-person process implies a mutual sharing of meanings resulting from experiences in knowing, thinking, or feeling. A person cannot share his experiences with another. He can only share the meanings those experiences have for him. Therefore, when an individual shares what his perceptions, his feelings, and his experiences mean to him, he is sharing part of himself. Sharing in this context is not the parcelling out of what is just or due, but the using, experiencing, enjoying, and enduring with or together. Each party is deeply concerned for the other's welfare.

Communication that is a sharing of meanings also implies that each gives something of himself to others with the intent to help, to encourage, and to facilitate the other person's being and becoming what he values. Some would assert that complete communication such as we have just described is rare indeed. In fact, if in his lifetime an individual meets two or three persons with whom he can communicate in this manner, he is extremely fortunate.[1] We propose that as more knowledge about how persons communicate is generated, the prospects of an increase in interpersonal communication as the sharing of deeper meanings will take place. In addition, persons may extend their ability to communicate in this penetrating manner to situations involving two or more persons.

---

1. Dean C. Barnlund, *Interpersonal Communication: Survey and Studies* (Boston: Houghton-Mifflin, 1968), p. 613.

A Participatory Process. Communication that is sharing personal meanings is a participatory process where the emphasis is on *we* as opposed to *you* or *they*.[2] The direction of communication is *with* as opposed to *at.* Participants who approach an interaction as mutual sharing do so with an expectancy and an enthusiasm that moves an interaction beyond the initiating stages and extends it in depth and breadth. There is a sense of trust that expects and evokes a response that can provide necessary information which in turn promotes further exploration and exchange. In order for the response to contribute to the quality of the interaction, there must be attentive listening by the participants. The silence of attentive listening is not the passive silence of boredom or indifference, but the silence of a sensitive action which serves to encourage and support.

Often a mutual sharing of thoughts and feelings uncovers a wide range of possibilities for discovering not only commonalities or opportunities for coming together but also differences or situations which require responsible action in previously uncharted or unfamiliar contexts. Persons engaged in mutual sharing are then faced with the challenge and responsibility of becoming *a part of* as opposed to *apart from,* and of *searching out* as opposed to *withdrawing.*

A Creative Process. Person-to-person communication in which meanings are shared is a potentially creative process. The expectations, responsibilities, and possibilities inherent in the process of communication contribute to the creative potential of the interaction. The nature and extent of this potential is further enhanced by the fact that expectations, responsibilities, and possibilities vary with participants and with the setting in which the interaction takes place.

An Ever-present Process. In further attempting to clarify our concept of person-to-person communication we need to recognize the ever-present quality of communication. Man is always communicating, even when he is silent. Where a person sits, how he walks, and how he looks at another person are examples of communication. In fact, the very existence of an individual—his life—can be viewed as communication.[3] In schools, by the postures students assume, by the expressions which accompany looks at the teacher, by the whispering which takes place

2. John R. Platt, *Perception and Change: Projections for Survival* (Ann Arbor: The University of Michigan Press, 1970), p. 112.

3. The existential approach to communication is discussed by Floyd W. Matson and Ashley Montagu, "Introduction: The Unfinished Revolution," in *The Human Dialogue,* ed. Floyd W. Matson and Ashley Montagu (New York: Free Press, 1967), pp. 1–11.

in quiet moments, students communicate vital and important messages.

Modes of Communicating.   Persons not only communicate all the time but they use several different modes or means of communicating. Writing, speaking, and bodily movements are ways of communicating meanings. Not only do modes or means of communication vary, but the ways and degree to which they are used also vary with individuals. Some persons are more skillful in using certain modes of communication, and some have a larger repertoire of communicative modes. The individuality of communicative modes further contributes to the creative potential of the communication process as well as to the complexities of it.

A Rich, Complex Process.   The last quality which characterizes the communication process is richness or complexity. The varied experiences persons have, the diverse ways in which they communicate meanings of experiences, and the depth with which persons interact contribute to the richness of the process. The richness or complexity we speak of can be compared to the form, flow, beauty, and pattern of a literary work or a painting. There are many elements which contribute to the work, but at the same time do not stand out as separate identifiable entities when the work is viewed as a whole.

The metaphor of a musical composition might also be applied. Many voices or parts contribute to the composition. At times some voices predominate while others play supportive roles. The fact that the individual voices or components can be identified contributes to the listener's or reader's understanding and appreciation of the work. On the other hand, identifying the parts does not have to destroy the mystery and beauty of the total composition. The same holds true for communication. We need to be able to identify and describe the components and how they function in different contexts, but we also need to maintain and preserve the beauty and wonder of this magnificent awe-inspiring phenomenon.

Prerequisites for Using Communication

In addition to understanding the nature and qualities of communication as a person-to-person process, an individual who utilizes communication to generate knowledge in the classroom setting needs to know: (1) what is encompassed in the verbal and nonverbal aspects of communication, and (2) why it is necessary to focus considerable attention on the nonverbal aspects.

Understanding verbal and nonverbal aspects

If the complete spectrum of communication is to be utilized in our attempts to generate knowledge in the classroom setting, we must include the nonverbal as well as the verbal modes of communicating. Communication goes beyond words. Total communication includes a person's nonverbal or unspoken language as well as his spoken utterances. Only when we see the relationship of the verbal and nonverbal aspects of communication can we say that our understanding of the process is such that we can use it in approximating knowledge in classroom settings.

Verbal Aspects. Verbal communication is commonly viewed as the use of the spoken and written word to convey meaning. Sounds and written symbols and their accompanying meanings are employed in the acts of listening, speaking, writing, and reading. When verbal aspects of the communication that occur during an interaction are the focus of attention, it is usually the oral or spoken utterances that are noted. When an individual reflects on the meaning that engaging in an activity has for his life he may communicate such information in written form, although he can also communicate it orally. In the event he writes his thoughts, the focus for analysis is his writing.

In listening for and recording oral or spoken utterances, an individual might note the following:

1. *How a Person Composes His Spoken Utterances*

   Does he raise questions, make statements, issue commands, or hypothesize about a situation?

   What is the pattern of his speech in terms of length of utterances? In what unique ways does he put words together?

   Does his vocabulary vary with the nature of the activity in which he is engaged?

2. *How a Person Interacts Verbally with Other Persons*

   With whom does a person interact?

   When in a group situation is he the initiator, the first one to speak, or does he tend to be a respondent much of the time?

   Does he interact predominantly with one person in a group? What characterizes the person with whom he interacts?

   Does he respond to questions addressed to him?

   How does he give directions to other persons?

   How does he follow directions given him?

3. *How a Person Uses Spoken or Written Language to Describe His Experiences or How He Feels about Them*

Does he speak in terms of the present, the past, or the future?

What proportion of his talk is related to any or each of these?

What kind of referent does he use in various interactions? (For instance, when or how often does he use cognitive referents such as, "I think," "I wonder," or "This is easy to figure out.")

Does he use emotional referents such as "I like," "I feel," or "I am unhappy"?

4. *How a Person Uses Spoken or Written Language to Generate Knowledge Himself and to Encourage Others to Do So*

How does he organize what he knows?

How does he describe the gaps in what he knows? How does he express his plans for finding answers to the gaps in his knowledge?

Does he ask questions, make statements, or raise problems that have leading-on power or that draw others into the search?

How does he respond to others' responses to his utterances?

What characterizes his response?

Answers to the above questions may require observation of accompanying nonverbal behaviors and noting the nature of the context. Also, it might be necessary first to describe aspects of oral communication, such as how a person structures his language and how he interacts verbally with others, and then apply this information to the broader question of how he generates knowledge. The latter requires combining basic information about a person's language.

5. *How a Person Changes in His Use of Verbal Language in Different Situations and Over Time*

How flexible is a person in his use of language in different contexts?

How does his language reflect his attitude and actions in a new or challenging context?

What patterns in a person's use of language are evident over a period of time?

The foregoing suggestions for examining verbal aspects of communication do not include techniques that are usually employed in a formal structural analysis of language often associated with linguistic analyses. Verbal language recorded in the classroom setting can be subjected to a more formal analysis if this would contribute to generating the kind of knowledge desired.

Nonverbal Aspects. There are many ways in which individuals can communicate nonverbally or without uttering words. A broad range of nonverbal behaviors is subsumed under body movement. Among these behaviors are movement of the body as a whole from one place to another, body stance, body position, and gestures including movement of the hands, arms, legs, and feet. Facial expressions involving the mouth, nose, forehead, and eyes are also included in this category of nonverbal behaviors. Presence, touching, how one dresses, the use of space (proxemics), and skin reactions such as blushing are also ways in which communication is accomplished nonverbally.

The use of space can be viewed from several perspectives. One can consider how an individual utilizes space when it is limited and when it is unlimited or how he utilizes space when he is alone and with other people.

Another aspect of nonverbal communication is paralanguage or intonation which accompanies verbal utterances. Intonation consists of pitch or the intensity with which a person speaks, stress or the degree of accent or emphasis he places on verbal utterances, and juncture or the pause between words. Sounds not directly associated with spoken words can also be included in paralanguage. Examples of these are laughing, sighing, yawning, and humming. Silence and volume are also aspects of nonverbal communication.

Additional means of communicating nonverbally include a person's use of time, the speed with which he moves, the duration of his movements, and the physical display of effort evident in his movements.

In observing nonverbal behaviors, it is possible to describe not only which behaviors are expressed, but also the degree or intensity with which they are expressed. The physical display of effort as exhibited in muscle tension and the number of times an individual returns to an activity might indicate the intensity or degree to which he expresses nonverbal behaviors.[4]

The same guidelines used for noting verbal behavior may be used in observing nonverbal. One could note the following:

1. *A Person's Repertoire of Nonverbal Behaviors*

   Does he employ many gestures?

   Does he use wide sweeping motions or smaller more narrow ones?

   Does he use a variety of body motions?

   Do certain gestures seem to accompany certain facial expressions?

---

4. The intensity with which a person expresses nonverbal behavior was one research focus of the Center for Young Children at the University of Maryland. Publications describing this research include *The Project on Involvement: An Interim Report* by Barbara Littlefield, June 1972 and *Identifying, Defining, Coding, and Rating Nonverbal Behaviors that Appear to be Related to Involvement: Project on Involvement Interim Report No. 2,* July 1973, by Jessie A. Roderick. Both reports are published by the Center for Young Children, College of Education, University of Maryland, College Park, Maryland.

Do his nonverbal behaviors seem to complement or contradict his verbal utterances?

2. *How a Person Interacts Nonverbally with Others*

Which nonverbal behaviors does a person use when he interacts with others?

Does he seem to use certain gestures, facial expressions when interacting with certain persons?

Which behaviors does he employ when initiating an interaction, when responding to another person?

At what pace does he interact nonverbally?

How close or how far away does he place himself when interacting with another person?

3. *How a Person Uses Nonverbal Aspects of Communication to Express His Reactions to, Interest in, or Feelings about His Experiences*

Which facial expressions are evident as he begins an activity or interaction, while he is engaged in it, and after he completes it or leaves it?

Which body movements, facial expressions, or gestures does he exhibit while engaged in a complex task?

Which does he employ in an easier task?

How long does he stay with an interaction?

Does there appear to be much display of physical effort, such as shaking of the arm in trying to manipulate some materials?

How often does he leave the interaction and then return to it?

Note: Judgments about the difficulty of the task should be in terms of the teacher's expectations for the learner as well as how the learner perceives it. If the teacher makes judgments, it is assumed he knows the learner.

4. *How a Person Uses Nonverbal Behavior in Generating Knowledge and in Encouraging Others to Do So*

Does he move from one activity or engagement to another and then remain at one for a period of time?

Does he look at another person engaged in an activity and then engage in a similar one, but in ways that are different from those he observed?

Does he combine materials or ideas in a variety of ways?

Does he use materials in ways other than those in which they are intended to be used?

Does he approach persons who are new to the situation and motion to them to join him in an activity?

Does he take his constructions to others and invite them to partici-pate in or to critique his work? (Constructions may be material ones or written creations.)

Do his nonverbal behaviors such as facial expressions, gestures, or larger body movements encourage others to become engaged?

Note: In these situations, as in the parallel verbal examples, informa-tion from several observations may have to be combined and informa-tion on verbal communication also considered in attempting to answer the questions.

5. *How a Person Changes in His Use of Nonverbal Communicative Behaviors Over Time and with Situations*

Does a person use different nonverbal behaviors in different kinds of situations?

If so, what are they?

When does he vary the nonverbal behaviors he uses within the same interaction? (For example, do the kinds of nonverbal behav-iors or the way in which they are exhibited change when another person either joins the interaction or observes it?)

Which persons seem to prompt a change in the person's nonverbal behaviors?

Over a period of time, does a person use more or less nonverbal behaviors, a greater variety of them, or does he seem to use a few rather consistently?

Many more questions can be raised in each of the categories suggest-ing how an individual uses nonverbal behaviors. The specific nature of these questions and attempts to generate knowledge about them in classroom settings depend again on the priorities that are set, the con-texts designed to facilitate the fulfillment of the priorities, and the procedures for obtaining feedback. In the next section are reasons for emphasizing the nonverbal aspects of communication to generate knowledge about change in students' skills in human processes.

Why Focus on Nonverbal Communication

A need exists to focus on nonverbal communication for several reasons. First, we have proposed that individuals cannot share experiences di-rectly but only the meanings these experiences have for them. We also propose that all aspects of experiences cannot be observed directly. What we observe and note is the language system individuals use to report their experiences.[5] Persons' reactions to and feelings about their experiences can be reported through nonverbal as well as verbal aspects of communication. If we ignore the nonverbal behaviors, we risk the chance of losing significant information about an individual's interactions. Often when attention is not given to what persons communicate nonverbally, we miss much of the *now* of an interaction or what is happening in the present.[6]

Second, since individuals do not always state their intent or describe their actions and feelings during an interaction, an understanding of nonverbal behaviors is crucial to explicating inferred internal processes such as decision making.

Other reasons for focusing attention on nonverbal behaviors relate to when persons use them and how nonverbal signals can supplement verbal utterances. Often, persons communicate intensely personal or deep feelings or meanings nonverbally but hesitate to do so verbally. An awareness of this characteristic of nonverbal communication can aid in understanding the contexts in which persons communicate deep feelings and the manner in which they are communicated. Nonverbal signals can also support, reinforce, or contradict verbal statements. The possibilities that an understanding of nonverbal behaviors holds for improving the quality of communication across cultures are many. La Barre contends that, ". . . kinesiology is . . . one of the most important avenues for better understanding internationally."[7]

Finally, in order to generate knowledge about what happens when persons interact with contexts in the classroom setting, it is necessary to employ procedures which enable persons to capture the evidences of the interaction as they occur or soon after. Observing persons in the process of engaging in activities is one way of accomplishing this. Since nonverbal behaviors are usually a natural and sometimes automatic part of the interaction and since they are readily observable, it makes sense to observe and record them as one way of generating knowledge about the interaction. When our knowledge of the nonverbal aspects of communication is combined with what we know about verbal communication, the gaps in our knowledge of the spectrum of communication are narrowed considerably.

The quality and depth of combined knowledge of verbal and nonverbal aspects of communication can be enhanced by efforts directed to-

---

5. Joel R. Davitz, *The Language of Emotion* (New York: Academic Press, 1969), p. 2.
6. The nonverbal as indicator of the *now* of interactions is discussed by Platt, *Perception and Change,* p. 60.
7. Weston La Barre, "Paralinguistics, Kinetics, and Cultural Anthropology," in *The Human Dialogue,* ed. Matson and Montagu, p. 481. In La Barre's discussion, kinesiology basically refers to nonverbal behaviors as discussed in this book.

ward determining congruency or the lack of it between the two aspects of communication. Congruency can be viewed as consonance between a nonverbal behavior and a verbal utterance that occur together or in close sequence. Congruency might also be treated as agreement between a recording of observed behaviors during an interaction and records of an individual's reflections on the experience. Means of recording information in both types of situations can be developed for use in specific contexts or settings.

The Challenge of Using Communication

Although it is possible to describe communicative behaviors and to organize the descriptions into guidelines or techniques which can then be employed in efforts to explicate inferred processes, this must be done with some understanding of the complexities inherent in the process of communication. These complexities do not render the task impossible, but they do have implications for the frame of mind with which the task should be approached and for the context in which the information achieved is judged and applied. The challenge presented by these characteristics of communication forces us to deal with the process in all its naturalness and humanness.

Since each person is a unique individual his interactions with others, with materials, or with ideas are totally unlike another person's interactions. The communicative behaviors expressed during these interactions are also unique to the person involved. The flow, depth, and changes in communication vary not only from individual to individual, but with the same individual over time and in different settings. This individuality of expression contributes to the unpredictability of human communication. Although a long-term study of one person's communicative behavior might reveal certain patterns, there is always the possibility and the expectation that deviations will and in fact should occur.

In addition to differences related to persons, we can expect differences in communication that relate to context. For instance, a verbal utterance or a nonverbal signal may mean different things in different settings. A communicative behavior can also mean different things at different times. An example of this point is the nonverbal symbol of a "V" made by the first two fingers. Over time the meaning changed from a victory sign to a peace sign. Utterances or symbols may also have different meanings when expressed by different persons. The "no" of a father can have a different meaning from the "no" of a sibling. An awareness of these context-related and person-related factors which account for some of the complexity of communication is vital to judging and applying knowledge gained through the use of communication.

That language can be a restricting element in our attempts to deal with the world constitutes another challenge to employing communication as a means of describing interactions.[8] The relationship between words and our perceptions is such that our vocabulary can influence what we perceive and how we organize what we see. It is also important for us to realize that a person's language may not reveal precisely how he feels or precisely what is happening as he is experiencing something. Often we use a limited set of basic communicative behaviors to organize and convey or report a variety of perceptions. Often we experience more complexity than we appear to express or convey through communication. These so-called limits of languages might complicate our efforts to utilize communication to infer internal processes, but they do not render the task impossible.

When our knowledge of communicative behaviors is used to help explicate inferred processes, the inference level at which we operate should be as low as possible. In other words, the gap between what is apparent to another person in terms of an individual's communicative behavior and how the other person judges this behavior to be an overt manifestation of an internal process should be as small as possible. Some examples in which the inference level begins at a very low, essentially zero level, and increases will help to clarify this principle. A person observed looking through several books announces that he is deciding which book to read. There is no need to infer his decision-making behavior. He has announced it. The inference level about a person's decision making increases when he is observed at the library running his fingers across the spines of books on a shelf. The inference level becomes even higher when a person is observed thumbing through a recent volume of *Books in Print.*

Noting verbal behavior probably results in making inferences at a lower level, but verbal utterances are not always honest, and as we noted earlier persons do not always decribe what they are doing. Nonverbal behavior is thought to be more honest and more spontaneous, but it is not as clearly "stated" as verbal and, therefore, the inference level tends to be higher. In addition, many nonverbal behaviors can occur simultaneously and with verbal utterances. In spite of these potential drawbacks, the spontaneous quality of nonverbal behaviors and the fact that they appear to be a more honest report of an experience

---

8. Joseph R. Royce discusses how language contributes to the encapsulation of man in *The Encapsulated Man* (New York: Van Nostrand Reinhold, 1964), pp. 36–44.

constitute two major reasons for employing them in the process of explicating inferred processes.

A final aspect of the challenge of using communication to generate knowledge about interactions can be seen in both a positive and a negative sense. Communication is not linear, but can be compared to a musical score. Many parts or voices are combined sometimes in harmony and sometimes in dissonance. At times one part or voice is heard above the others and at times two or more parts carry the predominant theme. So too with communication. At times the verbal aspects appear to be predominant with the nonverbal playing a supporting role or in some instances the verbal and nonverbal are in contradiction. When an individual utilizes communication to its fullest in his interactions with others, with materials, or ideas, the nature of the interaction can reflect all the intricacies and beauty of a symphony. Although these qualities might render analysis of communication difficult, they endow the process of communicating with flexibility, fullness, and challenge.

The chapter which follows includes specific procedures for developing knowledge-generating techniques. The development and use of these techniques are based on a knowledge of how communication can facilitate the process of achieving feedback. The nature of the techniques derived also reflects a concern for the person as discussed in the section on person-to-person communication in this chapter.

Suggestions for Further Reading

Anderson, Mary Lou S. *Touching: Communication During a Quiet Activity.* Center for Young Children Occasional Paper Number Eleven. College Park: University of Maryland, 1973.

Aranguren, J. L. Translated from Spanish by Frances Partridge. In *Human Communication.* World University Library. New York: McGraw-Hill, 1967.

Barbara, Dominick. "Nonverbal Communication." *Journal of Communication* 13: 166–73, September 1963.

Barnlund, Dean C. *Interpersonal Communication: Survey and Studies.* Boston: Houghton-Mifflin, 1968.

Berman, Louise M. "Communicating: The Sharing of Personal Meaning." In *New Priorities in the Curriculum.* Columbus, Ohio: Charles E. Merrill, 1968.

Birdwhistel, Ray L. *Kinesics and Context: Essays on Body Motion Communication.* Philadelphia: University of Pennsylvania Press, 1970.

Britton, James. *Language and Learning.* Coral Gables, Fla: University of Miami Press, 1970.

Cazden, Courtney B., Vera P. John, and Dell Hymes, eds. *Functions of Language in the Classroom.* New York: Teachers College Press, 1972.

Cummings, Susan N. *Communication for Education.* Scranton, Pa: Intext Educational Publishers, 1971.

Davitz, Joel R. *The Language of Emotion.* New York: Academic Press, 1969.

Duncan, Hugh D. *Symbols in Society.* New York: Oxford University Press, 1968.

Fabian, Don. *Communication: The Transfer of Meaning.* Beverly Hills, Calif: Glencoe, 1968.

Gerbner, George. "Communication and Social Environment." *Scientific American* 227: 152–60, September 1972.

Gerhardt, Lydia A. *Moving and Knowing: The Young Child Orients Himself in Space.* Englewood Cliffs, N.J.: Prentice-Hall, 1973.

Goffman, Erving. *Interaction Ritual: Essays in Face-to-Face Behavior.* Chicago: Aldine, 1967.

Goldmark, Peter C. "Tomorrow We Will Communicate to Our Jobs." *The Futurist* 6:55–58, April 1972.

Hall, Edward T. *The Silent Language.* New York: Doubleday, 1966.

Hastings, Donald W. and Glenn M. Vernon. "Ambiguous Language as a Strategy for Individual Action." *The Journal of Applied Behavioral Science* 7:371–75, May/June 1971.

Matson, Floyd W. and Ashley Montagu, eds. *The Human Dialogue: Perspectives in Communication.* New York: Free Press, 1967.

McCroskey, James C., Carl E. Larson, and Mark L. Knapp. *An Introduction to Interpersonal Communication.* Englewood Cliffs, N.J.: Prentice-Hall, 1971.

Montagu, Ashley. *Touching: The Human Significance of the Skin.* New York: Columbia University Press, 1971.

Platt, John R. *Perception and Change: Projections for Survival.* Ann Arbor: University of Michigan Press, 1970.

Roderick, Jessie A., with Joan Moyer and Ruth Spodak. *Nonverbal Behavior of Young Children as It Relates to Their Decision Making: A Report of Research Findings.* University Nursery-Kindergarten Monograph 5. College Park: University of Maryland, 1971.

Roderick, Jessie (Principal Investigator), Jacqueline Vawter (Associate Investigator and Author) and Others. *A Category System to Describe the Nonverbal Behavior of Teachers and Students: An Interim Report.* Center for Young Children Occasional Paper Number Two. College Park: University of Maryland, 1972.

Ross, Ramon R. *Storyteller.* Columbis, Ohio: Charles E. Merrill, 1972.

Smith, Alfred G., ed. *Communication and Culture: Readings in the Codes of Human Interaction.* New York: Holt, Rinehart and Winston, 1966.

8

Developing and
Using Techniques to
Describe Interactions

Perspective on Chapter 8

Theme: Sensitive and careful observation is critical to gathering information pertaining to a person's development in process-related skills.

Selected major points: (1) Events and behaviors occurring at any given moment in time can be recorded in a variety of ways. (2) Recording a person's behavior is a knowledge-generating technique particularly useful to curriculum developers.

As you read: (1) Think about your own situation and determine which of the observational techniques discussed would be most useful in helping you answer some of your immediate problems. (2) In what ways can colleagues work together in gathering observational data about a given classroom or setting?

In the previous two chapters we emphasized the importance of ascertaining what occurs when persons interact with contexts designed to develop process-related personal qualities. In this chapter we present guidelines for developing and using techniques which enable persons to obtain feedback on learners' interactions with contexts. Since students and teachers both participate in establishing process-related priorities and in designing contexts to fulfill the priorities, it is appropriate that these persons also participate in developing procedures for determining the degree to which the priorities are achieved.

Before specific knowledge about communicative behaviors can be achieved and used to infer internal processes, procedures and techniques for obtaining such knowledge must be developed. Recording in diary fashion what persons do and say during interactions with contexts is a basic approach to generating this kind of knowledge. However, complete and consistent reliance on diary-fashion recordings can be cumbersome and an inefficient, unproductive use of time. Therefore, it is important to recognize the value and use of diary-fashion recordings, but also to move beyond this method.

One way of moving beyond the diary-method is to derive from them techniques for describing an individual's behaviors during an interaction. Another is to derive self-reportive or reflective techniques to ascertain the meaning an interaction has for a person. These descriptions constitute a vital source of knowledge about progress in the development of process-related personal qualities and also support the need to generate additional knowledge in this area.

The importance of observation as a means of generating knowledge and ways it can facilitate describing interactions are discussed in the remainder of this chapter. Procedures for deriving other observational techniques from diary-fashion recordings are outlined and sample instruments presented. Also included are discussions of (1) the use of observational instruments already available; (2) reflection as a means of generating knowledge; and (3) the qualities that characterize knowledge-generating techniques designed to achieve feedback on progress in developing process-related personal qualities.

Observation: Foundation for
Explicating Processes

We propose that empirical data or information gained by sensory experience, in this case observation, is one approach to knowledge that persons responsible for what happens in classroom situations should recognize and employ. It should be recognized that thinking, feeling, and believing are also part of knowledge gained by observing.[1]

---

1. Ways of knowing that man uses in his search for reality and the relationships among them are described by Joseph R. Royce, *The Encapsulated Man: An Interdisciplinary Essay on the Search for Meaning* (New York: Van Nostrand Reinhold, 1964), pp. 11–29.

Observing in classroom settings is an appropriate procedure for answering questions about the development of personal qualities related to decision, involvement, and peopling. From diary-fashion recordings of observed interactions are derived techniques to describe communicative behaviors assumed to be overt manifestations of inferred processes.

The empirical approach to knowledge production becomes more important when it facilitates describing interactions that take place in a setting not contrived or distorted for information-finding purposes only. Interactions are recorded as they occur whether or not they parallel the expectations of persons who designed the procedures for describing what happens. Participants are not prompted or told how they should behave. They interact in terms of how they as individuals perceive the context.

Having established the value of observation as a means of ascertaining progress in process-related skills, we next examine how narrative descriptions can form the basis for devising procedures and techniques that facilitate describing persons' interactions with contexts.

Facilitating description of interaction

The possible flow from narrative descriptions to the development and application of observational guidelines is diagrammed in figure 8–1. Each box in the figure is lettered for reference purposes. As the arrows indicate, B (Observational Guidelines) is derived from A (Descriptive Narratives) and C, D, E, and F are applications of B.

Narrative Form. Box A in figure 8–1 outlines two purposes for directly recording observations in narrative form. The first is describing the range of behaviors observed in any context that has not been selected or designed to achieve a specified purpose. The second is describing behaviors observed in a context that has been designed or selected to encourage development of certain qualities.

Recordings of observations done for the two purposes described are written in narrative form as the observer sees or hears them. Recording in this manner implies that an observer watches a person or persons in the process of interacting with other persons or materials. Direct recordings may be made of live interactions within a classroom setting or of interactions on videotapes or movies. The term "direct" means that no short methods or formal instruments are used to focus and organize an observer's perceptions. Rather, observations are recorded in narrative or diary fashion. Special recording forms may be used, but narrative descriptions are recorded on them.

Describing the range of behaviors observed in an unstipulated context as stated in the first purpose is often an initial form of observation

FIGURE 8–1. *From Observations Recorded in Narrative Description to the Development and Utilization of Observational Instruments, Guidelines, and Coding Systems*

A

Observations Recorded in Narrative Description to

1. Describe the Range of Observed Behaviors in Unstipulated Context.

2. Describe Behaviors Observed in Context Designed or Selected to Encourage Development of Process-Related Personal Quality

B

Observational Instruments, Guidelines and Coding Systems Derived from Contents of Narrative Descriptions

C

Superimposed on or Applied to Narrative Descriptions of Interactions With Context Designed to Develop Personal Quality

D

Utilized in Describing Interactions with Context Designed to Develop Process-Related Personal Quality

E

Utilized in Designing Activity or Context in Which Person Interacts

F

Utilized in Designing Self-Reportive Techniques in Which Person Reflects on Activity and can be broad in coverage. The descriptions often capture the diversity of behavior persons exhibit.[2] These observations frequently deal with the broader setting and with the larger concerns of human interaction. The more all-inclusive nature of these broadly based observations can serve to stimulate questions that need to be raised when observing in more specified contexts and can aid in determining the kind of knowledge needed. They can also assist in providing handles for organizing the knowledge and in relating it to the larger concerns of the setting. An example of a broad observation is recording all verbal and nonverbal behaviors expressed.

A step toward a more specific mode of observation is recording only one aspect of communicative behavior, such as the nonverbal. Observation can be even more specific, such as focusing on designated groupings of nonverbal behaviors or a single behavior. Even though the focus may be narrowed, the person is still observed in the larger setting or unstipulated context.

Observation recorded in narrative form can also be used to describe individuals' interactions with settings or contexts that have been designed to encourage the development of process-related personal qualities. In this situation the purpose of observing is to obtain information which can be used to determine the degree to which the individual appears to be developing the personal quality the context was designed or selected to facilitate. In this case the narrative description is more focused and reflects what the observer knows about the purpose for the context. As a result, the knowledge generated relates primarily to the knowledge anticipated.

Observational Systems Derived from Narratives.   Some persons may choose to record all their observations in narrative or diary form. Valuable and pertinent feedback is achieved in this manner, but there are other ways the narratives can be used. Observational instruments, guidelines, or coding systems can be derived from them. The box lettered B in figure 8–1 represents this step in the flow from narrative descriptions to application of observational instruments.

An observational instrument is an aid to focusing and organizing what an observer sees. The instrument might be called a category system for observing a selected aspect of behavior such as teacher nonverbal behavior. Possible teacher nonverbal behaviors are grouped into

---

2. For a discussion of the need to describe diversity in all living things see Howard Ensign Evans, "Taxonomists' Curiosity May Help Save The World," *Smithsonian* 4:36–43, September 1973.

larger units or categories making it easier for an observer to look for and note behaviors that are subsumed under a designated category. Instead of writing in narrative what he sees, the observer can write the name of the category or a symbol representing it, or he can make a mark in a space opposite the name of a category. This type of observational system is often referred to as a coding system. The terms observational instruments and coding systems can be used interchangeably depending on the context. In this work, although we tend to use them interchangeably, coding systems can be viewed as somewhat more structured than observational systems in terms of formal categories, definitions, and directions for observing and recording. Directions for deriving and using observational instruments are given later in this chapter.

Using Observational Instruments.   Among the ways persons can apply observational instruments in developing curriculum are: analyzing narrative descriptions of interactions, recording learners' interactions with contexts designed to develop process-related personal qualities, designing activities or contexts which encourage growth in personal qualities, and designing self-reportive techniques. These applications of instruments are labeled C, D, E, and F, respectively in figure 8–1.

The first two ways of applying or using observational guidelines mentioned—analyzing narrative descriptions of interactions and describing in coded form interactions with context—are discussed in depth later in this chapter. Sample instruments are developed and procedures for employing them are described.

Specifics on how observational instruments can be used in designing contexts or activities and reflective techniques are *not* dealt with in this chapter. These uses can be inferred from the work as a whole. For instance, knowledge of the communicative behaviors a person exhibits in a certain context can provide direction for redesigning that context in terms of space, time, material, and ideational components. Specific knowledge gained by using an instrument focusing on space utilization, an aspect of nonverbal behavior, might influence the number of persons planned for and the placement of materials in an activity designed to increase skill in decision making. This same kind of information might provide direction for structuring self-reportive materials intended to reveal a person's reflections on how spatial conditions influenced his decision.

The reader is encouraged to note in the material on feedback and the suggestions for classroom applications found later in this book possibilities for applying observational instruments in designing contexts and self-reportive techniques. Guidelines for recording narrative descriptions of observations, analyzing them for content, and employing the resulting groupings or categories are presented in the sections that follow.

Recording narrative descriptions

A description of what transpires when an individual interacts with elements of the classroom setting can be accomplished by recording in narrative diary-fashion what the individual does and says. Although conceivably an observer can describe everything he sees and hears, it is often advisable to establish some observational focus. The nonverbal behaviors an individual expresses, his verbal utterances, behaviors he exhibits while engaged in a particular task, or the behaviors of several persons engaged in a given activity are examples of possible observational foci. No matter which facet of personal interactions with others, materials, or ideas the observer decides to describe, he should exert every effort to make his account objective and descriptive.

Separating descriptions of behaviors from possible interpretations of them can be accomplished rather easily. Interpretations can be placed in parentheses, or there can be a separate column entitled "Interpretations or Comments" included in the observational form. Figure 8–2 is an example of an observational form. A sample recording in which the observation focus was a child's nonverbal behavior is also included.

The observational focus for the above description is the nonverbal behavior the girl exhibits. In this instance, nonverbal behavior is defined as body movements, gestures, and facial expressions. Each nonverbal behavior is described in objective, descriptive terms. Since this is a broad focus, one that is relatively open and flexible in that the complete range of her nonverbal behaviors could not have been anticipated for this particular situation, the complexity, patterns, and exceptions to patterns can be caught. Important methodological procedures at this stage of knowledge generation include describing carefully all behaviors related to the observational focus as they occur and separating interpretations or subjective comments about the observations from descriptions of them.

How observations recorded in diary fashion are examined and utilized depends on the purpose of the observer. Selected guidelines for analyzing and organizing the content of narrative descriptions follow.

Analyzing the content of narrative descriptions

Content analysis as used in this book is the procedure by which categories or groupings are derived from descriptions of observed behaviors.

FIGURE 8–2. *Sample Narrative Description of Observed Behaviors*

Observation Recording Sheet

Child or
Youth_____Girl X_____

Grade or
Age Level_____Primary_____

Date of Observation_____

Time Begun _____

Observational Focus Nonverbal behavior of girl X   Time Stopped_____

Description of Setting (persons, materials, time of day, etc.)	Narrative Description of Observational Focus (subjective comments or interpretations are placed in parentheses)
Afternoon. Children in room are free to engage in activities of their own choosing. Teacher is talking with individual children who want to discuss their plans with her.	X walks to library corner and sits on the floor in front of a bookcase. She pulls out a book, drops it on the floor, looks back to where the teacher is, and reaches for another book. She leafs through that book, drops it on the floor and looks in the teacher's direction again. She reaches for another book and carries it over to a boy sitting at a table. She puts the book on top of a book he is reading. He picks up the book and hands it to her and pushes her away from him while pointing to his book. She shrugs her shoulders, bites her lip and walks to seat. She sits down and swings her foot back and forth while turning the pages of the book. She moves her lips. (She appears to want some attention or help in selecting a book she can read.)

Berelson defines content analysis as "... a research technique for the objective, systematic, and quantitative description of the manifest content of communication."[3] Kerlinger sees content analysis as more than a procedure for analysis. Rather, he says it includes procedures for observing which facilitate an individual's asking questions of the communications that persons have produced.[4] Most discussions of content analysis include the following as aspects of the process: (1) some written record of the communication or messages conveyed by persons; (2) a procedure for objectively and systematically examining and describing

3. Bernard Berelson, *Content Analysis in Communication Research* (Glencoe, Ill.: Free Press, 1952), p. 18.
4. Fred N. Kerlinger, *Foundations of Behavioral Research,* 2nd. ed. (New York: Holt, Rinehart, and Winston, 1973), p. 525.

the content or characteristics of the message or communication; and (3) the use of the analysis or examination to make inferences or answer questions that relate to the substance of the messages.

In the procedures for generating knowledge described in this book the messages or communications analyzed for content are the descriptive narratives of the individual's actions and verbal utterances during his interactions with the elements of context.

A person doing a content analysis of narratives can approach the task in one of two ways. He can examine the content with no preconceived ideas about which categories or groupings might emerge, or he can apply or superimpose on the narrative an overlay consisting of expected or desired categories or groupings appropriate to the observational focus. Both approaches are now discussed.

Content Analysis through Emerging Categories. When a person analyzes a narrative description for the purpose of determining which categories or groupings emerge, he tries to approach the analysis with no preconceived notions about which categories might emerge.

Selecting a unit as a basis for examining the content of a narrative is a first step in grouping or organizing the information in the narrative. In the sample observation in figure 8–2 on page 160, the observational focus is the nonverbal behavior of girl X. Since the purpose of recording the subject's behavior was to obtain a description of the range of nonverbal behaviors she exhibited, the nonverbal behavior is an appropriate unit to select in analyzing the description for categories or groupings of the unit that might emerge. A unit can also be selected after first scanning a narrative to determine which unit is appropriate to the observation focus and the purpose of the person doing the analysis.

Examining the narrative for examples of the selected unit is the next step. In this part of the analysis, each behavior that is an example of the unit is listed as it occurs in the narrative. When all illustrative behaviors are identified and listed, similar behaviors, or in the case of our example, nonverbal behaviors that appear to be like or related, are grouped into categories. For instance, there may be a series of nonverbal behaviors which seem to be in evidence quite regularly when a person is observed manipulating objects. These could be grouped together in a category or grouping called "Object Manipulation."

Behaviors or units that have been grouped and placed in one category should fit that category and no other. For example, nonverbal behaviors placed in the category of behaviors observed in manipulating objects do not fit a category of behaviors observed in contacting other persons. This implies that categories should be mutually exclusive. In addition, they should be exhaustive. There should also be a category into which each behavior or unit can be placed.[5]

Although the process of determining categories is approached objectively, there are personal factors which influence the decisions. Among them is what the person doing the analysis knows about the observational focus and the setting in which the observations are made, his knowledge of pertinent literature, and his experiences. It is important to recognize these factors and the possible impact they have on the analysis.

After groupings or categories are established they are labeled and described. In designating a label for a category, terms that are descriptive and representative of the behaviors or units in the category are selected. It is important to select terms that enable the person using the categories to readily distinguish one from the other. The category designation or label should denote the same meaning to many persons and should be readily conveyed.

The description accompanying the category or group name describes in brief what is meant by the label. For instance, if we named the category consisting of nonverbal behaviors evident in manipulating objects "Object Manipulation," a suitable description would be: hand, arm, and leg movements that are in direct contact with an object and that more or less affect the object. It is also helpful to include a few sample or illustrative behaviors in a category system or observational guideline. Illustrative behaviors for the category "Object Manipulation" might include kneading a lump of clay, pounding a hammer, and changing the ribbon in a typewriter.

In order to clarify the procedure described above, the narrative description in figure 8–2 on page 160 is analyzed below according to the outlined procedures. The *unit* selected is a nonverbal behavior defined as body movements, gestures, and facial expressions.

walks 1*	sits down 1
pulls out	pushes away
looks back 1	points
reaches	shrugs shoulders
leafs through	bites lip
carries to	swings back and forth (foot)
puts	turns (pages of book)
picks up	moves (lips)
hands to	drops

*When a behavior is just listed, it occurs once in the narrative. The numeral 1 after a behavior signifies that it occurs twice.

---

5. A discussion of the principles for grouping units into categories is found in Claire Selltiz and others, *Research Methods in Social Relations,* rev. ed. (New York: Holt, Rinehart, and Winston, 1959), pp. 391–401.

The next step in the content analysis is *grouping the units in categories.* As stated earlier, there are several factors which influence this step. Since some of them are personal and since the purpose for grouping the units into categories can vary, it is conceivable that there are several possible groupings or sets of categories that might emerge.

One way of grouping the behaviors listed above is according to parts of the body involved in the nonverbal behaviors. Groupings emerging from using this perspective and the labels or names assigned them are as follows:

Whole Body Movement
  walks
  sits down
  carries to
Head Movements
  looks back
Facial Movements
  bites lip
  moves lips
Leg and Foot Movements
  swings (foot) back & forth
Other Body Movements
  shrugs shoulders

Hand and Arm Movements
  pulls out
  drops
  reaches
  leafs through
  puts
  picks up
  hands to
  pushes away
  points
  turns (pages)

It is important to remember that these groupings are derived from a short narrative with a relatively small sampling of nonverbal behaviors. This is one reason for including a category named "Other Body Movements." With additional descriptions of observations in different settings and of different persons, a broader range of behaviors might be obtained and more definitive categories formed.

The *final step of describing and illustrating categories* can be displayed as shown in figure 8–3.

The category descriptions and illustrative behaviors in figure 8–3 represent one way of grouping the units (nonverbal behaviors) in the narrative description of the observation. These behaviors might have been grouped according to whether or not they appeared to be directed toward a person or a material or whether they were in response to the action of another.

Content Analysis through Superimposing Categories.   Another way of analyzing the content of a narrative description is to superimpose on the narrative a set of categories. In this approach, the content is analyzed according to the categories applied. The procedure also determines whether new categories need to be derived, existing ones revised, or changes in cate-

FIGURE 8–3. *Category Descriptions and Corresponding Illustrative Behaviors for a Set of Nonverbal Categories*

Category Description	Illustrative Behaviors
Whole Body Movement	
The body moves as a whole from one place to another or from one position to another.	Walks from one place in room to another, sits down, stands up, carries an object from one place to another.
Head Movement	
Movement of the head as a whole.	Turns the head, nods or shakes the head.
Hand & Arm Movements	
Movements of the hands or arms in contact with persons or materials or not in contact with anyone or anything.	Turns the pages of a book, reaches for a piece of paper, puts an arm around another person, points to an object or an area.*
Facial Movements	
Movements of parts of the face.	Moves lips, blinks eyes, raises eyebrows.
Leg Movements	
Movement of the leg and foot.	Swings legs, taps feet.
Other Body Movements	
Those movements not included in other categories.	Shrugs shoulders.

*Note that in some categories, illustrative behaviors not found in the sample narrative description are included. This is done to provide additional clarification of the category description and also to show how illustrative behaviors can be added after analyzing more narratives.

gory descriptions made. A miscellaneous category or grouping is usually included to catch those behaviors or qualities which were not anticipated and therefore do not fit the groupings applied. Further analysis of the miscellaneous category provides additional direction for revision procedures.

Some specifics related to analyzing narrative content by superimposing categories are the observation focus and the frame of mind with which the observer approaches the observation, the nature of the category system or stencil and how it is derived, and the major purpose of observing and analyzing the descriptive narrative in this way.

The *observation focus* of a narrative analyzed by superimposing categories on it can be somewhat narrow, such as the set of nonverbal behaviors an individual expresses in a setting. It can also be broader as related to a process or concept. In the latter, the focus may be verbal and nonverbal behaviors which appear to be overt manifestations of a mental process such as deciding or valuing the worth of others. Since in this book we emphasize the development of process-related personal qualities which are considered a broad and more complex focus for obtaining feedback, the major portion of the following discussion deals with analyzing descriptions of broad observation foci.

When more encompassing and complex foci are analyzed, *the mind set of the person applying the categories* is apt to influence the analysis. This can happen in several ways. Often the observer focuses on a context in which the personal quality related to the process is apt to be encouraged and familiarizes himself with the expected and desired categories. As a result, the leaps he makes in trying to establish a fit between the narrative description and the expected and desired categories applied tend to be larger than when the content of a narrative is more limited and analyzed with no preconceived notion of categories in mind. At all times the observer tries to keep inferences at a minimum level. Making judgments as close as possible to the time data are collected is one way of achieving this goal.

Up to this point we have focused on superimposing categories on descriptions of interactions that occur in a context designed or selected to facilitate growth in certain personal qualities. We have also suggested that persons applying category overlays to these narratives are familiar with the categories. Our purpose in giving special attention to this approach to analyzing narrative descriptions is to provide a readiness for the suggestions for classroom activities in chapters 9, 10, and 11.

It should be noted, however, that categories can also be superimposed on descriptions of interactions in a context with unknown characteristics or purpose. Also, the observer or the person superimposing the categories may be unaware of the derivation of and rationale for them. Under these conditions the descriptive information is probably more objective, but the value of this approach to the process of designing curriculum must also be considered. One needs to ask how this approach contributes to the ability to: (1) design contexts that facilitate the development of selected personal qualities; (2) understand that all of life can be seen through the framework of a certain process, but that some behaviors in certain situations tend to be more closely related to the process or appear to convey it more readily; and (3) derive categories or overlays useful in planning settings for learning. Observing with a knowledge of the purpose and the expected and desired categories might more readily help a person develop and utilize observational guidelines. At times a combination of both approaches to superimposing categories is fruitful.

Categories related to a process skill such as deciding that are superimposed consist of the major threads or elements inherent in the process.

These threads might be considered the components or aspects of a process or a larger construct. They are guideposts which facilitate a closer examination of the process and a description of behaviors that appear to be overt manifestations of the process. For example, some elements of decision making that could be part of a category system are the ability to predict outcomes, awareness of alternatives, and willingness to take risks.[6]

The sample categories in figure 8–4 on page 167 focus on an individual's investment of self in an interaction. The elements or aspects of this concept include duration, emphasis, penetration, and independence. In this model and in the decision model cited earlier, the elements are derived from observations of personal interactions, readings in the particular area and in related fields, one's own experiential knowledge, and one's view of humanity and how it contributes to the functioning of the larger society. The derivation of the overlay, and hence its form, can vary according to the purpose for which it was developed and what the person using it brings to the procedure.

In the analysis of a narrative description both with and without the use of overlays or stencils, we assume that the verbal and nonverbal behaviors of an individual can be viewed as overt manifestations of inferred processes. Second, we assume that overt manifestations have the potential for indicating how a behavior is performed or the degree to which an individual appears to invest himself or his energies in executing the behaviors. Third, we assume that indications of how a behavior is performed can be considered overt manifestations of a person's commitments related to his search for purpose in life. These assumptions underlie the sample categories or stencil described next.

The sample category grouping in figure 8–4 was derived according to the procedures and philosophy presented thus far. It is offered as a sample that has been applied once to the narrative description following it in figure 8–5. The results of superimposing the category overlay on the narrative description in figure 8–5 are shown in figure 8–6 (page 169). The primary purpose of the illustration is to outline one way of approaching the task. Readers are encouraged to derive their own procedures or revise ours. The categories when superimposed on a narrative description indicate how much of himself an individual appears to be investing in an interaction.

Figure 8–5 is a narrative description of the verbal and nonverbal behaviors of a person engaged in a group discussion. It is assumed that the observer has knowledge of the category groupings and that he

---

6. These skills related to decision making are discussed and examined in Joan Poultney and others, *Decision Making in Young Children: Part 2. A Report of Research Findings;* University Nursery-Kindergarten, Monograph 3 (College Park: University of Maryland, 1970).

FIGURE 8–4. *Categories to Describe an Individual's Investment of Self in an Interaction*

Category (Overlay Segment) and Description	Illustrative Behaviors
Duration Time spent in an interaction. (Includes indications of time spent upon returning to an interaction.)	Verbal statements such as: "I am going to continue working on this for several days until I finish." Nonverbal behaviors such as: Engaging in an interaction for an extended time period. Returning to an interaction one or many times.
Emphasis Overt display of stress or accentuation.	Verbal statements such as: "I meant it when I said it has to be done my way!" Nonverbal behaviors such as: Tremor in muscles. Whitening of knuckles. Change in pitch, stress, or accent in voice.
Penetration Overt expression of in-depth thinking, of engaging in interactions that have leading-on power, of moving beyond the givens in a situation and of utilizing several approaches, qualities and forces in an interaction.	Verbal statements such as: "That is an obvious kind of response, but what else might this person have been thinking?" "Why don't we divide into groups and each take a different approach to the problem?" Nonverbal behaviors such as: Furrowed brow. Manipulating puzzle elements in such a way that new puzzle is invented. Trying many ways to make desired construction.
Independence Overt evidence of risk taking, of initiating action and thought, and of engaging in the unexpected (in terms of the context or setting).	Verbal statements such as: "We must continue our efforts in spite of the pressures placed upon us by the administration." "We must begin to act now!" Nonverbal behaviors such as: A youngster approaching and engaging in an activity that had been planned for an older group. Walking to school alone after being once taken by older person.
Miscellaneous Behaviors which do not fit the overlay or categories in present form.	

FIGURE 8–5. *Description of Person Engaged in a Group Discussion*

Observation Recording Sheet	
Child or Youth____ Male X____	Group or Age Level____ Upper Secondary
Date of Observation _____	Time Begun ____
Observational Focus X's Verbal and Nonverbal Behaviors	Time Stopped ____

During a Group Discussion	
Description of Setting (Persons, materials, time of day, etc.)	Narrative Description of Observational Focus
A group of students is discussing the design of a proposal for a neighborhood museum. The proposal is to be presented to the Board of Directors of the Central Museum. Six students are present at this discussion, and Male X is among them. The student group has received a statement from the Board in which the structure of the proposed museum and the time and cost specifications are outlined. The group is reacting to the communication from the Board. (The students have been invited to participate in the planning of the museum.) The meeting is taking place in a conference room in the school.	X focuses his eyes on the chairman of the group the entire time he gives a summary of the Board's letter to the committee. At the end of the chairman's report X says, "We must move beyond concern about the basic structure, time, and cost specifications cited in this report to how we can help get neighborhood persons contributing to the directions this proposal might take. After all, it is to be their museum." X leans forward in his seat and clenches his fists as he talks. He continues, "I move we invite some persons from the neighborhood to attend our meetings. They can give needed direction. We should not be planning *for* them but *with* them." A discussion of X's points follows. Included in the discussion are comments related to the possibilities of alienating the Board if X's suggestions are followed as well as the fact that no one from that neighborhood has ever been invited to this school for the purpose of providing input and possible direction to a project. During this part of the discussion, X directs his eyes toward each speaker for the duration of his comments and grasps his pencil–his knuckles whiten. After 20 minutes of discussion a member suggests that another meeting be scheduled to which X replies, "We need to stay with this a bit longer today and try to take another look at this in another way."

selects a setting in which the indicated behaviors will most likely occur. It is also assumed that the observer makes a special effort to note those behaviors related to the categories that represent aspects of the process being studied.

Figure 8–6 illustrates the result of having applied the sample category groupings or stencil in figure 8–4 to the narrative description in Figure 8–5. The groupings of behaviors in Figure 8–6 resulted from superimposing the categories related to individual investment in an interaction on the description of verbal and nonverbal behaviors exhibited during a group discussion. Each time a behavior fitting the definition occurred in the narrative, it was listed under the appropriate category in the designated form.

In addition to being used to analyze the content of narrative descriptions of observed behavior, categories or stencil groupings can be used to record behaviors directly as they are observed.

Using category names or symbols

Categories or groupings derived initially from descriptive narratives or those revised as a result of applying them to such narratives can be used

FIGURE 8–6. *Form for Noting Results of Superimposing Category Stencil on Narrative*

Duration	Emphasis
X focuses his eyes on chairman for duration of the report.	X leans forward in his seat and clenches his fists as he talks. (Stress on *for* and *with* in following statement) "We should not be planning for them but with them."—grasps pencil—his knuckles whiten.
X directs eyes toward each speaker for duration of his comments—"We need to stay with this a little bit longer today . . ."*	

Penetration	Independence
"We must move beyond concern about the basic structure, time, and cost specifications cited in this report to questions of program and how we can help get neighborhood persons contributing to the direction this proposal might take." " . . . try to take another look at this in another way."	"I move we invite some persons from the neighborhood to attend our meetings."

Miscellaneous
"After all, it is to be their museum. They can give needed direction."

*Sometimes it is necessary to place part of a verbal utterance in one category or group and part in another. Also, when a behavior is repeated it need not be written twice. Hatch marks following the initial entry can represent additional occurrences.

directly to code observations. When category names or symbols are used, the observer writes on a tally sheet either the name of the category or a letter or figure symbol representing the grouping under which the observed behavior is subsumed. For instance, when an observer using the category grouping described on pages 163 and 164 sees a person exhibit a nonverbal behavior fitting the category Facial Movements, he does not describe the behavior in narrative form, but records the name of the category under which the behavior is subsumed. If he chooses, in place of the category name he can use a letter symbol such as F or a figure symbol such as

Recording category names or symbols instead of describing observed behavior in narrative form is coding. When a person codes behavior while observing it, there is no need to describe in narrative and then apply an overlay. However, it is also possible to code a narrative description or other forms of observational data.[7]

Coding behaviors using category names or symbols can vary in at least two ways: the coverage and the format for recording it. A broad range of behaviors may be observed by using all categories or groupings within a system. Or, a more limited range of behavior may be observed by using certain selected categories or even a single category. If we consider the categories on pages 163 and 164, all groupings might be employed during an observation, a core of categories composed of Leg Movements, Hand and Arm Movements, and Head Movement, or just the single category Head Movement. Decisions relative to this question are determined by the purpose of the observation, the time available to the observer, the individual being observed, and the ease with which the observer employs a technique.

The second way in which coding observations may vary is in the format employed in placing the category designations on a tally sheet. The selected category or group designation may be written in a column in the sequence observed. Two possible formats for recording in this fashion are shown in figures 8–7 and 8–8. Use of either method in figure 8–7 provides a record of nonverbal categories in the sequence in which they occur. Another format which might be employed when behaviors are recorded according to the category name or symbol calls for placing a mark in the column designating the category or grouping in which the observed behavior belongs. See figure 8–8 for an example.

In the mode of recording categories suggested in figure 8–8, a record of the sequence in which the behaviors occur is achieved by moving

---

7. For a discussion of coding see Selltiz and others, *Research Methods in Social Relations,* pp. 401–6.

FIGURE 8–7. *Possible Formats for Recording Using Category Names or Symbols*

Description of Context	Category	or	Description of Context	Category Symbol
	Head Movement			HM
	Leg & Foot Movement			LFM
	Hand Movement			HM

FIGURE 8–8. *Format for Recording Using a Mark in a Column Categories*

	Duration	Emphasis	Penetration	Other Categories?
1		X		
2	X			
3		X		
4			X	
5		X		
6	X			

down to the next horizontal line each time the behavior changes. In the example above, the first category observed was Emphasis (line 1), the next Duration (line 2), and so on.

Neither of the recording methods suggested in figures 8–7 and 8–8 in their present form reveals the occurrence of simultaneous nonverbal behaviors. It is possible that behaviors subsumed under a category such as Facial Movements can occur at the same time that behaviors in categories such as Leg and Foot Movements are exhibited. This phenomenon can be recorded by placing the symbol for a simultaneous behavior under and to the right of the first symbol. For example:

FM (bites or moves lips)
    LFM (swings foot back and forth)

In the example above a person is observed swinging his foot back and forth at the same time he is biting or moving his lips. There are other ways that simultaneity of nonverbal behaviors can be recorded. There are also additional notational adjustments and accommodations which must be made as observational situations and feedback techniques become more complex. We cite these examples as possible ways to handle some questions. Individuals need to adjust and invent in terms of their priorities, purposes, and interests.

Using category names or symbols to record observed behaviors often enables the observer to record more behaviors in a time period than he would be able to record in a descriptive narrative. On the other hand, limiting the focus of an observation to the categories of a system and recording only those behaviors subsumed in the categories might narrow the observer's scope and, as a result, the content of his recordings.

At times narrowing the observer's scope or perspective in terms of designated categories is an advantage. Using a specific group of categories enables the observer to sharpen his focus and obtain feedback related to personal qualities that a context is designed or selected to develop. Here is ground for testing and experiencing the unity among personal qualities deemed appropriate and desirable, a context or setting which is apt to encourage growth in these qualities, and feedback techniques that are designed to determine what happens when an individual interacts with the context.

Using brief descriptions or phrases

Often it appears necessary and appropriate to develop techniques which facilitate describing an individual's interactions with the context in terms other than designated categories. Although brief narratives are often used in these descriptions, the observation focus is usually more narrow than in observations where the narrative description as presented earlier in this chapter is employed. A form for recording descriptions in this manner is found in figure 8–9.

When employed to obtain the information desired, the observation guideline in figure 8–9 reveals which activities the learner engaged in during an 18–minute observation period, the sequence in which he engaged in them, and how long he spent at each activity. In this example, the context was designed so the learner would see in it opportunities to select from among several activities and to remain at any one of them for as long as he wished. The recordings on the observation sheet indicate the learner's choices and the amount of time he spent at each. The recordings also indicate whether or not the learner saw in the context what it was hoped he would.

The focus of the observation technique just described is an individual person. The focus of observation may also be the interest centers, activities, or work areas in a classroom. For instance, a teacher may want to know when and by whom a center such as materials and media related to a cross-national class project are utilized. Minor revisions in the observation guideline such as presented in figure 8–10 make it possible to obtain this information.

FIGURE 8–9. *Format for Recording Using Brief Descriptions*

Observation Guideline

Question or
Information Desired   Range of activities person engages in and

length of each.

Focus of Observation   Individual learner

Date _____   Time observation begins   9:30 A.M.

Time observation ends   9:48 A.M.

Learner Observed   5 year old

(Age is one way of identifying
person observed)

Activity in Which Subject Engages	Length of Time Engages in Activity	Observer Comments, Additional Notes, etc.
Painting	10 minutes	
Magnifying lens and seeds	5 minutes	
Painting	3 minutes	

Using the format in figure 8–10 to record observations during a day and over a period of days provides information relative to who frequented the center and when. If a teacher's purpose is to encourage learners to see opportunities for engagement in the cross-national center, the information achieved by employing the guideline in figure 8–10 contributes to his determining the degree to which his purpose is met. More in-depth feedback or knowledge about the use of the center is necessary to determine whether or not purposes related to engagement are met, but the information obtained by using the proposed observation guideline constitutes an initial step in this direction.

Additional knowledge which helps a teacher or learner determine the degree to which his purposes relative to engaging wholeheartedly in an interaction are achieved can be obtained by noting how often a person returns to a designated center. This information can be achieved by noting when the name of a learner first appears on the observation guideline, when it does not appear, when it does again, and so on. If persons who appear to be more actively engaged in an interaction tend to remain at it a longer period of time, knowledge or feedback reflecting this can also be generated. Figure 8–10 is a format useful in gathering information about how long persons engage in activities.

FIGURE 8–10. *Alternative Format for Recording Using Brief Descriptions*

Observation Guideline		
Question or Information Desired	Utilization of cross-national project center	
Focus of Observation	Cross-national project center	
Date_____ Time Observation Begins_____ Time Observation Ends_____		
Time of Day Observation Is Made	Persons Observed at the Center at a Specified Time	Comments
10:05	John, Esther, Louise, Dana	
10:30	John, Louise, David, Frank	

The observation guideline in Figure 8–10 can be further revised to generate knowledge relative to the personal interaction among individuals who are observed at the cross-national projects.

A tested instrument

The instruments or category groupings presented so far have not been widely applied in many different settings. However, instruments developed according to the procedures outlined in this section can be tested in a variety of contexts and revised accordingly. An example of a category system derived by using the procedures suggested in the preceding discussion and revised as a result of applying it in a variety of settings is the Pupil Nonverbal Category System. Figure 8–11 is an initial version of this system.[8]

When the Pupil Nonverbal Category System or one of the revisions is used to describe nonverbal behaviors that occur during an interaction, information about process skills is obtained. For example, the categories Movement toward People, Responsive Behavior-Positive, and Initiating

8. Subsequent revisions, descriptions of how the instrument has been employed, and findings are in the following publications: Jessie A. Roderick, with Joan Moyer and Ruth Spodak, *Nonverbal Behavior of Young Children as it Relates to Their Decision Making: A Report of Research Findings,* University Nursery-Kindergarten Monograph 5 (College Park: University of Maryland, 1971); Jessie A. Roderick (Principal Investigator), Jacqueline Vawter (Associate Investigator and Author), and others, *A Category System to Describe the Nonverbal Behavior of Teachers and Students: An Interim Report,* Center for Young Children Occasional Paper Number Two (College Park: University of Maryland, 1972).

Behavior-Positive are closely related to some of the major concepts dealt with in the discussion of peopling. Descriptive information derived by applying these categories to observations aids in explicating the process of peopling. Other categories in the system, such as Feeling Expression, Focusing Behavior, and Task Oriented, can provide descriptive information related to involvement. Selected categories may also be used to explicate decision making.

Summary

Illustrations of how persons can record their observations using category names or symbols representing them have been presented. We also discussed recording observations without using categories but rather a shorthand description.

Our discussion of developing observational techniques has dealt with recording in narrative description all behaviors observed, deriving categories from these descriptions, applying derived categories to narrative data, and applying categories directly as behaviors are observed. Also included was an instrument developed according to the proposed procedures and tested in a variety of settings. The individual is encouraged to select and utilize the procedure appropriate to his purposes.

If individuals do not wish to develop their own feedback techniques for specific learning contexts, they can choose from among instruments that are readily available. In the section which follows, we present some guidelines for selecting and using already-developed instruments.

Selecting and Using
Observational Instruments

In some cases the process of developing techniques for obtaining feedback may require more time, personnel, and experiential background than are readily available. Also, it is possible that within the range of observational instruments already developed there may exist one that provides the kind of feedback sought in a particular setting. Under these circumstances an alternative is to identify and use appropriate observational instruments developed by someone else.

Sources of observational instruments

Perhaps the most comprehensive listing of already-developed classroom observational instruments is found in *Mirrors for Behavior: An Anthology*

Pupil Nonverbal Category System

Recording Symbol	Category Description	Illustrative Behaviors*
H	Habitual Perfunctory acts performed automatically Mechanical personal acts	Hang up coat, take seat, wash hands, throw away milk cartons Mouth open, shrug shoulders, shake hair out of eyes, hands behind back
FE	Feeling Expression Facial expression of feeling Communicating with self Overt expression accompanying body movement	Bite lip, frown, grit teeth, smile Sing, hum Skip, run quickly, drag feet
FB	Focusing Behavior Observes, watches closely	Observe animal; look at teacher or child perform, give directions, or tell a story
P	Pause Stop in course of action	Stop in process of doing something, put head down
SB	Seeking Behavior Seeking approval, praise, help, recognition, permission, alternatives, ideas	Look around at people and/or situation; move from one object, place, person to another in quick succession. Look to teacher or children, tug on clothes of other person
IP	Initiating Behavior Positive Bodily contact in which child reaches out to communicate to show affection, to be friendly, to show interest in	Pat on back, tap on arm or shoulders, hug
IN	Initiating Behavior Negative Bodily contact in which child strikes out at another child or teacher for no apparent reason	Hit, push, kick, bite, pull hair, slap, spit at

Recording Symbol	Category Description	Illustrative Behaviors*
	Grabs toy and/or materials from another child or teacher	Snatch, tug, pull toy or material away from person
TO	Task Oriented Approaching and/or working at an activity and/or materials	Manipulate materials, objects, play game, demonstrate skill or use, point out objects, approach toy or equipment, return to task
W	Withdraw Remove self from situation, task or activity involving people and/or equipment	Move away from (leave) toys, activity, materials, equipment
MTP	Movement toward People Movement toward person or persons—to direct, initiate, join, praise	Walk to person or persons
RP	Responsive Behavior-Positive Positive response to directions, questions, commands, suggestions, invitations, gestures To emotional expressions (crying, shouting) To deliberate acts (putting arm around, shouting)	Share materials, perform activity, discontinue action, shake head "yes" Extend hand, self in help; walk over to, put arm around Accept toy, accept affection, snuggle up to
RN	Responsive Behavior-Negative Negative response to directions, questions, commands, suggestions, invitations, gestures To emotional expression (crying, shouting) To deliberate acts	Bodily contact, continue action, turn away Ignore, turn away, laugh at, point at Stomp feet, cry, attack, shake fist, clutch at material and/or toy
CJ	Cannot Judge Observer cannot make a judgment or child is out of view	

*Illustrative behaviors in this version of the Pupil Nonverbal Behavior Category System are those exhibited by three, four, and five year olds.

of Classroom Observation Instruments.[9] Volumes 1 through 14 describe or define categories for each system and give examples of illustrative behaviors. In addition, there is a summary page including information about the settings in which the system is used; the subject of observation such as teacher, pupil, or both; uses of the instrument as reported by the author in terms of research, training, and evaluation; methods of collecting data, coding methods and personnel required to code; category dimensions in terms of affective, cognitive, and activity; and coding units such as category change, time unit, and speaker change. Volume 15 is a summary of the first 79 category systems. Supplement volumes A and B contain a more complete description of selected observational systems.

Current information about classroom observation instruments is found in issues of *Classroom Interaction Newsletter,* also published by Research for Better Schools.[10] For other pertinent sources see the works of Beegle and Brandt, Coller, Goodlad, Jackson, Rosenshine and Furst, and Lindsey. Full bibliographic information on these works is found in the suggestions for further reading at the end of the chapter.

Since most sources describing observational instruments tell whether the focus is on teacher or learner behavior or both, it may not be too difficult to match behaviors in a category system with expected or anticipated classroom behaviors. On the other hand, it may be quite difficult to achieve a match between a designated context and the setting suggested for employing the category system. This might be viewed as an advantage in that the instrument can be used in a setting that has not been predetermined to a large degree. On the other hand, a lack of specificity in describing setting or contextual elements makes it difficult to (1) collect feedback on learner behavior that might be specific to a designated context, and (2) draw any conclusions as to the contributions that setting makes to the growth of the learner interacting with it.

Questions about using
observational instruments

When what we have been labeling as "already-developed" observation instruments are employed, questions raised about using them might include the following:

---

9. Anita Simon and E. Gil Boyer, eds., *Mirrors for Behavior: An Anthology of Classroom Observation Instruments,* Vols. 1–6 (Philadelphia: Research for Better Schools, 1967) (ED 029 833). Vols 7–14, *Summary* (ED 031 613) and *Supplement Volumes A and B* (ED 042 937) were published in 1970.

10. *Classroom Interaction Newsletter,* published once a semester. The mailing address is Classroom Interaction Newsletter, c/o Research for Better Schools, Inc., Suite 1700 Market Street, Philadelphia, Pa. 19103.

What does the information tell me?

Is it the kind of information I sought?

Is it in line with the purposes established by persons who are planning for, executing, and experiencing the interaction?

What additional or unanticipated information have I gained as a result of using the technique?

Does what I learned through using the instrument suggest the need to revise purposes, the nature of the context, or both?

Reflection: Helping Learners Explicate Processes

Although observation is a critical means of obtaining feedback about what transpires when a person interacts with materials, ideas, or other persons, feedback can also be obtained by reflection. In this process, persons are asked to think about the meaning an interaction has for them. As they reflect on an interaction, individuals can also project what might occur as a result of their interactions.

Definition

Reflection can be viewed as a thinking process in which a person ponders, recollects, or meditates not only on what is happening or has happened to him, but also on his feelings about the experience. Past and ongoing experiences or interactions can be the focus of reflective thinking as it is defined in this book. Reflection is a procedure by which the person thinks about or examines what he feels, knows, and experiences in order to increase what he knows and understands about himself and his relationship to the world. Reflecting is often considered casting light upon something. Information gained when an individual reflects on an interaction helps the individual and others cast light upon his interactions in a unique manner—from within the individual and from his perspective.

When personal reflections in the form of recordings or descriptions of an individual's thoughts or questions about an interaction are combined with records of that individual's behavior observed during an interaction, the result is feedback gained from two perspectives. When both types of feedback are obtained on the same interaction, information gained in one manner serves as a check on the other.

Obtaining feedback through reflective thinking is based on a view of man which embraces the idea that an individual brings to his interactions with settings a personalized orientation to the now, the past, and the future. The person synthesizes his experiences, thoughts, and feelings relative to these time settings. At times one time frame, past, future, or now, may predominate, but as a person experiences, feels, and thinks, all are brought to bear on the situation. In light of this view of man and the various time settings he experiences, it is appropriate and necessary to gather feedback by reflection as well as by observation.

Reflecting and observing: some contrasts

Reflecting is usually done after the person has engaged in an interaction, but it is also possible to engage in reflective behavior during an interaction. When this occurs, the time lag between acting and reflecting on the action is very short. An example of reflection in this sense is a person recording his thoughts while he is in the process of an interaction.

Although many techniques used to obtain feedback by reflection can be derived from those developed for observing, reflective techniques are often more personal. By this we mean that the person interacting is asked questions about his own verbal or nonverbal behaviors. He is asked to reflect on discussions or experiences *he* has engaged in or to recall *his* feelings about something *he* has experienced or observed. Also, at times he may reflect on another person's behavior or feelings as he appears to express them, but he does so from *his* perspective. For instance, he might be asked to reflect on how he thought the person seeking help from a welfare agency felt when after having waited all day he was informed the agency was considering no more cases that day. An individual might also be asked to describe how he felt when he observed or heard or read about the situation just described.

Reflective techniques for gaining feedback can also pose questions which require a person to assume a certain stance in response to a happening he has not experienced directly. In this case he is asked to project what he might do *if.* Asking an individual to reflect on another's interaction with a context by projecting himself in a similar situation is another way of reflecting on an interaction not experienced directly.

Whether information is obtained by observing or reflecting on an interaction, a major concern in recording the feedback is objectivity in describing what occurs. The chances for objective recording are probably higher for observation than for reflection.

In summary, the prime purpose of observation is to obtain a description of a person's behavior manifested during the process of engaging in an interaction. The prime purpose of reflection is to obtain a description of an individual's reconstruction of the interaction as he or others experienced it, his feelings about an interaction, and his impressions of the meaning the interaction might have for his future experience.

Qualities of Knowledge-generating
Techniques

Woven throughout our discussions of feedback and of the processes of deciding, involvement, and peopling are common threads. Among them are congruency between intent and action, close approximation to real life, a concern for the individuality and autonomy of the person, the development of experiences that are opening as opposed to closing in nature, and flexibility and diversity in thinking and doing. Ideas relating these concerns to information-finding techniques are presented next. The reader is encouraged to build upon our suggestions in terms of his own experience and situation.

Congruency between intent
and action

The word intent in the subtitle refers to curricular thrust, goals, purposes, or aims. Techniques for achieving feedback must be sensitive to and pick up information relative to the goals of process-oriented curricula. If the nuances of decision-making behavior or behaviors related to involvement and peopling are not picked up by using the technique designed for that purpose, revisions or a fresh start are in order.

Real-life approximation

The skills and personal qualities we propose are those which man needs to function effectively and productively in life, not in a contrived or artificial imitation of it. Experiences designed to encourage growth in these skills, and the feedback techniques employed during or after the experiences should also approximate the realities of life.

Trying to achieve a closeness to what actually happens in life implies a willingness to work with and at least temporarily accept the unfinished, the imperfect, or the undesirable. Knowledge-generating techniques which are sensitive to the imperfections of reality help persons see what actually occurs when the individual is encouraged to bring his impact to bear upon variables in the situation.

Concern for the person

Techniques need to be designed in such a way that persons are in control of the instruments instead of the instruments ruling the person and ultimately influencing all the decisions he makes.[11] This implies that the

11. For a discussion of the concept of man in control of tools as opposed to tools controlling man, see Ivan Illich, *Tools for Conviviality*, in World Perspectives, Vol. 47, ed. Ruth Nanda Anshen (New York: Harper & Row, 1973), p. 10.

person decides which techniques to employ, whether to use the complete instrument or part of it, and how to use it.

Persons involved in the learning experiences on which feedback is obtained should also have the opportunities to participate in developing and utilizing those feedback techniques. In this way, individuals can revise the instruments in terms of their experience with them and knowledge gained using them.

Another way in which the design of instruments can reflect a concern for the person is the inclusion of questions or categories which account for the unexpected or the unpredicted. When persons are alerted to watch for the unusual or the unexpected, they are apt to be more open and to seek new avenues or approaches which reflect their personal interests.

Finally, instruments which have been developed by persons who care about individuals are more flexible and diverse in terms of who can use them and how information gained by using them can be treated. Techniques are available for use by persons of varied degrees of experience and involvement. Parents, teachers, aides, and peers have access to techniques which help them organize and direct their search for new knowledge. The individual is able to choose the instrument that fits his purposes, interests, and skills. Flexibility also characterizes how the information gained is organized and analyzed.

In summary, knowledge-generating techniques which are characterized by a congruency between intent and action and a close approximation to real life and which reflect an interest in and concern for the person satisfy the criteria for techniques necessary to explicate the processes of peopling, deciding, and involvement.

In Retrospect

In this chapter we suggested ways that persons can develop techniques for describing what transpires when learners interact with contexts. Observation and reflection were presented as two major bases upon which feedback techniques can be developed. In addition, guidelines for selecting and using already-developed observational instruments were proposed. Finally, the qualities of knowledge-generating techniques necessary for achieving feedback on process-related qualities were outlined.

In the part which follows, we offer specific classroom suggestions for obtaining and recording feedback on decision, involvement, and peopling. The feedback techniques were designed to reflect the procedures and qualities recommended in this section.

Suggestions for Further Reading

Anderson, Mary Lou S. *Touching: Communication During a Quiet Activity,* Center for Young Children Occasional Paper Number Eleven. College Park: University of Maryland, 1973.

Beegle, Charles and Richard M. Brandt, eds. *Observational Methods in the Classroom.* Washington, D.C.: Association for Supervision and Curriculum Development, 1973.

Bellack, Arno A. and others. *The Language of the Classroom.* New York: Teachers College Press, Columbia University, 1966.

Berelson, Bernard. *Content Analysis in Communication Research.* Glencoe, Ill.: Free Press, 1952.

Brandt, Richard M. *Studying Behavior in Natural Settings.* New York: Holt, Rinehart and Winston, 1972.

Childress, Marilyn, Marian Greenblatt, and Robert Fessler. *Preliminary Investigation into Moral Behavior with an Emphasis upon Perception of Physical Contact by Five-Year-Olds.* Center for Young Children Occasional Paper Number One. College Park: University of Maryland, 1972.

Coller, Allan R. *Systems for the Observation of Classroom Behavior in Early Childhood Education.* Urbana, Ill.: ERIC Clearinghouse on Early Childhood Education, April 1972.

Eisner, Elliot W. "Emerging Models for Educational Evaluation." *School Review* 80:573–90, August 1972.

Flanders, Ned A. *Analyzing Teaching Behavior.* Reading, Mass.: Addison-Wesley, 1970.

Goodlad, John I., M. Frances Klein, and Associates. *Behind the Classroom Door.* Worthington, Ohio: Charles A. Jones, 1970.

Grant, Barbara M. and Dorothy Grant Hennings. *The Teacher Moves: An Analysis of Non-verbal Activity.* New York: Teachers College Press, Columbia University, 1971.

Hough, John B. and James K. Duncan. *Teaching: Description and Analysis.* Reading, Mass.: Addison-Wesley, 1970.

Illich, Ivan. *Tools for Conviviality.* In World Perspectives. Vol. 47, edited by Ruth Nanda Anshen. New York: Harper & Row, 1973.

Jackson, P. W. *Life in Classrooms.* New York: Holt, Rinehart & Winston, 1968.

Kerlinger, Fred N. *Foundations of Behavioral Research.* 2d ed. New York: Holt, Rinehart and Winston, 1973.

Lindsey, Margaret and Associates. *Inquiry into Teaching Behavior of Supervisors in Teacher Education Laboratories.* New York: Teachers College Press, Columbia University, 1969.

Love, Alice M. and Jessie A. Roderick. "Teacher Nonverbal Communication: the Development and Field Testing of an Awareness Unit." *Theory into Practice* 10: 295–99, October 1971.

McCall, George J. and J. L. Simmons. *Issues in Participant Observation.* Glencoe, Ill.: Free Press, 1969.

O'Gorman, Ned. *The Wilderness and the Laurel Tree: A Guide for Teachers and Parents on the Observation of Children.* New York: Harper Colophon, 1972.

Poultney, Joan (Project Director) and others. *Decision Making in Young Children: A Report of Research Findings, Part 2.* University Nursery-Kindergarten Monograph 3. College Park: University of Maryland, 1970.

Raths, James, "Teaching without Specific Objectives." *Educational Leadership.* 28: 714–20, April 1971.

Roderick, Jessie (Principal Investigator). *Identifying, Defining, Coding, and Rating Nonverbal Behaviors that Appear to be Related to Involvement: Project on Involvement Interim Report No. 2.* Center for Young Children Occasional Paper Number Twelve. College Park: University of Maryland, 1973.

Roderick, Jessie A. (Principal Investigator), Barbara Littlefield (Associate Investigator and Author) and others, *The Project on Involvement: An Interim Report.* Center for Young Children Occasional Paper Number Four. College Park: University of Maryland, 1972.

Roderick, Jessie A., with Joan Moyer and Ruth Spodak. *Nonverbal Behavior of Young Children as It Relates to Their Decision Making: A Report of Research Findings.* University of Nursery-Kindergarten Monograph 5. College Park: University of Maryland, 1971.

Roderick, Jessie (Principal Investigator), and Jacqueline Vawter (Associate Investigator and Author) and others. *A Category System to Describe the Nonverbal Behavior of Teachers and Students: An Interim Report.* Center for Young Children Occasional Paper Number Two. College Park: University of Maryland, 1972.

Rosenshine, Barak and Norma Furst. "The Use of Direct Observation to Study Teaching." In *Second Handbook of Research on Teaching,* edited by Robert M. W. Travers. Chicago: Rand McNally, 1973.

Royce, Joseph R. *The Encapsulated Man: An Interdisciplinary Essay on the Search for Meaning.* New York: Van Nostrand Reinhold, 1964.

Runkel, Philip J. and Joseph E. McGrath. *Research on Human Behavior: A Systematic Guide to Method.* New York: Holt, Rinehart, and Winston, 1972.

Selltiz, Claire and others. *Research Methods in Social Relations.* Rev. ed. New York: Holt, Rinehart and Winston, 1959.

Stevenson, Carol A. *The Development of an Instrument to Examine Teacher Influence on Decision Making Behaviors of Children Ages Three to Five.* Center for Young Children Occasional Paper Thirteen. College Park: University of Maryland, 1973.

Travers, Robert M. W., ed. *Second Handbook of Research on Teaching.* Chicago: Rand McNally, 1973.

Wagner, Jearnine and Cindy Herbert. *I See a Child: Learning About Learning.* New York: Anchor Books, 1973.

Webb, E. J. and others. *Unobtrusive Behavior: Nonreactive Research in the Social Sciences.* Chicago: Rand McNally, 1966.

Willems, Edwin and Harold L. Raush, eds. *Naturalistic Viewpoints in Psychological Research.* New York: Holt, Rinehart and Winston, 1969.

part four

Classroom
Application

Since curriculum is an applied field, any theories, hypotheses, ideas, or research proposals must be implemented or possess the potential for implementation if they are to be useful in school curricula or programs. Part four is written to invite the reader to develop, apply, and test out the concepts the authors have presented up to this point.

Format and Style

It should be noted that in these chapters an attempt is made to interrelate the ideas about persons found in part two, and ideas about recording and gathering information within context found in part three. Thus, the heart of each chapter consists of a statement of quality of context, statements about behaviors which might be evoked in each of the contexts, descriptions of specific contexts, and suggestions for recording feedback. (The reader is reminded that the term feedback as used in this work is defined broadly and is used primarily to facilitate ease and clarity in communication.) The subthemes of communicating, knowing, and dealing with social systems are also given attention although not within specific contexts.

A critical emphasis in this section is upon observing and recording feedback in curricular settings geared to any age level. Suggestions vary in emphasis, complexity, and purpose. The section highlights recording both anticipated and unanticipated behavior in order to build upon the spontaneous reactions of the learner as well as the preconceived ideas of the educator. It is this interplay between the spontaneous and the pre-planned that makes the thrust of this work different from many curricular writings.

It should also be noted that the information obtained through observation and other forms of record keeping is not intended to be judgmental in terms of standardization or developing norms. It is intended only to describe what is happening or what happened.

Both the second and third person are used in the suggestions for observing and recording feedback. At times suggestions are written for learners, at other times for teachers. Again, sometimes suggestions to teachers are included in guides for learners.

Application of Ideas
about Persons

The ideas about persons are derived in a fairly systematic manner from the chapters in part two. Although a suggestion for obtaining and recording feedback is not cited for every quality of behavior, most behaviors or groupings of them are repeated in this section of the book. The reader may wish to reread the sections on specific behaviors or qualities in part two as he attempts to work through the parallel suggestions for describing contexts and recording feedback.

Application of Ideas
about Context

Context or setting is a term used heavily in this work. What we are concerned about is the situation in which the person has the opportunity to interact and to grow in his capacity to demonstrate process-related skills. Information about growth in skills is gathered in context. Other ideas relative to context follow.

First, context can be structured in different ways. It can be carefully structured with a direct relationship between what the student is expected to learn and the modes for gathering feedback. Several illustrations of this type of structuring are found in chapter 10 on involvement. Context can also be structured so that a person can scan a range of possibilities and select from a number one that would have interest and value to the person carrying it out. Chapter 9 on decision has several illustrations of this type of context. Finally, context may not be in the school at all but in some segment of the larger community or world. In this case the context may be selected rather than structured. Chapter 11 on peopling is an example of this type of context.

Second, context actually exists in the eye of the beholder. Although education may structure and restructure environments, it is the learner who selects from the setting what he wishes to see.

Third, the assumption that educators should take into account the information they are gathering from learners and involve them as much as possible in developing or selecting contexts is implemented in many instances.

Application of Ideas about
Subject Matter and Skills

The essence of the content of the curriculum is derived from two sources: (1) the social dilemmas of the times placed in historical perspective, and (2) knowledge of skills necessary to understand one's own potential contribution to the resolution of the dilemmas of the times. Although no attempt is made to negate the traditional school subjects, an effort is made to highlight major concerns of the human condition and to arrange the learning situations in such a fashion that persons feel they can contribute to the improvement of it.

The ideas which follow are suggestions—not prescriptions. Adaptation and development of them, however, will assist in developing the kinds of citizens necessary for modern living.

9

Decision:
The What of
Living

Perspective on Chapter 9

Theme: The setting can be so designed that a person has an opportunity to learn behaviors related to the decision-making process.

Selected major points: (1) Specially designed settings in which attention is given to the nature of the activity and means of obtaining feedback are necessary if decision-making skills are considered an important part of the curriculum. (2) The characteristics of the decision-making process described in chapter 3 are discussed in terms of classroom application.

As you read: (1) Select several of the descriptions of contexts and the behaviors which they are designed to evoke. Adapt the activities to your own situation. (2) Which of the "packages" designed to help learners acquire decision-making skills seem especially workable or unworkable to you?

This chapter is written to assist the reader who wishes to implement some of the ideas presented in the earlier chapter on decision. Decision, it was stated, is so critical to adequate daily living that the schools need to plan directly for teaching this vital human function.

Attention in this chapter is given to contexts that provide opportunities for decision making as these contexts exist in the eye of the beholder or the learner, rather than in the eyes of context designers. Then consideration is directed to decision-making behaviors which might be developed in each context. The behaviors are those described in chapter 3. For each behavior at least one example is given of means to obtain and record feedback.

Contexts Facilitating Decision-making Skill

Among the characteristics of contexts where the learning of decision-making skills is prized are the following:

1. The learner sees within the context opportunities for considering concepts of free will and the self as locus for decision.
2. The learner sees in the setting two or more viable and attractive alternatives necessitating the pursual of one and the rejection of others.
3. The learner sees in the setting the necessity of utilizing the total self in carrying out a project which has worthwhileness for him.
4. The learner sees the context as inviting dynamic and flexible interaction with persons, ideas, time, and space.
5. The learner sees within the context opportunities to pause, reflect, and enjoy the playful.
6. The learner sees within the context the necessity to be morally responsible for the consequences of his decisions.

Where to Look for Evidences of Decision Making

If the teaching of decision making is a curricular goal, then attention needs to be given not only to the settings which encourage decision making, but also to obtaining feedback about the decision maker and his decisions; feedback about the impact of setting, situations, or contexts in which the person is operating. Such information serves two purposes: (1) to see whether what happened was in line with what was intended, and (2) to modify the conditions in some way so that the desired objective or a new one may be achieved.

Attention is given to the following topics as places for gathering information about decision making in a classroom: (1) the ideological context; (2) persons; (3) temporality; (4) orientation to space; (5) intervention; (6) infrequent or serendipitous data; and (7) the interrelationships of the previous six items.

The ideological context

A person must have "stuff" out of which to make decisions. The classroom, either through overt manifestations or through the inner workings of the human mind, contains a profusion of ideas. To the extent that ideas are available in books, media, a diversity of resource persons, or the planned sharing of individual knowledge a setting can be said to prize the ideological. Ideas enable the person to shape more skillfully the alternatives or to sharpen the already evident ones.

If an ideological context is prized, then modes of observing must accommodate the prevalent ideas, the modes by which ideas are generated, the storage and retrieval of ideas, and the means which individuals within the classroom utilize in dealing with ideas as they relate to their decision making.

Persons

A classroom context ordinarily contains persons who enter into another's decision making. For example, a classroom may be structured so that a diversity of ages, cultural backgrounds, and interests dwell within it. The need exists to assist the student to utilize wisely the variety of persons available in the classroom. Students need to learn what can best be explored with the teacher, with other adults, with a peer with interests similar to theirs, with an older or a younger student, with persons possessing skills different from their own.

If persons of different backgrounds are available in the classroom to strengthen the decision-making process of students, then observational tools need to focus on persons as they make decisions.[1] Peer-peer, teacher-child, and other adult-child relationships bear study in order to gain perspective on what is happening and to plan for next steps. The distances between persons, the rhythm of giving and receiving among persons, and the initiating and responding behaviors of persons have an effect upon decision. Information about these factors can be gathered

---

1. See Carol Stevenson, *The Development of an Instrument to Examine Teacher Influence on Decision Making Behaviors of Children Ages Three to Five,* Center for Young Children Occasional Paper Thirteen (College Park: University of Maryland, 1973).

through observation. Through interviews, questionnaires and open-ended techniques, students can be encouraged to reflect on what is happening. Observational data can then be checked against self-reports for congruity and insights relative to planning next steps.

In studying decisions within a classroom, one can look at the rhythm of the classroom—the pacing of activities; the timing of tasks in process; the "intruder," whether it be an idea or a person, into something a person has planned to do; and the unanticipated.

One can search for answers to questions such as the following:

Is attention given to accommodating the person who prefers to work in the morning or the afternoon?

Is "body time" given any credence or are persons deciding to carry out difficult tasks during peak periods of fatigue?

Are unanticipated persons or events accepted or rejected? Under what circumstances?

Observational procedures focusing upon sequencing of events, individual behavior patterns, or the problem of intrusion can give insight into how time affects decisions. Again, the coupling of observation with information from learners undergoing an experience provides valuable insights for planning next steps.

Space

If decision making is prized as a classroom goal, then attention needs to be given to the utilization of space. Is space within the classroom considered to be only unidimensional in its use? Or can the various pockets of space be utilized for a variety of purposes? Can space be divided up in various ways during the course of a day, week, or year? How do the arrangements of objects within a classroom affect a person's decision making?

Intervention

If decision making is prized, the concept of intervention probably needs more careful scrutiny. The notion that intervention on the part of peers can deter the development of certain cognitive factors has led Blank to propose that part of the program of the young child be in a tutorial setting.[2] On the other hand, many would propose that peer influence is extremely important in building knowledge about one's self and in

---

2. Marion Blank, *Teaching Learning in the Preschool: A Dialogue Approach* (Columbus, Ohio: Charles E. Merrill, 1973).

cultural knowledge acquisition.[3] Observational tools can help in answering questions such as the following:

Who should intervene in the decision-making process? For what purpose?

When is intervention a deterrent to and when is it useful in the decision process?

Infrequent events

The practice and habit of observation can enable the school to be sensitive to questions they are not asking, but perhaps should be. Individuals can ponder why infrequent events occurred when they did and whether the setting should be modified in such a way that they will occur again. The infrequent event can be a source of new insights for creating environments which stimulate more creative decisions on the part of students.

Interrelationships

Obviously more than one factor needs to be studied if we are to obtain adequate data to enable better understanding of the decision-making process. Thus, it would appear that attention needs to be given to looking at several of the preceding items concurrently to obtain adequate information about decision. Further insights can be obtained by coupling observation with open-ended techniques such as participating in interviews or answering open-ended questions.

Context, Behaviors,
and Recording Feedback

In this section an attempt is made to interrelate the statements about context with some of the behaviors of decision making discussed in the previous chapter. Not all the behaviors are considered as they relate to context, but hopefully enough illustrations are given so that the person can take other decision-making behaviors and plan contexts that foster them.

Basically, the remainder of the chapter follows an outline which first states the quality of the context followed by a behavior the context may

---

3. Willard W. Hartup, "The Needs of Young Children and Research: Psychosocial Development Revisited," *Young Children* 12:129–35, April 1973. Also see Eric Mount, Jr., *Conscience and Responsibility* (Richmond: John Knox Press, 1969).

evoke. This is followed by a brief description of where data may be gathered and a suggestion for recording feedback. The suggestions are proposed with recommendations of how to record what is happening for purposes of gaining knowledge upon which to plan next steps. It should be noted that the statements of context, behaviors, and suggestions for recording feedback are not geared to any one age level. Again, the ingenuity of the teacher is tapped to adapt the suggestions to the situation in which he finds himself.

Free will and self as locus

Quality of Context: The learner sees within the context opportunities for considering concepts of free will and self as the locus for decisions.

BEHAVIOR A: The learner is aware that he possesses free will within a society which simultaneously has restricting and releasing elements.

Description of Context: A table and chair with paper and pencil are available.

Recording Feedback: For 20 minutes each day over a period of a week, record everything you do. You may get a friend to record for you. Now analyze your activities in terms of these questions:

Which of the activities were you able to plan?

Which ones were planned for you?

How did you feel about each of the activities?

To what degree do you feel you have control over what happens to you?

In situations which you feel are planned for you, what aspects of your life can you still control?

To help gain a perspective on your responses, make a line. At one end place the events in your life over which you have little control. At the other end place the areas over which you feel you have much control. Place the remaining events on the line where you feel they belong.

---

little control   much control

Now think about how you might gain more command of your life. List ideas about what you can change in order to gain a greater sense of freedom. List areas you cannot change but in which you might alter your attitude.

BEHAVIOR B: The person indicates that he has courage to act even in the face of the contingencies of life.

Description of Context: Paper and pencils are placed on a table or beside a comfortable chair.

Recording Feedback: Make a list of the ten things in life that you dread most. Examine your reasons for dreading these areas. How do the items on the list affect your decision making? Are there items that a courageous person might delete from the list?

Dealing with alternatives

Quality of Context: The learner sees in the setting two or more viable and attractive alternatives necessitating the pursuit of one and the rejection of others.

BEHAVIOR A: The decision maker can identify the alternatives or options and can describe the ethical and moral values which are inherent in the pursuit of each of the options.

Description of Context: A comfortable chair is located near a table on which a variety of books about occupations are placed. Paper and pencils are available.

Recording Feedback: Identify three different kinds of work which a person might undertake.[4] Consider such opportunities as concert guitarist, forest ranger, member of hockey team, cancer researcher, minister, truck driver—the list is endless. On a sheet of paper write the occupations and under the list indicate the values which you think a person should hold in order to enjoy each of the occupations. Now try to ascertain which of the occupations is most in line with your basic values. If the values of the occupations which you have selected are incongruent with what you consider important, keep going through the process of selecting occupations and listing values inherent in them until you find at least two occupations which are compatible with what you feel is important in life.

4. Richard Saul Wurman, ed., *The Yellow Pages of Learning Resources* (Philadelphia: Group for Environmental Education, 1972).

BEHAVIOR B: The decision maker, in order to pursue alternatives wisely, learns to reject some alternatives so that he can devote time and energy to the selected alternative.

Description of Context: Quiet music is playing in an attractive setting.
Recording Feedback: Think about a decision you have made recently.

What were the alternatives available at the time?

Are there some you wish you could have pursued?

What might have been the outcome if you had pursued one or more of the rejected alternatives?

Are there some areas in which you feel conflict because of having rejected an alternative?

How do you deal with such conflict?

Context providing possibilities for involvement of self

Quality of Context: The learner sees in the context the necessity of utilizing the total self in carrying out a project which has worthwhileness for him.

BEHAVIOR A: The person developing increased sophistication in the process of decision making needs to learn how to give simultaneous attention to such factors as the following:

> multiple communications
> garbled messages
> the "who" should make the decision
> competing desires for the same resources
> problems of ambiguity

Description of Context: A church, a political meeting, or a meeting of a community organization provides a good setting to work on the activity.

Recording Feedback: Attend a few meetings of a church or community organization in which some controversial issue is being discussed and in which you may play an active role. Make notes of what transpires in the meeting. After the meetings, superimpose the following categories on your notes:

multiple communications simultaneously taking place in the meeting

messages which appear to be garbled

discussions about who will make the decision

competing ideas for the same resources

problems of ambiguity

Since you are playing an active role in the decision process, ask someone to record diary-fashion what you do in the discussions. Then conduct a content analysis of the diary. What categories emerge which give you some idea as to the degree to which you involved your total self in the project?

BEHAVIOR B: The person makes decision to ... rather than searches for freedom from ...

Description of Context: A quiet place with paper and pencil provides a good setting.

Recording Feedback: Take a sheet of paper and make two columns. At the top of the left-hand column write *"Decision to ..."* At the top of the right-hand column write *"Freedom from ..."* Think back on your life during the past week or month. List activities which resulted from decision to ... thinking and those which resulted from freedom from ... thinking.

Take a new sheet of paper and make two columns. Label one "Decision to ..." and the other one "Freedom from ..." As you go about your work for the next two days try to make "Decisions to ..." rather than search for "Freedom from ..." Record them in the appropriate columns as close to the time of the decision as possible.

Description of Context 2: A classroom is arranged with a choice of variable activities. Talk with a child about what he would like to do during a period that he is in school. Now give the child 20 minutes to select an activity.

Recording Feedback: Record what you hear and see the child doing. Compare what the child said he would like to do with what he actually does. How did what he said he wanted to do differ from what he actually did? Did the child try to free himself from something or select an activity of interest to him?

Context as inviting flexibility

Quality of Context: The learner sees the context as inviting dynamic and flexible interaction with persons, ideas, time, and space.

BEHAVIOR A: The person is flexible in his interaction with ideas, persons, time, and space.

Description of Context: A classroom over a period of a few days has a number of different visitors representing different occupations, racial backgrounds, nationality groups, and ages.

Recording Feedback: Observe how individuals interact with a number of persons representing a variety of age levels, socioeconomic backgrounds, occupations, race, nationality, and so forth. Make a chart to record your observations which looks something like this:

Person's Name	Visitor	Questions asked by person	Comments made by person	Nonverbal reactions such as (touching, facial expressions, tonal reactions, movements, silences)

From the information, try to determine whether the learner interacted with the visitor in a flexible manner. What varieties of behavior did the learner exhibit? Discuss with the learner your analysis of how he interacted with persons within the context.

BEHAVIOR B: The person can develop a new framework for dealing with ideas when an old framework no longer accommodates the idea with which he is dealing.

Description of Context: A group of teachers are gathered in a work center in a school.

Recording Feedback: Assume that you are a teacher who is moving from a self-contained classroom to a team teaching situation. Through the use of observation, try to gather information about what happens in a learning situation in order to gain ideas about possibilities for your own classroom behavior.

Develop further the observational instruments below by (figure 9–1) adding categories which you feel are pertinent.[5] (You can refer to chapter 8 for specific guidelines in developing instruments.) Then try the observational instruments in a team teaching situation.

Observe a situation in which the teachers are interacting frequently with each other. Make a slash each time you see one of the stated behaviors on the part of either teacher. Add any other pertinent categories.

5. A useful observational system for observing interaction among teachers and also among children is the "Revised Pupil Nonverbal Behavior Category System," in Jessie A. Roderick with Joan Moyer and Ruth Spodak, *Nonverbal Behavior of Young Children as It Relates to Their Decision Making: A Report of Research Findings,* University Nursery-Kindergarten Monograph 5 (College Park: University of Maryland, 1971), pp. 26–28. A version of this system is included in chapter 8.

FIGURE 9–1. *Observational Instrument*

Teacher-Teacher Interaction

Verbal Behavior	Teacher A	Teacher B
Questions		
Initiates		
Responds		
Makes Statements		
Other		
Nonverbal Behavior		
Large sweeping gestures		
Small gestures		
Smiles		
Grimaces		
Close in space		
Distant in space		
Other		
Congruence Between Verbal		
and Nonverbal		
Cite instances where you feel there is incongruence between verbal and nonverbal behavior		

Pause

Quality of Context: The person sees within the context opportunities to utilize pause so that it contributes to his own physical, emotional, and mental well-being.

BEHAVIOR: In order to heighten his own mental and physical health, the person sees humor in situations, engages in physical exercise, participates in activities which utilize mental processes but which are unrelated to the points of decision, and engages in pleasurable changes of pace.

Description of Context: A book for recording one's activities is conveniently located in a comfortable setting.

Recording Feedback: Over a month's period, engage in as many out-of-the-ordinary kinds of activities as you can think of. Keep track of the ones from which you derive pleasure. Go back and analyze why you received pleasure from these activities.

Develop a plan for your own work which incorporates the playful. Are you able to carry out the repetitive and the uneventful activities more easily if you plan for play? What aspects of your on-the-job activities give pleasure? How do your requirements for play differ from your best friend's?

Now plan your next month's activities, incorporating the knowledge you have generated about yourself. Keep a diary. Each day note the anticipated and the unanticipated in terms of what contributes to your relaxation and change of pace.

Responsibility for consequences

Quality of Context: The learner sees within the context the necessity to be morally responsible for the consequences of his decisions.

BEHAVIOR A: The person learns to be responsible for his actions.

Description of Context 1: The unmarried father or mother of an unborn child is talking with an adult.

Recording Feedback: Talk about and record responses of a parent-to-be about the following questions:

What must be considered relative to the health care of the mother and unborn child, financial support, the possible long-term consequences of immediate actions, the possible raising of the child, personal growth of parent or parents?

What are the responsibilities that must be given attention if one is to bring a child into the world?[6]

Description of Context 2: In a classroom are groups of materials about significant persons.

Recording Feedback: Study the life of a person who has made a contribution to a field of study. You could read about this person, analyze a film about him, examine his personal papers, or interview him.

How early in life did he define what he wanted to do?

What circumstances led him to define this vision for himself?

What action did he take in order to carry out his life purpose well?

Were there deterrents to his carrying out his tasks the way he wished?

What kinds of persons made contributions to the person along the way in terms of moral support, material, or other types of resources?

Did the person carry out responsibilities as he defined them?

---

6. For discussion material relative to early childrearing, contact the consortium on Early Childbearing and Childrearing, Child Welfare League of America, Inc., Washington, D. C.

Did the person for the most part feel that he was in the mainstream of life?

At what points did he feel isolation?

At what points did he feel the companionship of others?

Was the person responsible for the consequences of his actions despite circumstances?

BEHAVIOR B: The person decides to make service an integral part of his life.

Description of Context: At a table are papers and pencils.

Recording Feedback: Describe how one serves in terms of giving and receiving in a familiar field. How does what one receives enrich what is given in the field you have chosen?

What kind of rhythms is it necessary to establish in life if one wishes to lead a life of service? Make three columns on a sheet of paper with the following headings: Area of service, Giving, Receiving. Indicate the rhythm of giving and receiving in two or three different areas of service.

Now go out and observe somebody who leads a life of service. Record what you see, making columns using the following headings: "Activity in which subject engages"; "Length of time engages in activity"; "Comments—special notations on verbal or nonverbal behavior while engaging in activity." Analyze the information for overt evidences of service.

BEHAVIOR C: The person works through the problem of accountability in terms of the following: (1) the persons to whom one will be accountable; (2) the bases or criteria for accountability; and (3) means of gathering data for what one chooses to be accountable.

Description of Context: At a table are paper and pencils.

Recording Feedback: Select an area of your life in which you feel you have some choice. The area might be related to your family, your work, or your recreation. With whom do you interact in that area? Is there a person to whom you wish to be at least partially accountable? Perhaps you wish to be responsible only to yourself. Once you have decided to whom you will be answerable, determine what the purposes will be in the area and the criteria that you will establish for your own behavior. Now decide what means of gathering data about the achievement of your own goals you will use. Perhaps if you select a person to whom to be particularly accountable, this person can help you achieve feedback on how you are accomplishing your purposes.

One way might be to gather information under columns with the following headings: "Person assisting in accountability (for example, teacher, friend, another student)"; "Criteria (for example, carries task through to completion, or selects an alternative that can be carried out)"; "Evidence (for example, completes home work before going to town, or looks at several books before deciding which one to read)"; "Next Steps (for example, plans for friend to discuss homework and finds person with whom to talk about book being read)."

Context Contributing to Communicating, Knowing, and Social Systems

In addition to developing skill in processes related to decision making, the context can contribute to skill in communicating, knowing, and dealing with social systems as these areas relate to decision. Attention is now directed toward specific behaviors that might be developed in contexts which foster those skills. The quality of context is not given specific attention in this section.

Decision and communicating

BEHAVIOR A: The person, in order to make decisions which encompass as much of the data as possible, learns to consider communication as a total process.

Description of Context: The context includes three groups: a club or organization in which you are involved, a group of young children, and another group of your choice.

Recording Feedback: Visit three different types of groups and attempt to understand the communication processes in these groups as they relate to decision making.

In gathering information, you might wish to use certain of the following categories of CODE (Categories for the Observation of Decision-making Elements).[7] (see Appendix). This system involves verbal and nonverbal categories, such as Attending, Focusing, Predicting, Choosing, Informing, Extending, and Appraising. It is possible to code more than one person at a time.

After you have gathered information about the total communication process as it related to decision on the three kinds of groups, see if you can find likenesses and differences in the three groups.

---

7. Stevenson, *The Development of an Instrument.*

BEHAVIOR B: The person, realizing that not all decisions are stated, makes only tentative judgments about what he perceives to be the decisions of others.

Description of Context: A videotape is being shown of a person in the process of making a decision.

Recording Feedback: Study a videotape of a person in the process of decision making. Turn off the sound and describe the motions, facial expressions, gestures, and so forth, that seem to characterize the person.

BEHAVIOR C: The decision maker indicates an awareness of both seen and unseen factors that he and persons he knows consider in their decision making.

Description of Context: Two friends are observing and recording each other's behaviors as they engage in decision making.

Recording Feedback: Make two columns on a piece of paper. Label one "Unseen Factors," and the other "Seen Factors." Observe a person in the process of making a decision. List all the seen and unseen factors you think the person considers in his decision making. What clues do you have that the person seems to consider the unseen factors?

List the seen and unseen factors that affect your own decision making. Ask a friend to make a similar list about you. Does a list that you make about yourself stack up with a list a friend makes about you? What does the comparison of the two lists indicate about your own communication?

Decision and knowing

BEHAVIOR A: The person is aware of a variety of ways in which persons come to know and are able to assess the relative worth of different forms of knowing for decision making.

Description of Context: Paper and pencil are on a table.

Recording Feedback: List the advantages and disadvantages of utilizing primarily "personal knowledge" in the decision-making process. Under what conditions is personal knowledge useful in decision making? Under what conditions should other forms of knowing be utilized? What is the relationship of observation and reflection to personal knowledge?

BEHAVIOR B: The person is willing, under certain circumstances, to go beyond his knowledge in his decision making.

Description of Context: A paper and pencil are near a chair.

Recording Feedback: List some situations in which you took a leap and made a decision without adequate knowledge. What decisions turned out well as a result of your leap? What decisions poorly? Can you generalize at all about kinds of decisions which necessitate adequate information and those in which a leap may be useful?

BEHAVIOR C: The decision maker allows himself to wonder about gaining knowledge, its interrelationship, and its usefulness in problem solving in making more creative decisions.

Description of Context: A nearby school, city, family, or organization can serve as the setting.

Recording Feedback: Study an aspect of the neighborhood (school, city, family) in which you live or work. Walk around and describe various attributes of the area.

Now take each of the attributes and ask this question: I wonder what would happen if this attribute were changed to ... Which of the changes might be worth implementing?

Decision and dealing with social systems

BEHAVIOR A: The person makes thoughtful decisions about what he will give in terms of the social system.

Description of Context: Paper, pencil, comfortable chairs and a friend are nearby.

Recording Feedback: Make a list of the talents you feel you possess. Now consider institutions to which you belong such as the school, family, club, or organization. Make a list of some of the needs of the institution.

Seek to become engaged in a project which utilizes your talents. Ask a friend to jot down how you help meet the designated need of the institution. What do you learn about yourself and how you give?

BEHAVIOR B: The person can deal with the limiting circumstances which prevent his carrying out a decision in a manner that he might like.

Description of Context: The setting is a mock planning council meeting.

Recording Feedback: Assume you are on the planning council for a new town. Your committee has three major projects: (1) to define the plan for the new town, (2) to get the plan evaluated and modified; and (3) to modify the plan in light of the criticism.

Ask an observer to make notes about what is happening. How do the various planning committee members deal with the limiting factors which are present as a result of the evaluation?

In Retrospect

The suggestions which have been developed to provide learners opportunities to gain skill in aspects of decision making are by no means exhaustive. One purpose of the chapter was to assist the reader in seeing the relationships to classroom practice between the earlier chapter on decision and the section on feedback techniques. A major emphasis within the chapter has been upon obtaining and recording feedback relative to decision-making behaviors. Next, attention is given to classroom practices which might provide opportunities for persons to grow in their capacity to become involved.

Suggestions for Further Reading

Blank, Marion. *Teaching Learning in the Preschool: A Dialogue Approach.* Columbus, Ohio: Charles E. Merrill, 1973.

DeNues, Celia. *Career Perspective: Your Choice of Work.* Worthington, Ohio: Charles A. Jones, 1972.

Featherstone, Joseph. *Schools Where Children Learn.* New York: Leveright, 1971.

Goodlad, John I., M. Frances Klein, and Associates. *Looking Behind the Classroom Door: A Useful Guide to Observing Schools in Action.* Worthington, Ohio: Charles A. Jones, 1974.

Horowitz, Sandra, and Louise M. Berman, ed. *Decision Making in Young Children: A Report of Research Findings, Part I.* University Nursery-Kindergarten Monograph 2. College Park: University of Maryland, 1971.

Kissinger, Joan. *A Process Curriculum for Five-Year-Olds.* Center for Young Children Occasional Paper Seven. College Park: University of Maryland, 1973.

Maryland State Department of Education. *Goals and Needs of Maryland Public Schools.* Baltimore: Maryland State Department of Education, 1972.

Mount, Eric, Jr. *Conscience and Responsibility.* Richmond: John Knox Press, 1969.

Perin, Constance. *With Man in Mind: An Interdisciplinary Prospectus for Environmental Design.* Cambridge, Mass.: MIT Press, 1970.

Poultney, Joan (Project Director) and others. *Decision Making in Young Children, A Report of Research Findings, Part 2.* University Nursery-Kindergarten Monograph 3. College Park: University of Maryland, 1970.

Roderick, Jessie (Principal Investigator), Jacqueline Vawter (Associate Investigator and Author), and others. *A Category System to Describe the Nonverbal Behavior of Teachers and Students: An Interim Report.* Center for Young Children Occasional Paper Number Two. College Park: University of Maryland, 1972.

Stevenson, Carol A. *The Development of an Instrument to Examine Teacher Influence on Decision Making Behaviors of Children Ages Three to Five.* Center for Young Children Occasional Paper Thirteen. College Park: University of Maryland, 1973.

University of Wisconsin-Milwaukee. *Inquiry and Decision Making in the Campus School.* Final Report. January 1968 (Mimeographed).

VonHaden, Herbert I. and Jean Marie King. *Educational Innovator's Guide.* Worthington, Ohio: Charles A. Jones, 1974.

Wurman, Richard Saul, ed. *Yellow Pages of Learning Resources.* Philadelphia: Group for Environmental Education, 1972.

10

Involvement:
The How of Living

Perspective on Chapter 10

Theme: In order to help persons acquire skills inherent in the process of involvement, settings can be specially designed for learners, and information obtained about growth in this process.

Selected major points: (1) This chapter contains suggestions for practical applications of the skills pertaining to involvement that are described in chapter 4. (2) Settings for involvement can be created and the phenomenon studied in contexts designed for various age groups and within a number of disciplines or interdisciplinary fields.

As you read: (1) Try to create a context and figure out how you would gather information relative to a skill you consider important to involvement. (2) After reading two chapters on involvement as a critical curriculum thrust, what do you think about directly planning for teaching it?

Since involvement is a major process giving depth and richness to a person's existence, those responsible for curriculum in the school must determine how the process can be taught and learned. How can the school facilitate an individual's becoming involved in interactions which are *personal* in the sense of providing opportunities for him to incorporate his ideas, *enduring* in that they have leading-on power, and *meaningful* in that they help him see purpose and intent as well as the complexities, depth, and wholeness inherent in them?

In this chapter we propose some ways of answering this question. After a discussion of the elements of context as they relate directly to the process of involvement, specific qualities of context which encourage involvement are described. Then learner behaviors anticipated as a result of a person's interacting with the context, descriptions of contexts, and suggestions for recording feedback are described.

Context Related to Involvement

This section examines elements of context that facilitate a person's becoming involved for reasons he deems appropriate and to the degree he wishes.

Patterns of human interaction

Whether a learner functions better alone, with another person, or in a group should be considered in determining a personal context that facilitates involvement.

Are there opportunities for the person to be absolutely honest with himself and others?

Is there opportunity to be engaged with others in situations where persons are not labeled and grouped according to ability or achievement test scores?

Are there opportunities for sharing with others? for praising and for encouraging others?

Can a person see opportunities for personal growth and satisfaction?

Vehicle for interacting

Some individuals tend to become more deeply involved when working mainly with ideas or cognitive concerns. Others become involved when emotions, actions, or materials form the predominant basis for interaction. Persons should be able to see in the setting some vehicle inviting involvement.

Nature of realia or materials

Although the nature of materials is not the sole determinant of a learner's interactions, it is important to recognize that materials can be facilitative or restrictive. Some materials do not lend themselves to a learner's creating newness with them. Such materials should not be included in a context in which the learner is expected to perceive opportunities for inventing or creating something new. On the other hand, some persons need to see a concrete end result of their involvement. In such cases, there should be materials which lend themselves to being built upon, extended, or preserved if the individual so desires. Sometimes it is important for a learner to produce a product which does not change or to know what happens to his product.

Time and space

Sustained involvement requires flexibility in the time and space requirements of individuals. Individuals vary in the amount of time and space they need to become involved and in how they utilize these elements of context. Persons are more apt to become involved in short- and long-term pursuits if at times they can apply their own concepts of time and space to their interactions.

Presence of others

The presence of a person who does not interact with an individual can have an influence on his involvement. The influence may be positive or negative, direct or indirect. The presence of a person may be a model to emulate or a reminder of rules, constraints, or opportunities for expanding. This presence may encourage self-confidence or function as a catalyst to self-denigration.

A Rhythm of Involvement and Noninvolvement

The rhythm of the ebb and flood tides is evident in many forms of life, and man is no exception. Fluctuations in the rate of body processes, in emotional states, and in climatological factors are natural influences on the rhythm of a person's life. The degree of intent and purpose with which man pursues his interests and responsibilities also varies, thereby suggesting that learning contexts designed to encourage involvement must allow for varying kinds and degrees of involvement. At times this can include no involvement at all. Perhaps the learner needs to see in some contexts opportunities for less intense interactions and more opportunities to reflect and gain a perspective which reveals the incongruous and the humorous. Opportunities for marginal involvement can lead to more intense involvement at a later or more appropriate time. Persons responsible for involvement in a classroom setting should also concern themselves with finding out how much newness individuals can experience without being overwhelmed and as a result not become involved at all.

Descriptions of learning contexts which encourage progress in personal qualities related to involvement are not applicable to all learners. Each learner perceives within the context opportunities for him, a unique individual, to interact. Also, each learner sees within the context possibilities for establishing a relationship between the activity and his life experiences.

We can assume that persons will approach a carefully designed context in different ways. Those who approach life with an air of expectancy will probably become involved quite readily. Those who do not approach life in this manner may need satisfying experiences to help build positive expectations of themselves and others. Having engaged in satisfying experiences, these persons are more apt to adopt an approach to life that is increasingly characterized by a hope and belief in what they can do. All persons need experiences in which they see and act on opportunities for becoming involved in a personal, meaningful, and enduring way.[1] The knowledge generated through our attempts to achieve feedback helps us determine whether hopes and expectations are fulfilled as learners become increasingly involved in contexts they deem worthy.

Qualities of Contexts
Facilitating Involvement

The following qualities of contexts are derived from the preceding discussions of the elements of context and from the material in an earlier chapter on involvement.

1. The learner sees the context as inviting and encouraging him to engage wholeheartedly in an interaction as opposed to merely tolerating it.

---

1. An example of using observation to describe interpersonal contacts of different kinds of children in open environments is reported by Patricia Minuchin and Debra Klinman in *Children's Styles and Open Environments: A Study of Different Kinds of Children in Open Classrooms*. (Mimeographed.) This paper was presented at the meetings of the Orthopsychiatric Association, Atlanta, Georgia, March 1976.

2. The learner sees in the context opportunities to engage in experiences that have holding and leading-on power and are characterized by flow or ongoingness.
3. The learner sees in the context opportunities to create new knowledge in ways that are unique to his learning style.
4. The learner sees in the context opportunities to develop agreed-upon or established meanings but also meanings that are not predetermined but which grow out of the interaction of personal qualities, ideas, and materials.
5. The learner sees in the context opportunities to utilize as many facets of his life and environment as possible or appropriate in accomplishing a goal.

Contexts, Behaviors,
and Recording Feedback

The qualities of contexts stated above, anticipated behaviors of persons who interact in the contexts, and suggestions for generating knowledge about what actually happens during these interactions are presented in the remainder of this chapter. The following illustrations are planned to be used by teachers, supervisors, college or university students, as means of helping them think through teaching the personal qualities described as part of involvement. The illustrations can serve as preludes to other kinds of activities and feedback-gathering devices which interested persons might develop. The illustrations can also be tried out in classrooms with teachers, children, supervisors, and others, in order to gain practice in establishing contexts and gathering feedback related to specific skills.

Context inviting wholehearted participation

Quality of Context: The learner sees the context as inviting and encouraging him to engage wholeheartedly in an interaction as opposed to merely tolerating it.

BEHAVIOR A: The person sees and realizes his own sense of power in terms of what he can do and how much control he has in a situation.

Description of Context: The setting consists of a variety of reading materials.
Recording Feedback: Observe a person selecting reading material.

What indications did the person give that he was sure of his ability to accomplish the task? For instance, did he proceed without looking to someone else for guidance or without requesting help?

Did he move to more complex materials without first trying all the possible prior and less complex ones?

Was he able to select materials that he was capable of reading but which also appeared to provide him with some challenge?

Answers to these and other pertinent questions might be recorded as shown in figure 10-1.

FIGURE 10-1. *Observed Behaviors in Selecting Reading Materials*

Learner_____ Nature of task observed_____			
Aspect of Behavior	Observed Yes No		Comments
Looks at someone else during task			
Asks another person for help			
Moves immediately to more advanced materials			
Selects materials somewhat more complex than those he had been selecting			
Additional aspects			

As a check on your observations, you could ask the person to reflect on his experience and answer the following questions:

Did you feel the need to seek help, direction, or advice from someone else while you were engaged in the task (in this case, selecting reading materials)?

Were you confident that the task or aspect of it that you chose to work on was one that you were capable of handling?

At what point did you feel you had control over the situation?

(Add other questions that you or the learner might want to raise.)

BEHAVIOR B: The person approaches an interaction with the attitude or belief that his purpose will be achieved because he has the capacity to accomplish it.

Description of Context: There are opportunities for persons to lead a discussion group under two different conditions: (1) an individual volunteers and (2) the role is delegated.

Recording Feedback: (1) Observe a person who has volunteered to lead a group discussion of a current crucial issue such as drafting a statement supporting the need to assure quality housing for elderly persons on a fixed income. As you observe, record the following aspects of behavior.

A. *Posture, Facial Expressions, and Body Movements* which seem to indicate a confident or expectant attitude.

B. *Timing* or a balance of initiating behaviors, pauses, and responding behaviors.

C. *Vocabulary and Intonation* including language of purpose and intent and references to sources within the group including self as well as intonations suggesting enthusiasm.

FIGURE 10–2. *Sample Coding Sheet*

Aspect of Behavior Suggesting Belief or Confidence in Ability	Behavior Observed (✓)	Comments
Posture, Facial Expression, Body Movement		
Timing		
Vocabulary and Intonation		
Other Aspects		

A coding sheet for this activity might look like figure 10–2. The checks indicating observed behaviors provide some indication of the leader's confidence in his ability to accomplish a task. *Note:* A major purpose of obtaining and recording feedback in the manner proposed is to identify behaviors that appear to be indicators of involvement. The observation foci of Timing, Posture, Facial Expression, Body Movement, and Vocabulary and Intonation are only suggestions. We need to make many observations comparing and contrasting the behavior of individuals in a context designed or selected so that the learner sees in it opportunities to approach an interaction with the belief that he can make a difference.

Also note which aspects of behavior described in A, B, and C were evidenced by a person who did not volunteer to lead a discussion group but did so at the direction of another with the focus of the discussion being predetermined. The format for the coding sheet could be the same as that used in observing a person who had volunteered to lead a discussion of a problem of interest to him.

How does the feedback obtained in both settings compare? What does the feedback suggest about the leadership of persons who become involved voluntarily and those who are designated or asked to become involved?

Context inviting ongoing involvement

Quality of Context: The learner sees in the context opportunities to engage in experiences that have holding and leading-on power and are characterized by flow or ongoingness.

BEHAVIOR: The person moves beyond the givens of a situation and searches for more complexity and challenge.

Description of Context 1: There are available topical materials of varying levels of complexity.

Recording Feedback: Note the content and difficulty level of printed matter a learner consults in his search for information about one of his interests. As his search progresses, note whether the publications he consults become significantly more complex in their treatment of the subject. You might seek answers to questions such as the following:

What is the nature of the main ideas or concepts he selects for consideration?

How do the ideas he selects from earlier sources compare with those from sources consulted later?

What characterizes the thinking or questions prompted by the readings?

In order to answer these questions, ask the learner to keep a record of the publications he reads for information. You might use a form with the following column headings: "Title," "Main Idea or Concept," and "Further Thinking or Questions." In columns to the right of the publication title, the learner can state the main idea or concept he focused on and further thinking or questions sparked by these ideas.

You and the learner can then discuss the progression of his reading and the flow and direction of his thinking prompted by it. (Note: This context description can be modified to include nonprint media.)

Description of Context 2: The setting contains materials that are designed so that one would expect certain identifiable constructions to emerge. An example would be a kit containing materials to construct a cardboard wagon or a house.

Recording Feedback: Observe a child working with a set of materials such as those described in context 2. As you observe, try to answer the following questions:

Does he try to assemble the materials in different ways, thereby appearing to test the flexibility of them in various combinations?

Does he add to or elaborate on what might be the expected construction or products?

Does he make elements or parts to add to those already in the set?

Answers to these and other questions you might raise can be recorded on a sheet on which the questions are written and spaces provided for written comments or checks. You can observe the child at the same activity at different times or in different activities. You might also observe different children at the same activity and compare your observations.

Creating individualized knowledge

Quality of Context: The learner sees in the context opportunities to create new knowledge in ways that are unique to his learning style.

BEHAVIOR A: An involved person creates knowledge in a variety of ways that are unique to him.

Description of Context: The larger context consists of at least three different kinds of settings. There may be a setting or activity in which the learner interacts with materials; one in which he interacts with a small group of persons; and one where the interaction is with a large group of persons.

Recording Feedback: Observe a learner in three different settings such as those described above. Indicate whether the person appears to be highly involved or minimally involved. Describe those behaviors which seem to indicate high and low degrees of involvement. For possible indications of involvement, see categories on page 167. (These categories include Duration, Emphasis, Penetration, and Independence.) As you examine the information recorded in this manner, determine whether there are any behaviors that occur in more than one setting. Also identify behaviors that occur in one setting only. What clues does this information give you and the learner about his interactions with different settings? Which factors in the settings might have encouraged his development and use of his unique way of interacting?

You might record feedback on a coding sheet similar to the one shown in figure 10–3.

FIGURE 10–3. *Observed Behaviors Indicative of High or Low Degree of Involvement*

Nature of Interaction	Verbal		Nonverbal	
	High Involvement	Low Involvement	High Involvement	Low Involvement
Interaction with Material				
Interaction with Small Group of Persons				
Interaction with Larger Group of Persons				

BEHAVIOR B: The person goes beneath surface issues and creates knowledge that reflects his personal interests, thinking, and concern for others.

Description of Context: The setting consists of films of persons from various cultures or from different parts of a country engaged in their daily activities.[2] These activities might include obtaining food, producing goods, taking care of the young or the old, engaging in school-related activities, doing handicraft work, or entertaining themselves or others.

Recording Feedback: Observe films such as those suggested and note the following:

Facial Expressions: Describe the face in terms of the mouth (smile, pursed lips,) eyes (wide open, lids lowered), brow (furrowed, smooth).

Body Stance: Describe the body in terms of posture (erect, hunched over, etc.).

General Body Characteristics: Describe the body in terms of slimness, obesity. Describe the muscles, joints, and skin texture if possible.

Vision Focus: Describe eye focus in terms of whether or not vision is directed toward what the person is doing or toward aspects in the setting that seem to facilitate his involvement in the task.

---

2. An appropriate film is "Hunger in America," a CBS report. The film was produced in 1968 and is 52 minutes long. It focuses on different parts of North America, and may be obtained from the University of Indiana or the University of California. This and other sources of information on the world food problem are found in Jayne C. Millar, *Focusing on Global Poverty and Development: A Resource Handbook for Educators* (Washington, D.C.: Overseas Development Council, 1974). A section on films entitled "Hunger: A Growing Problem" is found on pp. 594–96.

Pause in Action: Indicate if there are long pauses between engagement in an activity or parts of it. Does the learner return to the task or interaction after the pause?

Movement from One Place to Another: Describe how a person moves from one place to another. (Does he move quickly, slowly, haltingly, etc.?)

Distraction: Describe the individual's response or lack of it to distractions. (Does he turn his head or eyes in the direction of the distraction? Does he return to the task at hand after the interruption?)

Completing a Task: Describe what a person does when he has completed a task or interaction. (If he has constructed or created something, does he smile, hold it off to examine it, place it down carefully?)

Response to Others: Describe how a person responds to individuals who approach him directly for help or to evidences that another individual needs help.

Other Aspects of Behavior: (Which questions would you raise to facilitate gathering information about behaviors that appear to be related to the involvement of the persons you observe?)

There are cultural differences in how persons overtly express what they are doing and how they feel about it. Also, similar nonverbal behaviors have the potential for communicating different meanings in different communities. Because of this fact, persons describing the behavior of individuals in these films must be careful not to generalize. We also recognize that nutrition is probably not the only factor that contributes to how involved an individual appears to be in an interaction. A recording sheet for use in this recording might look like figure 10–4.

FIGURE 10–4. *Recording Sheet*

Description of the setting and task or interaction in which person is involved: _____	
Behavior or Body Characteristics	Description
Facial Expressions	Lips pursed, brow furrowed

After observing several film sequences and recording behaviors according to the suggested guidelines or categories, group your observations. You might be able to group cultures according to the adequacy of their food supply. Compare your descriptions of persons in cultures where the food supply is adequate with those in cultures where the food supply is known to be less than adequate. What differences and similarities did you note?

BEHAVIOR B: A person engages in interactions in such a way that he generates knowledge about himself and how he interacts with the various facets of his environment.

Description of Context: The setting consists of many ways to find out what people do for a living and how they feel about their work. Included are opportunities to observe persons at work, to interview them, and to read what the worker and others have written about particular jobs.

Recording Feedback: Ask individuals with different jobs to write a short essay for you, or you can interview them and record their responses. You can also read published materials about work.[3] As you examine these different accounts, look for statements which indicate the following:

What an individual likes about his work.

What he hopes to gain by working.

Why he is doing the work he is.

What kinds of satisfactions or meanings he is seeking in his work.

Whether he wants to become involved in his work.

The kind of involvement that appears to be a result of his own doing or choice and that which is a result of other persons directing him.

After you have studied accounts of how others make a living and how they feel about their work, try to analyze your own work, school, or hobby experiences. You might want to use the same focal points for analysis you used in examining accounts of others' work experiences. It might be necessary to look at other points as you focus on your personal experiences.

How did your analysis of the written accounts of what others do for a living and how they feel about their work help you study what *you* do and how *you* feel about your work, hobby, or learning experiences?

Developing emerging meanings

Quality of Context: The learner sees in the context opportunities not only to develop established meanings but also to develop meanings emerging from the interaction of personal qualities, ideas, and materials.

---

3. A comprehensive source of descriptions of jobs and how individuals engaged in them feel about their work is Studs Terkel, *Working: People Talk About What They Do All Day and How They Feel About What They Do* (New York: Pantheon Books, 1974).

BEHAVIOR: A person brings to interactions his own personal meanings, and as a result his actions and thoughts are not
always dictated by predetermined structures and meanings.

Description of Context: The setting consists of possibilities for persons
to use language in the following ways: to discuss how to deal with
terrorism in a community, to plan and develop a project, and to increase
vocabulary or improve in the use of language rules through formal
lessons. Some of these activities are determined by the teacher and some
by learners.

Recording Feedback: Observe a learner in a situation in which the
emphasis is on employing language to explore possible ways of dealing
with a situation or to design a project. Using the categories in figure 9.1
on page 198, code the verbal and nonverbal behaviors the learner exhibits during this discussion. What does the feedback suggest about the
involvement of the person in this type of experience in which the
primary function of the language is to solve a problem?

Observe a learner in a situation in which language is used primarily
for the purpose of increasing vocabulary or improving the use of language rules.[4] .How does the feedback obtained in this activity compare
with that obtained in the earlier setting?

Observe in those settings where purposes for employing language are
determined by learners. Which verbal and nonverbal indicators of involvement are evident when learners determine the purpose for employing language? Compare and contrast the feedback obtained in a
context in which learners determine purpose with that in which teachers determine purpose. What does the comparison suggest about the
nature of involvement of learners interacting in these settings?

Utilizing facets of life and the environment

Quality of Context: The learner sees within the context opportunities to
utilize as many facets of his life and environment as possible or appropriate in accomplishing a goal.

BEHAVIOR A: An involved person approaches an interaction from
many different perspectives applying his senses and personal meanings in the process.

---

4. A longitudinal study of disadvantaged children and their first school experiences
revealed a need to provide youngsters with experiences in which they can learn to use
language in ways that help them solve problems. Virginia C. Shipman of the ETS Early
Learning and Socialization Group directed the study. This suggestion for obtaining and
recording feedback was prompted by a summary of the study in *ETS Developments* 21:1,
5–6, Spring 1974.

Description of Context: The setting consists of a table and materials for constructing a collage.

Recording Feedback: Observe the learner constructing a collage and note how many different times he groups and regroups the materials on the collage background. Try to answer questions such as the following:

Does he feel the material, rotate it in his fingers, or seemingly test it out in other ways in terms of touch or tactile properties?

Does he stand back and view the collage and then return to work on it once again?

Does he talk about patterning, texture, and organization in other contexts, thereby suggesting that he sees and looks for these qualities in his environment beyond the confines of his collage?

Do you notice any change in how he organizes materials after he has had certain experiences?[5]

Feedback related to these questions can be recorded by writing "yes" or "no" after each question, or by constructing a checklist such as the one shown in figure 10–5.

FIGURE 10–5. *Observation Checklist*

Observing How a Learner Approaches an Interaction			
Learner _____ Activity _____			
Date	Aspect of Behavior	Observed (✓)	Comments
	Groups and regroups materials/elements		
	Handles materials (rotates, etc.) before placing them		
	Stands back, views creation, returns to work on it		
	Talks about textures, patterning organization in other contexts		
	Obvious change in grouping, combining of materials after a particular experience		
	Other aspects		

5. Guidelines and suggestions relative to the arts in a program for young children can be found in Robert D. Hess and Doreen J. Croft, *Teachers of Young Children* (Boston: Houghton Mifflin, 1972).

BEHAVIOR B: A person employs many personal qualities and environmental forces to move his thinking and actions from the
simple to the complex and from himself to the larger
world.

Description of Context: Persons are given the opportunity to eat two
kinds of meals on two different days. After each meal they engage in
an activity or task.

Recording Feedback: Observe persons engaged in an activity after they
have eaten a breakfast consisting of foods such as cereal, fruit, eggs,
bacon, toast, butter, jelly, and milk or cocoa. (Persons whose regular diet
consists of these foods often eat them in unrestricted amounts.) You
might use the observational categories in the system described on page
167 in chapter 8. (These categories include Duration, Emphasis, Penetration, and Independence.)

At another time observe these same persons engaging in an activity
after they have eaten a breakfast consisting of a cup of diluted tea, a
crust of bread, and a small bowl of rice. Utilize the same observational
categories you used when you observed them after they ate a breakfast
consisting of foods described in the first part of this activity. Add
observational categories which give additional information about this
situation and delete inappropriate ones.

Compare and contrast your observations of the involvement persons
exhibit after eating both kinds of breakfasts.

What does the feedback generated from this activity suggest about
the possible relationship of nutrition and the nature of an individual's
involvement?

Ask individuals who have eaten both breakfasts to reflect on their
experiences by answering questions such as the following:

After which breakfast did I feel more like staying with an activity?

After which breakfast did I seem to tire more easily?

After which breakfast did I exert more energy in trying to complete
a task?

Or, you might ask persons to answer some general questions such as:

Did I feel different after the two types of breakfast?

Was I more satisfied with my involvement in school-related activities after one of the breakfasts?

What might this experience help individuals understand about: (1)
the involvement of persons who must live on a limited diet, and (2) our
specific responsibilities related to the worldwide problem of starvation
and how we can become involved in carrying them out?

Involvement and Communicating,
Knowing, and
Social Systems

Context as we define it can also contribute to the development of skills in communicating, knowing, and dealing with social systems. The suggestions which follow should be viewed as ones that focus *primarily* on the skills of communicating, knowing, and dealing with social systems, and how these skills relate to involvement.

Involvement and communicating

BEHAVIOR: The person can see how authors use verbal and nonverbal aspects of communication to indicate how involved their characters are.

Description of Context: Books such as fiction and biography are available for reading.

Recording Feedback: Carefully scrutinize a passage, then list the nonverbal actions and verbal utterances an author ascribes to characters in order to convey commitment or high involvement.

Involvement and knowing

BEHAVIOR A: The person reaches into his past to gain perspective on the knowledge he generates about himself and others during his interactions with persons and ideas.

Description of Context: The learner has opportunities to write about a particularly meaningful personal experience.

Recording Feedback: Ask the learner to reflect on his writing in terms of the following:

What happenings, feelings, or experiences in your past are reflected in your writing? What in your past does your writing recall to you?

Which aspects or parts of your writing do you appreciate more than others? Why?

What indications of your personal involvement are evident in your writing?

What have you learned about yourself and how involved did you become in a task as a result of writing and reaching into your past?

BEHAVIOR B: The learner sees possibilities for creating knowledge in a variety of ways.

Description of Context: The setting consists of many activities such as building blocks, house corner, books, construction materials.

Recording Feedback: Sutton-Smith proposes that types of children's play correspond to four ways of knowing. They are imitation, exploration, testing, and construction.[6] Observe a learner interacting with persons and materials during what might be called free-play or choosing time. Describe what the learner does and categorize his play in terms of the type of knowing that seems to be the predominant mode of learning employed. For example, if you are observing a girl dressed in a costume and "walking" a tight rope on the floor, you probably would categorize this action as imitation. There is most likely some testing and exploration involved also, but the major emphasis appears to be imitation.

Observe this child in a variety of contexts and activities and categorize her interactions accordingly. A coding sheet which might be used is shown in figure 10-6. Recording over a period of time and in different activities will provide some clues as to whether the learner is creating knowledge in a variety of ways.

FIGURE 10–6. *Sample Coding Sheet*

Child _____ Observation Focus	Use of Modes of Knowing

Date	Activity Description	Type of Knowing

Involvement and dealing with social systems

BEHAVIOR A: The person is able to assess whether or not a group or organization values purposive behavior.

Description of Context: The setting is a place where persons are engaged in creating an object or product such as stained glass windows or clay pots.

Recording Feedback: Observe the persons engaged in making the object and indicate how involved they are. You might use the observation categories suggested on page 167.

What in the setting seemed to encourage persons to become deeply involved? What seemed to discourage involvement?

---

6. Brian Sutton-Smith, "Child's Play: Very Serious Business," *Psychology Today* 5:67–69, 87, December 1971, p. 87.

You might have an opportunity to talk with one of the workers about their involvement. Then you could compare your observations with what the person had to say about his involvement.

BEHAVIOR B: The learner is able to help another clarify how his involvement can further the efforts of an organization or group of persons.

Description of Context: The setting consists of an opportunity to talk with a person who is deeply involved in the work of an organization such as the World Council on Curriculum and Instruction.[7] The purpose of this organization is to foster cross-national consideration of curriculum problems.

Obtaining and Recording Feedback: You might ask questions such as the following:

What prompted your initial interest in this group?

How does the work of the organization complement your life purposes?

At which point or points did your interests move more in the direction of the larger world community?

How has your work toward this cross-national goal helped you to better understand yourself and others?

In Retrospect

In this chapter we elaborated on some of the specific characteristics of context that facilitate a learner's becoming involved. We also made suggestions for obtaining and recording feedback on what transpires when persons interact with contexts designed or selected to encourage involvement. We speak of *suggestions* hoping that the reader is encouraged to develop activities and procedures appropriate to *his* situation. We move next to suggestions for helping learners increase their skill in peopling—the *why* of living.

Suggestions for Further Reading

Berman, Louise M., ed., and Staff. *Toward New Programs for Young Children: Program and Research Possibilities.* University Nursery-Kindergarten Monograph 1. College Park: University of Maryland, 1970.

---

7. Information about the World Council on Curriculum and Instruction can be obtained by writing WCCI, Executive Secretary, Teachers College, Box 171, Columbia University, New York, N.Y. 10027.

Ivey, Allen E. and Stephen A. Rollin. "A Behavioral Objectives Curriculum in Human Relations: A Commitment to Intentionality." *The Journal of Teacher Education* 22: 161–65, Summer 1972.

Kissinger, Joan. *A Process Curriculum for Five-Year-Olds.* Center for Young Children Occasional Paper Seven. College Park: University of Maryland, 1973.

Millar, Jayne C. *Focusing on Global Poverty and Development: A Resource Handbook for Educators.* Washington, D.C.: Overseas Development Council, 1974.

Raskin, Marcus G. *Being and Doing.* New York: Random House, 1971.

Roderick, Jessie (Principal Investigator). *Identifying, Defining, Coding, and Rating Nonverbal Behaviors that Appear to be Related to Involvement: Project on Involvement Interim Report No. 2.* Center for Young Children Occasional Paper Number Twelve. College Park: University of Maryland, 1972.

Roderick, Jessie A. (Principal Investigator), Barbara Littlefield (Associate Investigator and Author), and others. *The Project on Involvement: An Interim Report.* Center for Young Children Occasional Paper Number Four. College Park: University of Maryland, 1972.

Terkel, Studs. *Working: People Talk About What They Do All Day and How They Feel About What They Do.* New York: Pantheon Books, 1974.

11

Peopling:
The Why of
Living

Perspective on Chapter 11

Theme: The school can provide or create settings in which persons can learn to join with others in exciting, mutually satisfying ventures.

Selected major points: (1) Based on the peopling behaviors discussed in chapter 5, this chapter presents suggestions for settings and ideas for observing and recording feedback. (2) The major purpose for helping persons learn to live with others and gather systematic feedback relative to their interactions with others is to assist them in feeling comfortable in sharing life with persons representing a diversity of backgrounds and interests.

As you read: (1) What problems relative to peopling have not been treated in the two chapters in this book on the topic of person-person relationships? (2) What settings in your locale would be fruitful places to study peopling?

Whatever the strengths or weaknesses ascribed to the common school, it is a meeting place. As such, it is a significant resource where

225

the young can gain new insights about themselves and others as they engage in collaborative efforts. Basically, persons are learning to people when they can join with other individuals in executing mutually satisfying rather than only competitive ventures. It is our thesis that persons should acquire skills related to cooperating, showing concern, and caring.[1] These skills can and should be planned for in school programs if persons are to achieve the learnings necessary for a life of inner contentment and outward service.

In this chapter attention is first directed to notes on contexts that facilitate peopling. Then follows a list of specific characteristics of contexts believed to facilitate peopling. The bulk of the chapter is devoted to ways of recording feedback relative to behaviors which may be developed through interacting in contexts designed for peopling.

Contexts for Peopling

Peopling demands contexts that invite the development of complex skills as they pertain to being aware of, identifying with, and showing compassion for persons both close to and distant from the immediate space of the student. Settings may be specially selected or created. Places to look for peopling include, but are not limited to, the following: the ideological context, persons, temporality, space, intervention, and infrequent events.

The ideological context

Obviously, if one of the purposes of the curriculum is to assist persons in enhancing the scope and depth of their relationships with others, one way to foster this is to plan for experiences in which persons are given new information relative to involvement with others. People are seen not as strangers to be ignored or avoided, but rather as exciting sources of contact who can enrich self and others. Encountering persons, hearing from them, talking with them, reading about them, observing them provides a wealth of information about persons. In turn, this information helps strangers become sources of involvement, comfort, and means of gaining perspective for one's self and others.

---

1. For a review of research on instructional theories based upon differing goal structures, see David W. Johnson and Roger T. Johnson, "Instructional Goal Structure: Cooperative, Competitive or Individualistic," *Review of Educational Research* 44:213–40, Spring 1974.

The context for peopling includes multiple and diverse settings, for the more one can see others in their own surroundings, the more exact knowledge one can acquire about others—what they do, how they feel, how they decide, what they care about, what they aspire to and long for, what they feel they can contribute to life, and what hinders their own well-being.

In addition to first-hand encounters with a diversity of persons, the stuff of peopling can also be found in the telling painting or photograph, the moving short story, the compelling sociological or psychological theory or study, or the sensitive history of a person or group of persons. The ideas for peopling come not from vast compendia of inert information, but rather from insightful persons willing to give of themselves or to communicate in some form telling aspects of the human condition.

Persons

A source that provides a context for peopling includes the persons with whom the individual has planned direct encounters. These persons include teachers and other school-related personnel, peers, work-study personnel, persons in selected settings to which students go for specific purposes, parents, older and younger persons, and all the individuals who have the potential for making a contribution to the student's life.

Persons can be viewed by looking at what is obvious—roles or professions. They can also be viewed in terms of their more subtle characteristics such as their initiating and responding behaviors, their willingness to share, to make an impact, their modes of decision making, their characteristic ways of feeling and expressing their feelings, their strengths and handicaps, their willingness to count for something, their inclinations to take a stand and to follow through on it, and their willingness to tilt, stretch, and reach.

Temporality

Temporality includes the person in times past, present, and future. If the person is to build upon his past and provide within the present an adequate heritage for the future, then modes of establishing settings and gathering feedback need to provide for these three time dimensions. Probing the life of an historical character, considering alternative futures of persons, and analyzing moment-of-now behaviors all need to be part of the opportunities for learning and growing. Data-gathering techniques can focus on observing persons and groups of persons over time as well as at a specific moment.

Space

Persons concerned about peopling must look for ways to transform pockets of space into settings which invite the stranger to make himself known and which change persons from entries on statistical tables to persons about whom biographies can be written.[2] In a world which is becoming increasingly crowded, persons may feel that they cannot form intimate relationships with many in their life-space, and as a result tend to isolate themselves in spaces too small to accommodate others or too large to come to know those who pass through.

The challenge for those who people is to enclose spaces so that participation in the lives of others is invited. For example, the large old house turned into a school may have spaces conducive to a relaxed informality with others. Small neighborhood city parks can be constructed so that they serve as gathering places for persons in nearby dwellings. Studios taping broadcasts for satellites can serve as centers where space in one part of the world is linked with space in another through human interaction. Lounges where students can engage in discourse with others invite more peopling than sterile halls where no talking is allowed.

Space can be friendly or unfriendly. In the search to unite distant persons through our advanced electronic media and the attempt to facilitate psychological proximity among neighbors, peopling is fostered.

Intervention

How one person intervenes in the life of another affects people. The person concerned about peopling seeks to use words that denote to the other person that he counts, that what he says and does matters. He seeks to minimize aggressiveness and maximize friendliness. Words that encourage another person to go on, invite an individual to pursue one of his interests or concerns more deeply, or help a person feel optimistic about himself are examples of interventional techniques facilitating peopling.

On the other hand, words that cut into another's train of thought, denigrate his life style or color, or push another to change his course of action when he does not wish to be redirected are examples of intervention which deters peopling.

---

2. For a discussion of space as it relates to persons in the urban setting, see Lyn H. Lofland, *A World of Strangers: Order and Action in Urban Public Space* (New York: Basic Books, 1973).

Persons concerned about peopling consider the consequences of intervention before taking action. Such intervention is thoughtful and sensitive. An attempt is made to anticipate its effect on the person before intervention is enacted.

Infrequent events

Despite the interest of certain curriculum planners in providing experiences which invite a high level of involvement, the bulk of the student's life is probably spent in situations which do not make major kinds of impact on him. Much of his school learning is about content which he has had little part in selecting and is sequenced in ways of little interest to him. Therefore, the potential impact of certain infrequent events should be heightened. For example, if peopling is of concern, then the student's reaction to a person with a powerful sense of presence should be noted and highlighted. Unusual group situations should be noted, analyzed, and broadened where possible. Infrequent events should be used as opportunities to develop learnings not inherent in frequent, but sometimes mundane, events.

Contexts Facilitating Peopling

In chapter 5, attention was given to six qualities which might characterize persons skilled in peopling. Contexts can be specifically designed or selected to foster these qualities. The contexts are seen from the vantage point of the learner and may be described as follows:

1. The learner sees the context as one in which persons are viewed as co-equal but as possessing diverse gifts.
2. The person sees the context as one which invites reaching out to other persons in time and space.
3. The person sees the context as one in which a variety of kinds of contact can be established as he reaches out to give to others.
4. The person sees the context as one in which he can establish his own criteria for knowing when to reach out to another with the intent of changing him and when to reach out to show concern and support.
5. The person sees in the context the opportunity to solve problems relative to peopling.
6. The person sees in the context the opportunity to use his own presence powerfully.

Contexts, Behaviors, and
Recording Feedback

The next section is a consideration of contexts, behaviors, and suggestions for recording feedback. The context descriptions are basically
restatements of the characteristics of context identified in the first part
of this chapter. The behaviors parallel closely those developed in chapter 5. The reader might want to select from the many suggestions for
recording feedback those most pertinent to his situation.

The following illustrations may be adapted by college or university
students, teachers, or supervisors to fit the situation. The situations to
which the feedback techniques may be applied include day-care centers,
elementary, middle, or secondary school classrooms, university or college classrooms and settings in which adults work together to gain
added expertise in dimensions of peopling.

Diverse gifts but co-equal persons

Quality of Context: The learner sees the context as one in which persons
are seen as co-equal but as possessing diverse gifts.

BEHAVIOR A: The person sees other persons as works of art, some of
the qualities lending themselves to description, and others
transcending verbal analysis.

Description of Context: The setting is a comfortable room where a
person may sit alone or with others. Paper and pencils are on a table.

Recording Feedback: Either singly or in small groups answer the question: What is man? Be factual, fanciful, and as far-ranging as possible.
For example, man is a creature who can construct vehicles to fly in outer
space for months and is a creature who buys bread and then burns it
in the toaster. Arrange the items on the lists in categories. Which items
are more difficult to describe?

Then, answer the question: Who am I? and categorize the responses
according to universal, national, and individual characteristics. Answer
the question on several days and see how the responses change. Discuss
universal, national, and individual characteristics. Which ones were
more difficult to describe?[3]

Make a list of three qualities that are frequently mentioned and three
that are infrequently mentioned in response to the "Who am I?" ques-

---

3. This item adapted from David Wolsk, *Workshop for Associated School Teachers*
(Hamburg: UNESCO Institute for Education, 1972). Mimeographed.

tion. Ask a friend to observe you and check the number of times he sees the qualities in you.

BEHAVIOR B: The individual can give appropriately so that discomfort is not felt by the receiver.

Description of Context 1: The setting contains a table and chairs. On the table are books and catalogs of things to make, do, or buy.

Recording Feedback: Try to think of an appropriate gift for someone you know. Make or buy the gift and give it to the person. Record the receiver's verbal and nonverbal reactions to the gift. What did you learn about giving through this experience?[4]

Description of Context 2: The context is one in which books are available about persons with problems. Other appropriate settings would be hospitals or nursing homes.

Recording Feedback: In the short story "Region of Ice," Joyce Carol Oates recounts the fate of a troubled university student who indicated to his instructor in numerous ways that he needed help.[5] Ultimately, he took his own life. Think about the degree to which one can give the gift of taking on the hurt of another. To what degree should one give the gift of assuming responsibility for one who cannot seem to manage his own life?

Visit someone you feel is in difficulty. While you are with that person, think about emotional, social, intellectual, or material gifts that might make life easier for that person. What kinds of gifts might have meaning? Why?

Ask a teacher or a peer to record verbal and nonverbal behavior when you try to give an appropriate gift to someone in trouble.

BEHAVIOR C: The person recognizes and prizes the diversity of purposes and gifts people possess.

Description of Context 1: Settings may include the places of work of a carpenter, a lawyer, a teacher, a plumber, an automobile mechanic, or a gardener.

Recording Feedback: Try to get a brief apprenticeship in two or three different occupations. While you are working in each occupation, try to answer each of these questions:

---

4. For a variety of suggestions relative to doing for others, see Mary Renaud, ed., *Bringing the World into Your Classroom,* Curriculum Series Number Thirteen (Washington, D.C.: National Council for the Social Studies, 1968).

5. Joyce Carol Oates, "In the Region of Ice," in *Live and Learn: Stories about Students and Their Teachers,* ed. Stephanie Spinner (New York: Macmillan, 1973), pp. 176–200.

What are the characteristics of the contexts in which persons in the particular occupations work? For example, how is space enclosed? What kinds of tools are necessary to the job?

Study the language of the persons in the job. What are the characteristics of any specialized vocabulary peculiar to the job? Do the persons in the occupation rely heavily on verbal discourse, utilization of statistical methodology, or manual dexterity to accomplish their tasks?

What values do you think characterize the persons who enter each given occupation?

What gifts do persons need in each of the occupations? What have you observed about the attitude toward giving in each of the occupations?

Description of Context 2: The setting may be the workplaces of any occupation such as actor, plumber, teacher.

Recording Feedback: Teachers can observe students working as apprentices in various occupations. Before observing, teachers and students might list some critical components of the occupation. While observing, teachers might indicate whether any of the components contained in the observational guide in figure 11–1 are made by teachers or students.

FIGURE 11–1. *Observational Guide*

Occupation: Pharmacist	
Item	Frequency (check each time noticed)
Kinds of questions asked by pharmacist	
One correct answer	
Those requiring creative thinking	
Managerial Skills	
Organizing items in store	
Organizing personnel	
Organizing records	
Qualities relating to giving	
Give advice on drugs	
Give advice on other items	
Other? List	

Description of Context 3: The setting is a quiet place with paper and pencils available.

Recording Feedback: After you have gathered as much information as you can about a variety of occupations, reflect on the personal qualities needed in each occupation.[6] Write a brief paper on the occupations you think might be appropriate for you. Give reasons for your selection. What gifts that you have seen do you prize?

Reaching toward others in time and space

Quality of Context: The person sees the context as reaching toward others who are in different arrangements in time and space.

BEHAVIOR A: The person reaches out to others in space.

Description of Context 1: The context is a group of persons from a number of different lands who are talking. The setting might be in a school, organization, playground, or church.

Recording Feedback: Talk with someone whose family comes from another country. You might discuss your feelings about your families, attitudes toward the countries from which you come, ideas about school, what you would like to do in the future. During these conversations, teachers may observe the conversation using an observational system which they may adapt from figure 11–2. Then teachers might want to compare the behaviors of persons from two different parts of the world when the contact is both frequent and infrequent. If a heterogeneous population is available in the school, observations can be made there. If a mix does not exist in the school, then teachers may want to visit a school which has an integrated population, a migrant population, or a foreign population to gain insights about the orientation of children to other persons representing different backgrounds. Does continuous contact make a difference in how children and youth relate to individuals from different parts of the world?

Description of Context 2: The context may be any institution where people work. Some institutions which might be interesting to study in terms of the people who work in them are the following: museums, art galleries, music studios, armed forces offices, hospitals, clinics, schools of architecture, radio and television studios, newspaper offices, courts, jails, offices of public welfare.[7]

---

6. A useful source of ideas relative to various occupations is George Borowsky and others, *Yellow Pages of Learning Resources* (Philadelphia: Group for Environmental Education, 1972).

7. For a discussion of community institutions and what children can learn from them, see Marcus G. Raskin, *Being and Doing* (New York: Random House, 1971), pp. 349–51.

FIGURE 11-2. *Observational Guide*

Observing Persons from Different Cultures		
	Person A	Person B
Nature of Verbal Communication	Make a slash each time you hear or see one of the following:	
Questions		
Responds		
Initiates		
Neutral statements		
Positive statements		
Negative statements		
Others?		
Nature of Nonverbal Communication		
Moves or tilts toward person		
Moves or tilts away from person		
Gestures broadly		
Gestures narrowly or no gestures		
Smiles		
Frowns		
Ideas:	Please list in order of discussion	
Future Plans: Check one		
Plans made for future encounter		
Plans not made for future encounter		

Recording Feedback: In the institution, plan three steps: (1) observe; (2) probe through questions, reading, etc.; and (3) participate in the actual work of the institution.

To guide you in your work, try to answer the following questions:

What is_____doing now?

How does_____function?

Who is involved?

Who runs_____?

Who supports and carries out directions?

Who benefits? What are the benefits?

How did_____originate? Why?

How are minority groups being represented? Cared for?[8]

Now analyze your own thoughts and feelings relative to your participation. Have any of your involvements in these projects made you a more caring, responsive, knowing, responsible individual? Why?

BEHAVIOR B: The person reaches out to others in time.

Description of Context: A busy or rural street where people congregate provides a good place to observe "life on the street."[9]

Recording Feedback: Record what you see when you look at places where people congregate. Do you see forms of behavior which seem to be peculiar to any specific age groups? Now think back and see if you can recall from your knowledge of history persons who exhibited behaviors you have just seen. Why do some modes of behaving seem to persist in history? What behaviors seem to be observable in any generation?

Establishing degree of giving

Quality of Context: The person sees the context as one in which a variety of contacts can be established as he reaches out to give to others.

BEHAVIOR A: The person is aware that he relates to the few and to the many in different ways.

Description of Context: The context is one in which a group of friends may interact or work alone.

Recording Feedback: Make a list of four persons you know. One person should be a good friend and a second one a casual acquaintance. The

---

8. Ibid., adapted.

9. Francis P. Hunkins and Patricia F. Spears, *Social Studies for the Evolving Individual* (Washington, D.C.: Association for Supervision and Curriculum Development, 1973), p. 6. In this work Hunkins and Spears suggest that "life on the street" should be the starting point for considering all other information.

remaining two persons may be any two you wish. Now fill out the chart in figure 11–3.

FIGURE 11–3. *Interaction Chart*

Quality Answer the questions for each person	Person 1 Name:	Person 2 Name:	Person 3 Name:	Person 4 Name:
a. How long have you known this person?				
b. In what capacity do you know this person—friends, family, etc.?				
c. If something were troubling you, would you tell this person?				
d. Does this person tell you about his concerns?				
e. What kinds of things do you give or might give to this person?				
f. What kinds of things does or might this person give you?				
g. Do you and this person participate in similar activities?				
h. Do you want to know this person better? Why?				

Try to get someone to observe you while interacting with one or more of the persons you have named. Ask them to record what they see on certain of the above items. Items "c" through "h" lend themselves to gathering observable information.

Now compare your information with that of your observer's. What have you learned about how you relate to persons you know with varying degrees of intimacy? What might you do differently as a result of engaging in this experience?

BEHAVIOR B: In his day-by-day behavior the person indicates an increased amount of moving toward people or love and a decreased amount of standing off from people or indifference.

Description of Context: Churches, social centers, organizations, or any place where ethnic or cultural groups meet for specified purposes provide useful contexts.

Recording Feedback: Record the following for one place which you visit: the percentages of persons from different cultures or ethnic groups who frequent the place, the purpose for which the group gathers, the activities, and nature of group interaction.

Draw up a plan for integrating this group more fully in the life of the community. Do you think your plan will work? Why?

BEHAVIOR C: The person can engage in cooperative as well as individualistic giving.

Description of Context: The setting is a museum, church, club, or other organization which community persons have shaped. An example would be the Anacostia Museum, Washington, D.C., a place in which neighbors can think about the community and act on their ideas. The people decide who runs the museum, what goes into it, and what problems will be dealt with in it. It is evolutionary rather than static. Things in process as well as finished products are part of the museum. Children have the opportunity to work side-by-side with a specialist creating within a given field.

Recording Feedback: If a setting similar to the one above can be found, study the nature of giving within the institution or organization. What tasks are performed by individuals alone and which ones are performed by individuals working in concert? What seem to be the qualities of persons who work well alone and those who work in collaboration with others?

Make an observational instrument to capture qualities of cooperative giving. Look at evidences of nonverbal and verbal behavior which seem critical to this concept. You might want to look for indications of: (a) awareness of subtle changes in human behavior; (b) action on the possible rather than constant negation of it; (c) willingness to let another feel success; (d) willingness to act on principle; (e) ability to see the frameworks of other persons in the group; (f) ability to listen and really hear what others are saying. Try to use your observational guide in a setting in which it seems pertinent.

Now think back on your own behavior. What qualities of cooperative giving do you feel you possess? After you have listed the qualities, teachers may gather information about your performance in situations which warrant cooperative giving. Then the information gathered can be analyzed by you and your teacher.

BEHAVIOR D: The person can give comfort when appropriate.

Description of Context: A table is available with paper and pencils.

Recording Feedback: Make a list of things that can be done for a person who is bereaved. Then decide how to accomplish these tasks in an encouraging, joyful manner. What verbal and nonverbal behaviors might be characterized as encouraging or joyful? To assist in discovering such behaviors, record in diary fashion and conduct a content analysis. See pages 159–174 for guidelines for this activity.

Giving and changing

Quality of Context: The person sees the context as one which is basically supportive, but as also offering the opportunities for him to change if he so desires.

BEHAVIOR: The person develops a way of behaving which is basically supportive of others, but which simultaneously is open to personal change and to providing opportunities for others to change.

Description of Context: The setting is a classroom in which two teachers are working together. One teacher is responsible for the children. The other teacher can scan the classroom and reflect on how she feels about trying to change the behavior of students.

Recording Feedback: During the process of scanning the classroom and reflecting, the teacher can try to answer the following questions:

How accepting am I of students and the behaviors they bring to class? How do I know?

What are the kinds of behaviors I cannot tolerate?

What kinds of opportunities do I make available for students to examine their own behavior?

What opportunities are available for students to give feedback to each other?

Do I provide an environment where it is safe to try on new behaviors?

What kinds of feedback do I give when a person tries on a new behavior but decides to revert to previous patterns?

Solving problems

Quality of Context: The person sees in the context opportunities to solve problems relative to peopling.

BEHAVIOR A: The person has a repertoire of means of establishing contact with another person.

Description of Context 1: The setting is a room where one can sit and think and where he can also interact with other persons. A person is available to be an observer-recorder.

Recording Feedback: Think about ways to initiate communication with another person. Among the ways which might be useful in reaching some persons are the following:

Exchange of recipes	What one most likes to do
What irks the person most	What one likes to do least
Shortages—paper, gas	Tall tales
Dream houses	Ways of relaxation
City sidewalks and their uses	Favorite music
	Favorite artist
Favorite part of the country or world	Favorite theologian
	Favorite styles
What one appreciates most	Other
What makes a person sentimental	

Once possible points of contact have been identified and tried, ask a participant-observer to give feedback on what transpired. Analyze whether one's approach to giving is in line with what one intends to do for and with other persons.

Description of Context 2: The setting is a place where the individual can be on his own and also has the opportunity to interact with persons from other lands.

Recording Feedback: Think about the problems of engaging in mutually enhancing activities with persons from another culture. For example, try to record or role play what might be the dinner conversation among members of a family in a country in which you are interested. What might be the topics of conversation? How might the conversation be the same or different from a dinner conversation of persons in your country? If you were to be a guest of the family in the foreign country, what "gifts" might you bring to create a readiness for contact? What topics might you discuss and which ones might you avoid? What areas do you feel you would have to develop more fully before you could be a comfortable guest in the country which you have selected? What gifts do you now possess that would be useful if you were to visit the selected country?

Now observe a situation in which persons from two different countries are interacting. Record what they say and conduct a content analysis of your material.

BEHAVIOR B: The person sees in the context opportunities to cross barriers in terms of his relations with persons.

Description of Context: The setting is a place with writing materials that is conducive to reflection.

Recording Feedback: Conduct an inventory of the kinds of persons with whom you have had an opportunity to interact with any degree of frequency or intimacy. You may keep the record daily, weekly, or monthly. One way of keeping the record might be to fill out a form such as the one in figure 11–4 on each contact and then to compile a summary check from the individual forms.

What have you learned about yourself through this inventory? Are there groups of persons you want to have more contact with as a result of what you have learned? Do you feel it is important to break barriers in your relationships with others? Why?

BEHAVIOR C: The person can convert adverse influences in an environment to positive ones.

Description of Context: The context is a room in which information about drugs and drug pushers is being taught to children. The same group of children is being taught in two blocks of time. Emphasis is on what the community can do to help drug pushers change their habits or to assist children and/or youth if they are caught in a situation in which they are being urged to be a party to the drug habit. The lessons involve outreach into the community. The lessons may also involve manipulating various materials related to drugs, viewing various audiovisual materials, engaging in student-initiated collaborative or individual projects.

Recording Feedback: Record the verbal and nonverbal behaviors of two children during the two work periods. Later, take the same two children

FIGURE 11–4. *Inventory of Personal Contacts*

	Check one item in each category	Describe degree of intimacy in relationship when appropriate	Idea for getting feedback about relationship; discuss where appropriate
Age of contact Peer Younger than self Older than self			
Geographical home Own town Own state Another state Another part of world			
Race Same as self Different from self			
Religion Same as self Different from self			
Ways of thinking Same as self Different from self			
Occupation			
Other things you wish to remember			
Purpose of contact			
Number of contacts			

into the community where they have the opportunity to observe either drug pushers or the effects of drugs. Again, record the children's verbal and nonverbal behavior. What do their gestures, words, facial expressions tell about the meaning of their learning? Do the children or youth take any initiative in changing adverse circumstances in the community to more positive ones?[10]

Do you note changes in behavior in your observations? Can you account for the changes? Do you think children or youth can better handle adverse circumstances as a result of these experiences? Why?

10. For a discussion of teaching about drugs in city schools, see Mary Rowe, *All Kinds of Love—In a Chinese Restaurant, West Portugal Day Care Center, New York* (Washington, D.C.: U.S. Department of Health, Education and Welfare/Office of Education, 1970).

The power of presence

Quality of Context: The person sees in the context an opportunity to use his own presence powerfully.

BEHAVIOR: The person searches for opportunity to utilize his presence
                powerfully.

Description of Context: The context is a classroom in which persons of different ages and backgrounds are interacting.

Recording Feedback: Set up a classroom so that children or youth can choose another person with whom to work on a topic of mutual interest. What transpires between the persons? Study what happens between peers. Also study how students tend to utilize the teacher and/or other adults.

At some point arrange to have grandparents, resource persons from the community, young children, or parents available. Record what happens when persons are free to establish interaction with another in any way they see fit.[11]

Keep a log of yourself as a teacher in a setting in which students are free to choose those with whom they wish to work. What do you do to indicate that you are accessible?

How can a teacher utilize time in meaningful ways when there are many persons for whom his presence is significant and important?

Peopling and Communicating

Communicating is a human process critical to the central ideas of this work. Consideration is now given to certain interrelationships between peopling and communicating.

Language as a vehicle

BEHAVIOR: The person can utilize language in a direct, honest manner
                even though he attempts to make his language appropri-
                ate to his audience.

Description of Context: The setting is a meeting—at school, in a play group, at church.

---

11. For a discussion of how to arrange environments so that persons can utilize presence in various ways, see Willard J. Congreve and George J. Rinehart, eds., *Flexibility in School Programs* (Worthington, Ohio: Charles A. Jones, 1972).

Recording Feedback: Tally the language of persons in a meeting. Title one column "Masked" language and the other column "Candid" language. Title a third column "Not Sure." As persons speak, tally what they say. After the meeting is over, see if you can think of the clues you received which caused you to tally as you did. To what degree does congruence between verbal and nonverbal behavior make a difference as to whether you hear language as masked or candid?

Integrating meanings

BEHAVIOR: The person can identify with other persons to the degree that he can integrate meanings with them during the interactive process.

Description of Context: The setting contains a table, a tape recorder, writing equipment and two persons engaging in a conversation in which they are trying to arrive at a common understanding.

Recording Feedback: Tape record a conversation between you and another person about a designated topic. After you have listened to the tape of your discussion, tally what you hear using headings such as the following: major points of each of the speakers, unpredictable comments, points of agreement, points of disagreement, new meanings common to both persons.

When is it important to attempt to integrate meanings in conversation? When is it important for persons to think alone? How should persons handle the unpredictable when the intent is to integrate meanings?

Mass media and tilting

BEHAVIOR: The person can utilize the art and linguistic forms projected by the mass media to enhance his own knowledge about tilting toward others.

Description of Context: The context is a media center, a library, or a classroom where the student has the opportunity to study a noteworthy person as he is projected in a variety of media, such as newspapers, television, and advertisements.

Recording Feedback: What potential do you see for media distortion of the image of a noteworthy person.[12] What potential exists for presenting a realistic image of the person?

---

12. Teachers may wish to supplement an assignment such as the one just mentioned by having students read Joseph Fletcher Littell, ed., *Coping with the Mass Media* (Evanston, Ill.: McDougal, Littell, 1972).

After you have conducted your study of the potential of the media to project images of the person, make two lists: the utilization of media to harm human contact, and the utilization of media to improve the quality of human contact.

Peopling and Knowing

If persons are to develop skill in peopling, it is necessary for them to gain knowledge unique to this area. They need to gain knowledge about self, the process of making attributions, contexts, and ways of knowing and sharing ideas with others.

Self-knowledge

BEHAVIOR: The person seeks to gain increased knowledge about himself.

Description of Context: The setting contains writing materials and a teacher or friend.

Recording Feedback: See if you can list traits about yourself which would fall into each or any of these categories. You may add some categories if you wish.

Creative interests or potential

Aspirations and values

Attitudes toward power

Questions I have

Feelings of affection toward others

Desire for power

Directions I wish to take

Deep hurts or quirks that may keep me from pursuing my goals

After you have made your list of traits, ask a teacher or friend to observe you for a period of time to record incidents related to each of the traits. Then check the two lists—your perceptions of your traits and your friend's observations. What likenesses and differences do you see in the lists? Why? What additional knowledge did you gain about yourself?

Attributions

BEHAVIOR: The person is aware of the bases upon which he makes attributions to other persons.

Description of Context: The setting is an embassy, a classroom, or a social organization where persons from other lands are in attendance.

Recording Feedback: Engage in a discussion with persons from other lands relative to characteristics of the American people. Tape record this discussion if possible so that you can go back and study it from various perspectives. On what basis do persons from other lands attribute attitudes, beliefs, values, and behaviors to Americans? Do you have any hunches why the attributions were made? What suggestions do you have for changing people's perceptions if you feel the attributions are inadequate or incorrect?

Try to think about the criteria you use in attributing thoughts or ideas, feelings, perceptions, or values to other persons. Write down some questions you might ask others or statements you might make to help check your hunches. Try out your ideas. Do you think you see persons more accurately if you check out tentative attributions?

Understanding context

BEHAVIOR A: The person in his interactions with others indicates that he is aware of persons and objects within his setting.

Description of Context 1: The setting is a classroom in which an observer is keeping a diary.

Recording Feedback: It has been said that persons pass through our schools untouched and untouching. Keep a diary-type record, 20 minutes in length, of a person in the classroom. Indicate what he touches and who or what touches him. Then consider the following question: What within the context contributes to a sense of touch or to a lack of it?[13]

Description of Context 2: The context is the lower income section of a city.

Recording Feedback: Study your town or city or some portion of it. Find an area in which low income persons live. Scan the newspapers and other forms of advertisements to see if you can find differences in how persons eat and live in that section of town as compared to a more affluent part.

Plan an interview schedule and utilize it with a person in the selected part of town. On your schedule, include questions relative to nutrition,

---

13. For a category system to note observations relative to touching, see Mary Lou S. Anderson, *Touching: Communication During a Quiet Activity,* Center for Young Children Occasional Paper Number Eleven (College Park: College of Education, University of Maryland, 1973).

housing, medical care, schooling, and recreation. Try to get at feelings and values as well as facts. What did you learn about differences in settings or contexts?

Description of Context 3: The classroom contains many materials, such as newspaper clippings, films, posters, and audiotapes relative to the food crisis.

Recording Feedback: No specific assignment should be given to students about the use of these materials although they should be located in convenient, accessible places.

Study how students use the materials by employing an observational guide with these headings: "Name of child," "Looks at materials," "Reads or listens to materials," "Does something with ideas in materials immediately," "Does something with ideas in materials at a later time."

BEHAVIOR B: The person can utilize the spontaneous and the fresh in the context as well as the more static elements.[14]

Description of Context: The context is one in which old and new materials are evident.

Recording Feedback: Study a classroom setting in which persons are engaging spontaneously in an activity. Make notes of new interests or revitalized old ones that seem to emerge. Why do you think this happens? What new plans might develop as a result of what transpired during a spontaneous activity? How do persons tend to see each other when spontaneity is evident? What evidence do you have to support your statements?

Knowing others

BEHAVIOR A: The person can determine points about which others feel free to express themselves as well as those areas which they repress.

Description of Context: The setting can be a classroom, a home—any place where one person has the opportunity to observe another over a period of time.

Recording Feedback: Observe someone for ten-minute periods several times during a week. Jot down what the person talks about. Each time a person goes back to the same topic, put a check. After a few days, go back and list topics about which the person did not speak but which

---

14. David Hawkins talks aptly of the use of the spontaneous and the accidental in the classroom in a telling article, "How to Plan for Spontaneity," in *The Open Classroom Reader,* ed. Charles E. Silberman (New York: Vintage Books, 1973), pp. 486–504.

might have been appropriate within the setting. Can you make some guesses as to why some topics were discussed several times and others ignored?

BEHAVIOR B: The person comes to know persons representing a variety of ages, backgrounds, and skills.

Description of Context: The setting is a place where a student has an opportunity to know and work with another person.

Recording Feedback. Arrange for students a series of experiences that provide the opportunity to come to know persons representing a variety of backgrounds. One way of insuring that children have a range of persons with whom they can interact is to plan for teaching so that students have opportunities for "skill exchange," "peer matching," and "reference services to educators-at-large."[15] Encourage students to gather feedback relative to how they come to know different kinds of persons. Students may want to work in pairs or trios, taking turns gathering information about each other.

Places to look when gathering feedback are:

How or when an individual talks while doing his work.

The different ages and socioeconomic backgrounds of those engaged in a selected activity.

The transmission of information in tasks in which that is the chief purpose.

The feelings people express as they go about their work or as they converse with new acquaintances.

What does one learn about the person and the person in relation to his work? How do the settings in which you observed persons seem to affect them? What evidence do you have to support your statement?

Reflecting shared ideas

BEHAVIOR: The person demonstrates the ability to develop and share ideas with others.

Description of Context: The setting contains two persons, a tape recorder, and writing materials.

---

15. For a development of this point, see Ivan Illich, "Education without School: How It Can Be Done," in *Farewell to Schools???*, ed. Daniel U. Levine and Robert J. Havighurst (Worthington, Ohio: Charles A. Jones, 1971), pp. 35–38, 40.

Recording Feedback: Find a colleague who has an interest similar to yours.[16] Plan a project together. Tape record some of your discussions. Now go back and analyze the discussions in terms of idea development. Make an instrument on which you indicate each new idea and what each contributed to the development of it.

Peopling and
Social Systems

Self-serving/other-serving

BEHAVIOR: The person can channel his energies in such a manner that he simultaneously can be self-serving and other-serving.

Description of Context: The setting is a classroom in which students have a degree of choice.

Recording Feedback: Study two students in a classroom over a period of time. Look for such qualities as freedom to make decisions, commitment, involvement, spontaneity, freedom to contribute ideas, willingness to assess ideas. As you record, note when you see these qualities and whether they are in situations in which the individual is primarily self-serving, other-serving, or both. What kinds of situations seem to contribute to a person's being self-serving and other-serving simultaneously?

Self-authority/ institutional authority

BEHAVIOR: The person is able to balance his personal sense of authority with that of others and the authority of institutions.

Description of Context: The context is a group of persons engaged in a discussion about the relationship of personal authority to personal freedom and about the authority of various persons and institutions.

Recording Feedback: Pull out the key points in the discussion and see if you can develop a statement relative to the relationship of personal authority to the authority of others and that of institutions.

While you are engaging in this activity, ask a third person to observe your interaction. The person should record diary fashion what is transpiring and then see if a critical analysis of the material yields categories

16. For a description of paired endeavors among the young, see *Model Programs, Childhood Education, The Micro-Social Preschool, Vineland, New Jersey* (Washington, D.C.: U.S. Government Printing Office, 1970), pp. 6–11.

relative to the nature of personal authority and individual authority. What are the points of congruity and incongruity between the activity of the two participants and the categories of the observer?

In Retrospect

In this chapter attention has been given to opportunities for acquiring certain skills for peopling that schools can make available to their young. The last chapter considers some jumping-off points persons might want to consider if they are interested in reality-based or process-oriented curriculum.

Suggestions for Further Reading

Anderson, Mary Lou S. *Touching: Communication During A Quiet Activity.* Center for Young Children Occasional Paper Number Eleven. College Park: University of Maryland, 1973.

Bolam, David, Director. *Exploration Man: An Introduction to Integrated Studies.* Schools Council Integrated Studies. London: Oxford University Press, 1972.

Carswell, Evelyn M. and Darrell L. Roubinek. *Open Sesame: A Primer in Open Education.* Pacific Palisades, Cal.,: Goodyear, 1974.

Congreve, Willard J. and George J. Rinehart, eds. *Flexibility in School Programs.* Worthington, Ohio: Charles A. Jones, 1972.

Cronbach, Lee J. *Essentials of Psychological Testing.* 3d ed. New York: Harper & Row, 1970.

Engle, Shirley H. and Wilma S. Longstreet. *A Design for Social Education in the Open Curriculum.* New York: Harper & Row, 1972.

Epps, Edgar A., ed. *Black Students in White Schools.* Worthington, Ohio: Charles A. Jones, 1972.

Goulet, Denis. "An Ethical Model for the Study of Values." *Harvard Educational Review* 41: 205–27, May 1971.

Hawkins, Frances Pockman. *The Logic of Action: From a Teacher's Notebook.* University of Colorado, Mountain View Center for Environmental Education, 1969.

Heston, Lilla, Joy Littell, and Sarah Solotaroff, eds. *Brotherhood.* Evanston, Ill.: McDougal, Littell, 1972.

Hunkins, Francis P. and Patricia F. Spears. *Social Studies for the Evolving Individual.* Washington, D.C.: Association for Supervision and Curriculum Development, 1973.

Johnson, David W. and Roger T. Johnson. "Instructional Goal Structure: Cooperative, Competitive, or Individualistic." *Review of Educational Research* 44: 213–40, Spring 1974.

Kenworthy, Leonard S. *The International Dimension of Education.* Washington, D.C.: Association for Supervision and Curriculum Development, 1970.

King, Edith W. *Educating Young Children—Sociological Interpretations.* Dubuque, Ia.: Wm. C. Brown, 1973.

————. *Worldmindedness: The World: Context for Teaching in the Elementary School.* Dubuque, Ia.: Wm. C. Brown, 1971.

Littell, Joseph Fletcher, ed. *Coping with the Mass Media.* Evanston, Ill.: McDougal, Littell, 1972.

Lofland, Lyn H. *A World of Strangers: Order and Action in Urban Public Space.* New York: Basic Books, 1973.

Lyon, Harold C., Jr. *Learning to Feel—Feeling to Learn: Humanistic Education for the Whole Man.* Columbus, Ohio: Charles E. Merrill, 1971.

Miel, Alice and Peggy Brogan. *More than Social Studies: A View of Social Learning in the Elementary School.* Englewood Cliffs, N.J.: Prentice-Hall, 1957.

Miles, Matthew W. and W. W. Charters, Jr. *Learning in Social Settings, New Readings in the Social Psychology of Education.* Boston: Allyn and Bacon, 1970.

Pittel, Stephen M. and Gerald A. Mendelsohn. "Measurement of Moral Values: A Review and a Critique." *Psychological Bulletin* 66: 22–35, 1966.

Raskin, Marcus G. *Being and Doing.* New York: Random House, 1971.

Renaud, Mary, ed. *Bringing the World into Your Classroom.* Curriculum Series Number Thirteen. Washington, D.C.: National Council for the Social Studies, 1968.

Robinson, Donald W., ed. *As Others See Us: International Views of American History.* Boston: Houghton-Mifflin, 1969.

Savary, Louis M., S. J. with others. *Listen to Love: Reflections on the Seasons of the Year.* New York: Regina Press, 1973.

Silberman, Charles E., ed. *The Open Classroom Reader.* New York: Vintage Books, 1973.

Spinner, Stephanie, ed. *Live and Learn: Stories about Students and Their Teachers.* New York: Macmillan, 1973.

Taylor, Harold. *The World as Teacher.* Garden City, N.Y.: Doubleday, 1969.

Townsend, Alan and Geoffrey Hartley, eds. *Communicating with Others,* and *Living Together,* Units 2 and 3. Teachers' Guide. Schools Council Integrated Studies. London: Oxford University Press, 1972.

Trickett, Edison, J. and David M. Todd. "The High School Culture: An Ecological Perspective." *Theory into Practice* 11: 28–37, February 1972.

Wigginton, Eliot, ed. *The Foxfire Book.* Garden City, N.Y.: Doubleday, 1972.

Wurman, Richard Sal, ed. *Yellow Pages of Learning Resources.* Philadelphia: Group for Environmental Education, 1972.

12

Epilogue

Perspective on Chapter 12

Theme: For the person who wishes to implement the ideas developed in this book, certain jumping-off points are suggested.

Selected major points: (1) A first jumping-off point is raising questions relative to gathering data pertinent to process-related skills. (2) If the curriculum is seen as providing opportunities for persons to develop process-related skills, then attention should be given to preparing personnel and encouraging collaboration among various persons concerned about the learner.

As you read: (1) What additional jumping-off points do you consider important? (2) What can be done within existing curricula to help persons become more process oriented?

When individuals establish curricular priorities related to personal qualities; when they design or select settings in which the qualities can develop; and when they achieve feedback on learners' interactions with the settings, certain jumping-off points, new thresholds, or unanswered questions can be expected to emerge. We propose three broad areas in which these points can occur.

The first area includes two concerns: (1) the nature of questions that emerge in the development of a living-based curriculum, and (2) procedures for judging progress in process-related personal qualities. The second area deals with the broad preparation of persons to implement the curricular thrust of this work. The third area relates to collaboration in generating knowledge about process-related skills.

Point 1:
Raising Questions and
Making Judgments

The nature of questions prompted by approaching curriculum in the manner we propose and procedures for judging progress in process-related skills have not been explored to any degree thus far in this book. A brief discussion of these two points follows.

Raising questions

Those questions which emanate from, as well as stimulate efforts to develop a living-based curriculum are likely to be characterized by clarity, specificity, and objectivity. The careful statement of priorities related to personal qualities and the precise descriptions of settings purported to facilitate progress in these qualities help one not only identify a range of anticipated outcomes but also raise questions about them. For instance, instead of asking generally how a person seems to be progressing in his concern for others, one might ask: What did the person do when confronted with a situation in which three children were hurt? If the teacher is interested in a student's decision making, he might establish a context in which viable choices exist and ask the question: Did the student recognize the alternatives in the situation? By what process did he select from among them? How did he evidence his ability to live with the consequences of his decision?

Another procedure related to a living-based curriculum which prompts clear, specific, and precise questioning is obtaining feedback on what transpires when persons interact with settings. Earlier we spoke of clarity and precision in establishing goals related to personal qualities and in selecting or designing settings that encourage progress in these qualities. When feedback techniques designed to generate knowledge about personal qualities are used to describe interactions with settings or to record learners' reflections or experiences, the resulting feedback is also more specific and to the point. Persons having access to such feedback can raise additional pertinent, clear, and precise questions.

Questions related to a curriculum designed to develop process-oriented persons are also more directly related to the nature of the curriculum experiences. There is a unity or congruence between what is proposed and attempted and the questions raised about these proposals and attempts.

To this point we have maintained that persons engaged in developing and implementing a living-based curriculum will, by virtue of the specifics inherent in this approach, operate at a new threshold or jumping-off point where increased clarity and specificity in questions are apparent. Questions evolving from the processes inherent in the development and implementation of a living-based curriculum might include the following:

What if the learner does not see in the context those opportunities for progressing in a process-related personal quality that the individual who selected or designed the context anticipated he would?

What seem to be the implications of this problem for redesigning or reselecting a context?

In what ways does observed or reported behavior differ from anticipated behavior? How does the person responsible for the setting deal with the unanticipated?

What seem to be the implications for obtaining more suggestions from the learner about designing a context necessary to accomplishing his purposes?

What does an interaction that differs from an anticipated one suggest about individual perception?

What kind and how much intervention, if any, is appropriate for a learner in a particular setting?

Which specific learner behaviors provided the impetus for applying a specified intervention by the teacher?

What does the feedback achieved indicate about stages or degrees of growth in process-related skills and personal qualities?

What does charting or mapping interactions with various settings over a period of time suggest about possible stages or degrees of growth?

What kinds of behaviors appear to be related to settings which have different emphases?

What changes are evident in teaching skills as a result of raising specific questions about a particular approach to curriculum development?

The reader is encouraged to raise questions pertinent to his own situation in terms of curricular priorities, procedures for encouraging development of them, and means of achieving feedback. The sample questions above are offered as a stimulus to asking questions about what was anticipated and what occurred. These and other questions can aid in welcoming and handling the serendipitous as well as the planned.

In summary, persons who engage in procedures related to developing and implementing a living-based curriculum are able to examine critically their efforts and to raise clearly stated, specific questions about them. The questions raised also facilitate the generation of knowledge about anticipated and unanticipated outcomes. Making judgments about progress toward objectives is a natural follow-up of raising questions about progress. Some basic concerns related to judging progress are discussed in the next section.

Making judgments about progress

Raising questions about efforts to encourage progress in process-related skills discloses the need to develop and utilize appropriate feedback techniques. In turn, the knowledge generated by employing feedback techniques provides a basis for making judgments. Because people are constantly making judgments, they need to reexamine the procedures by which they make them. Persons prepared to approach curriculum development in the manner described in this book will most likely operate at the cutting edge in the area of judging progress. Those persons can be expected to (1) scrutinize the process by which they use feedback to arrive at judgments about progress; (2) explore more deeply the possibilities for employing judgment in the various aspects of curriculum development; and (3) rethink their attitudes toward the role of judgment in evaluating educational experiences.

The process by which judgments about a curricular approach are made can be broad or more narrow in scope, depending on the particular situation. Defined broadly, the judgment process can include the priorities which give direction to curriculum development.[1] Although at some time the process should be examined in its entirety, factors in each situation determine the beginning focal point or the aspect receiving more attention. In this discussion we place major emphasis on examining the process by which feedback can be used to arrive at judgments about learner progress. The intent is not to minimize the importance of other steps in judgmental procedures, but rather to follow through on the importance we have assigned in this work to observation and reflec-

---

1. For a discussion of a more broadly defined view of the judgment process see Samuel Messick, "Educational Evaluation as Research for Program Improvement," *Childhood Education* 46:413–14, May 1970.

tion as means of obtaining information about more than terminal paper and pencil products.

Using Feedback.   Once feedback has been obtained either by describing a person's interactions or by asking him to reflect on his experience, we must ask what the knowledge generated says. What does it tell us about a specific learner's interaction with a specific context? How does it help us determine whether the learner has made progress? To what degree and in which direction has he done so? What does it tell us about what constitutes satisfactory or desirable growth for a learner in a specified context?

In attempting to answer these questions, we are called upon to make judgments based not only on the feedback obtained, but also on our knowledge of the setting and the learner and on the priorities we have established. In a curricular approach which values the individuality and unpredictability of a learner, the most we can hope to achieve is refined judgments about the change or movement a person exhibits as he interacts with specified contexts. In so doing we move away from general judgments based primarily on feelings and from tight categorizations and labelings. This move requires a critical examination of possible means of making more refined judgments based on observational information. It also requires the involvement of persons who can live with tentativeness, with change, and with the freedom to establish their own goals and can take steps to achieve them.

Since process-related personal qualities can present more complexities of implementation than might be expected in a curriculum emphasizing a given body of subject matter, the task of making judgments is also more complex. As in the development and utilization of feedback techniques, there is much working and reworking of attempts to develop ways of refining judgments.

Using Bases.   One way to refine judgments of learner progress contained in observational records and reflective responses is through the use of bases for making comparisons and eventually judgments about that progress. In this context a base is an identifiable and relatively stable foundation upon which comparisons might be made. An example of a base is an individual's current behavior compared to his behavior over a period of time. Although "foundation" might suggest inflexibility, it is hoped that judgments made using base as defined will not be rigid or linear. A base merely provides a more concrete standard or point of reference in making comparisons. Such comparisons can lead to more refined judgments.

When a base is used to facilitate making comparisons and subsequently judgments, the base selected, the priorities established, the contexts designated, and the feedback procedures employed must be related. Perhaps the closest relationship exists between the base and the feedback techniques. For example, if a feedback technique provides information relative to the number of verbal utterances an individual makes in a particular context, it is appropriate to assume that a workable base would be defined in terms of an objective point of reference such as the number of utterances per time unit. If a feedback technique is specific in terms of the behavior of a particular age group, then an appropriate base includes a reference to that age group. Comparing feedback achieved with points of reference along a base enables us to make judgments in terms of comparisons such as *more than, less then,* or *the same as;* or in such terms as *high, moderate,* or *low.*

In another instance, if we rate feedback in terms of a base such as "individual's behavior compared to how other persons of a similar age act in a similar situation," we can judge whether the behaviors described are the same as, somewhat different from, or totally different from behavior expected of persons of a similar age engaged in a similar activity.

Another way of using a base to judge a learner's progress is to focus on obtaining feedback about a specific quality or characteristic of behavior such as penetration (see chapter 8). A base such as "individual's behavior compared to behavior of individuals of similar age" can be employed to arrive at judgments about behaviors indicative of penetration. Judgments can be made in terms of whether or not the feedback obtained suggests that when compared to the behavior of persons of similar age, the observed penetration is more intense, the same as, or less intense.

There are many ways one might approach the task of judging learner growth or progress toward developing the skills of a process-oriented person. Persons engaged in making these judgments might want to explore the following bases to determine whether or not they are workable in a particular situation.[2]

1. Individual's behavior as it appears to be generated by the potentialities of materials, space, area.
2. Individual's behavior compared to behavior of individuals of similar age.

---

2. Specific information about the use of these particular bases is found in Jessie A. Roderick, *Identifying, Defining, Coding, and Rating Nonverbal Behaviors that Appear to be Related to Involvement: Project on Involvement Interim Report No. 2* (College Park: Center for Young Children, University of Maryland, July 1973).

3. Individual's current behavior compared to his behavior over a period of time.
4. Individual's behavior compared to how people in general tend to act in a similar situation.
5. Objective point of reference (i.e., number of motions per time period or unit).

Defining and using bases for comparison is one way persons operating at the cutting edge of the judging aspect of curriculum development might proceed. Our experience tells us that more and more questions emerge during this kind of exploration, and as a result new jumping-off points and thresholds emerge. Also, seeking ways of arriving at more refined judgments discloses the need to develop more appropriate instruments for generating feedback. Improving our skills in making judgments can also have a positive impact on the priorities we establish and the quality of the contexts designed or selected to encourage growth in them. In addition the leaps we make can be better defined in terms of their parameters and of the implications they have for a living-based curriculum.

Point 2:
Personnel Preparation

The curricular emphases proposed in this book are a bit irregular in terms of what one would probably find in practices around the world today. Although schools feel some commitment to having children and youth become involved, make wise decisions, and people, other subjects or emphases frequently have higher priority than the ones we are recommending. Hence, if the assumption is accepted that the suggested curricular emphases are critical ones, then a need exists to prepare persons to consider, develop competence in, and apply the thrusts presented in the previous pages.

A topic which has been touched on but not adequately treated is the preparation of persons to implement the major recommended components. Although no attempt is made to develop a sequential program either at the in-service or pre-service level, some areas are suggested where skill is needed for persons to implement curricula based upon the premise that the schools can assist in developing more adequate persons. It will be noted that we are not proposing courses, but rather experiences which might lead to the creation of environments for children and youth in which process-related skills can be learned. As stated earlier, basic to an adequate implementation of living-based programs are persons who desire to collaborate in developing the thrust of this book.

Familiarity with process

First, persons interested in assisting in implementing curricula in which process skills can be learned need a familiarity with the processes of deciding, becoming involved, peopling, dealing with social systems, communicating, and knowing. In addition, persons need to explore concepts in such areas as valuing, thinking, creating, and other areas closely related to those skills.

No one course or group of courses at this time is probably going to give an adequate background in these basic human processes. The preparation of persons, therefore, should include stimulating a vital hunger to explore areas of study such as the humanities, the social sciences, and the natural sciences in order to formulate new insights and understandings, hypotheses, and questions relative to the process-related person. Since human nature lends itself to increased probing, the preparation of persons should create the need to turn to a variety of sources for fresh understandings about the person and how he functions. Thus, one dimension of personnel preparation is the encouragement of an excitement about the complexity of persons so that individuals become aware of the many facets of human nature.

Observing

A second skill that should be included is that of observing in a variety of ways. A large portion of this book has been devoted to methods of obtaining and recording feedback. Feedback techniques are based on the premise that one can and should observe closely, carefully, and through various colored lenses. A number of observational techniques have been discussed in earlier pages. A program of studies might invite the person to examine his own modes of perceiving. Subsequently, he might gain competence in utilizing the systems or partial systems discussed earlier and in creating new ones appropriate to the process skills on which he wishes to focus. Skill in observation is central to making judgments. Without means of achieving plentiful, useful, and pertinent information one cannot plan adequately for teaching process skills.

Furthermore, information gathered through skilled observation enables the person to think more fully about himself and others. Careful observation of basic human processes, coupled with refined judgmental skills relative to using the observational material are essential if the curriculum worker seeks to utilize the wealth of information he can gather from students in planning classroom experiences.

Creating educational milieus

A third skill necessary for persons interested in developing process skills is that of creating educational milieus. Educational milieus can be of two types: (1) pre-arranged settings designed to provide the student with an encounter which highlights skills of a process-oriented person, and (2) contexts which are relatively open but which possess the likelihood that students will learn some living-based skills. One context is more particularized than the other, but both types are necessary to learn the variety of skills the sensitive, responsive person must possess.

What is and what ought to be

Fourth, persons need to differentiate between what is and what ought to be, and to develop competence in moving from one to the other. The realities need to be sifted through the filter of one's value construct in order to plan appropriate next steps in curriculum development.

What is types of information can be gathered through careful observations. Ideas relative to *what ought to be* can operate at two or more different levels. The first is in terms of an ideal without reference to a specific person or situation. The second is in terms of what appear to be the best next steps for a particular person or situation. Through a careful understanding of both the nature of the individual and what he can become and the skill of observation and achieving feedback, one can make the leap from what is to what seems to be the best choice for action.

Moving from utilizing feedback to gather information to planning for next steps based upon the data involves an internalized knowledge of the various process skills and of the real situation including students, materials, space, and time. The preparation of persons should involve the actual demonstration of the ability to synthesize and apply the concepts presented in this book in real-life situations.

Particularized preparation and involvement

The curricular designs about which we have been concerned necessitate a shift in thinking about who should be involved in teaching. When one moves toward curricula which attempt to highlight the person, including idiosyncratic as well as common dimensions of personality, teaching becomes exceedingly complex. When one focuses only upon the mastery of a given body of content with little attention to the person, teaching is easier but devastating to the full development of the person. In the curriculum orientation we are proposing, there is need to draw more persons into the instructional process to observe, to establish environments for learning, and to record the interactions between learners and their contexts.

In the next few paragraphs attention is given to persons who can assist in the instructional process and the types of tasks to which they might devote time and energy.

Classroom Teacher. The classroom teacher is the key person in designing curricula to enhance process skills. He needs background in literature on process skills and a desire to implement them in teaching. He needs skill in observing, knowledge of how to find and create a variety of educational milieus, and skill in utilizing feedback for planning next steps.

Since the classroom teacher by himself probably cannot do all that is expected in curricula designed to foster process skills, he needs to administer and coordinate the efforts of others who work with him in the classroom. In addition, he needs to keep adequate observational records of what is actually happening in the classroom.

In situations in which a team approach to teaching exists, it may be that one or more members of the team develop special expertise in one or more processes or in the development and utilization of feedback systems. The development of expertise can be useful in the collaborative process of planning learning contexts. By emphasizing both breadth and depth in members of the team, those responsible for teaching can insure commonality and diversity as they tackle the challenge of helping to develop more process-oriented persons.

Aides, Students, Parents. Persons who aid in the classroom may develop certain types of specialized expertise. For example, many parents, students, or aides can be trained to use a particular observational instrument. Others might become skilled in preparing specialized materials pertinent to teaching a particular human skill. Since the utilization of equipment such as videotape machines, tape recorders, and cameras can supplement and enhance the gathering of observational data, older students or aides might develop skill in its operation. In brief, paraprofessionals, parents, and students can acquire particularized skills necessary to the implementation of curricula based upon developing vital human processes.

Supervisors, Administrators, Curriculum Coordinators. Professional personnel responsible for overseeing and coordinating instructional programs can best enhance curricular designs based upon the development of process skills by providing a climate in which persons are encouraged to explore, to collaborate, to gather observational data about their students, and to select or create educational milieus in line with the behaviors emphasized in the curriculum. Those instructional personnel not directly responsible for teaching children can play a vital role in strengthening living-based curricula if they seek to provide a setting in which the total staff can act as a community searching for new knowledge about persons and school programs. This means that every person serving in a supervisory or an administrative capacity must insure that the setting is such that persons do not build walls around themselves, but rather share fully in developing school programs appropriate to today's world.

Summary. We need to give attention to new topics in the preparation of persons. These topics include qualities of persons who are flexible, searching, and energetic in their approach to life; developing expertise in observation, selecting and creating appropriate educational contexts; and utilizing what *is* in order to help design what *ought* to be.

In addition, a variety of persons including teachers, parents, students, aides, curriculum workers, and administrators can develop expertise related to process-oriented curriculum.

Point 3:
Collaborating across Barriers

Persons who engage in the various aspects of developing a living-based curriculum are most likely to act upon a range of possibilities for collaborating with others. Collaborating is working together in a joint effort and is characterized by sharing mutual interests, concerns, and responsibilities. Barriers can be physical ones of space or distance or constructions such as classroom walls.[3] There can also be psychical barriers such as fear of the unknown, inability to communicate across cultures or groups, and insecurity about sharing one's ideas and questions.

We believe that there are certain aspects or facets related to developing a living-based curriculum that function as facilitators in collaborative efforts. Achieving feedback in the form of descriptions and reflections on visible and audible experiences is one facet that might

---

3. Dreeben comments on the fragmentation classroom teachers experience in the school. A contributing factor is spatial isolation and the influence this has on teacher activities. For further development of this idea see Robert Dreeben, "The School as a Workplace," in *Second Handbook of Research on Teaching,* ed. R. M. W. Travers (Chicago: Rand McNally, 1973), pp. 450–73.

encourage a broader sharing of learnings and ideas. Such sharing can occur when a teacher is invited to observe and record in a colleague's classroom or to talk with learners who work primarily with another person. When means for achieving feedback are developed and utilized on a cooperative basis, and when there is concrete information used as a basis of sharing, individuals are apt to spend more time in this endeavor. By working together in developing, using, and discussing these techniques and the knowledge generated, barriers of insecurity, indifference, and unconcern can be lessened.

The emphasis on the person germane to developing a living-based curriculum can also facilitate collaborative efforts if persons in different roles are encouraged to work together. Each person involved shares in the responsibility for planning, executing, and evaluating the experiences. A team teacher, an aide, a community consultant, a curriculum supervisor, or a student may at one time or another be part of collaboration.

Barriers caused by differences in orientation toward teaching can also be crossed during collaboration. Persons who approach teaching from one perspective might be interested in looking at another approach if they have descriptive information about their own approach and that of another. Individuals from different parts of the world with common curricular concerns might also collaborate more readily if they generate knowledge about their experiences as they and learners engage in them. The feedback resulting from this process can form the basis for exchange on a personal level.

It is highly possible that collaborative efforts which stem from the kinds of experiences described will result in a broader dissemination of knowledge. Such dissemination encourages persons to look more carefully at what they are doing in their own classrooms and to share accounts of experiences and thoughts related to the process of knowledge generation. Short papers, monographs, or newsletters can be disseminated. Written means of collaborating can result in a forum for the exchange and enrichment of ideas across many kinds of barriers.

Throughout this work we have emphasized the importance of persons having opportunities to make decisions, to become involved, and to people. Does it not seem reasonable to expect that individuals who have been prepared to develop curriculum as we describe it will be more likely to see and act upon opportunities for collaborating? And does it not seem reasonable to expect that through collaborative efforts, persons will focus more attention on the very critical dimensions of living such as making wise decisions, becoming involved in worthwhile enterprises, and showing concern for persons of all kinds? No one can do the job or experience the satisfactions alone. But the job must be done if persons are to have the necessary skills to insure their own well-being while simultaneously contributing to the well-being of others.

Suggestions for Further Reading

Anderson, Robert H., ed. *Education in Anticipation of Tomorrow: The Lamplighter Seminar.* Worthington, Ohio: Charles A. Jones, 1973.

Berman, Louise M. and Mary Lou Usery White. *Personalized Supervision: Sources and Insights.* Washington, D.C.: Association for Supervision and Curriculum Development, 1966.

Berman, Louise M. *Supervision, Staff Development and Leadership.* Columbus, Ohio: Charles E. Merrill, 1971.

DeVault, M. Vere, ed. *Research, Development and the Classroom Teacher Producer/Consumer.* Washington, D.C.: The Association for Childhood Education International, 1970.

Dreeben, Robert. "The School as a Workplace." In *Second Handbook of Research on Teaching,* ed. by R. M. W. Travers. Chicago: Rand McNally, 1973.

Eisner, Elliot W. "Emerging Models for Educational Evaluation." *School Review* 80:573–90, August 1972.

Fuller, Francis F. "A Conceptual Framework for a Personalized Teacher Education Program." *Theory into Practice* 13:112–22, April 1974.

Hartup, Willard W. "The Needs of Young Children and Research: Psychosocial Development Revisited." *Young Children* 12:129–35, April 1973.

Horowitz, Sandra. *From Theory to Practice: A Personal Diary of a Teacher of Young Children.* Center for Young Children Monograph 6. College Park: University of Maryland, 1971.

Joyce, Bruce and Marsha Weil. *Models of Teaching.* Englewood Cliffs, N.J.: Prentice-Hall, 1972.

Joyce, Bruce and Marsha Weil, eds. *Perspectives for Reform in Teacher Education.* Englewood Cliffs, N.J.: Prentice-Hall, 1972.

Smith, Robert G. and others. *A Program for Young Children Based on Process Skills: Examples of Practice.* Center for Young Children Occasional Paper Number Nine. College Park: University of Maryland, 1973.

Yamamoto, Kaoru, ed. *The Child and His Image: Self Concept in the Early Years.* Boston: Houghton-Mifflin, 1972.

appendix

CODE
Categories for the Observation of
Decision-making Elements*

CATEGORIES	DEFINITIONS
1. Attending	This category indicates attention or inattention or request for attention by the teacher or child.
a. Listening-Watching	One or more actors focus on speech or activities by apparent listening-looking.
b. Not Responding	The teacher or child does not respond to a request, suggestion, or direction.
c. Responding-Indicating Delay	A response is made by an actor that indicates his action will be postponed.
d. Requesting Attention	The teacher or child solicits the attention of another.
2. Focusing on a Problem	This category is concerned with the recognition of a problem or problem situation by the teacher or child.
a. Identifying a Problem	One or more actors indicate a problem situation.

* Thi

264

CATEGORIES	DEFINITIONS
b. Requesting Identification of a Problem	The teacher or child asks another to identify a problem or problem situation.
3. Assisting	The teacher or child offers, provides, or requests help or solace (human or material resources) during interaction.
a. Offering Assistance or Comfort	An actor offers assistance or comfort to another person.
b. Giving Assistance or Comfort	An actor provides assistance and/or comfort to another.
c. Requesting Assistance or Comfort	An actor solicits assistance or comfort from another.
4. Informing	This category depicts statements of facts or personal beliefs (or lack of either) by the teacher or child.
a. Stating Facts or Opinions	An actor relates factual information or personal feelings or beliefs.
b. Requesting Facts or Opinions	The teacher or child solicits factual information or personal feelings/beliefs from another.
c. Not Knowing	An actor does not have an answer or opinion to a question directed to him.
5. Extending	These are statements or questions by the teacher or child that request or provide additional thought, clarification, or explanation. These remarks usually follow statements coded in other categories.
a. Elaborating	The teacher or child adds information, clarifies, or explains previous comments or actions.
b. Requesting Elaboration	An actor solicits further information, clarification, or explanation.
6. Prescribing and Describing	This category includes giving and requesting a course(s) of thought or action by the teacher or child.
a. Suggesting a Course of Thought or Action	An actor recommends one thought or action. Suggesting statements usually include such words as "perhaps," "might," "suppose," etc.

CATEGORIES	DEFINITIONS
b. Suggesting Alternative Courses of Thought or Action	An actor proposes more than one thought or action. Imperative statements by children may be coded in this sub-category when they follow requests for suggestions.
c. Directing a Course(s) of Thought or Action	The teacher or child commands another to follow a prescribed thought or action. Teacher statements using imperatives are always coded in this sub-category.
d. Requesting a Possible Course (s) of Thought or Action	An actor solicits one or more possible suggestions from another/others.
7. Predicting	The teacher or child states or requests statements of future consequences and/or outcomes. This behavior goes beyond stating opinions (which are concerned with past and present thoughts and actions).
a. Stating Predictions	An actor foretells the consequences or outcomes of ideas or actions.
b. Requesting Predictions	An actor solicits the hypothesis/hypotheses of others.
8. Intending-Choosing	This category includes statements by the teacher or child of intentions. It also encompasses actions resulting from intentions, suggestions, or directions.
a. Stating Intent	The teacher or child states his intention to select or not select a thought or action.
b. Requesting Intent	An actor solicits the intention or plan of another.
c. Following Through	The teacher or child acts on his stated or unstated intent, or on the suggestions or directions of another/others.
d. Not Following Through	The teacher or child does not act on his own intent or the suggestion or direction of another. (If he is responding to a suggestion or direction, he declares that he does not want to act.)
9. Appraising	This category includes all teacher or child assessments of thought and action of self and others.
a. Approving	An actor confirms or approves his or other's feelings, thoughts, or actions. Non-verbal actions such as a nod accompanied by a smile and/or gesture indicating approval are coded here.

CATEGORIES	DEFINITIONS
b. Accepting	This sub-category indicates a passive or neutral appraisal of feelings, thoughts, or actions. Repeating the statement of another, or describing what another is doing or has done, without value judgment is coded here. Behaviors such as a nod or value-lacking utterance ("uh-huh," "Okay," etc.) are included if no specific evaluation is perceived.
c. Disapproving	An actor disconfirms or disapproves his or other's feelings, thoughts, or actions. The sub-category may include negative head-shaking, frowning, hitting, verbal utterances such as "yuk."
d. Requesting Appraisal	The teacher or child solicits the assessment of another/others concerning their feelings, thoughts, or actions.
10. Mystifying	These are behaviors by teacher or child that cannot be recorded in the foregoing categories.
a. Interacting Behavior that Cannot be Seen or Heard	These behaviors occur in an interactive situation, but cannot be coded in categories 1–9 because they are inaudible or out of the observer's vision. This sub-category includes incomplete statements that do not convey meaning. Nonsensical comments are also coded here.
b. Interacting Behavior that Cannot be Coded	These behaviors occur in an interactive situation but cannot be coded in categories 1–10a.